An Offering of Light

Healing with Jyorei, Natural Agriculture, and Art

An Offering of Light

Healing with Jyorei, Natural Agriculture, and Art

Roy Gibbon & Atsushi Fujimaki
with Gerard Rohlfing

Revised Edition

SHUMEI AMERICA PUBLICATIONS

Medical Disclaimer

The information in this book is based on published and unpublished sources. The purpose is for educational and research purposes only and should not be construed as giving medical advice. The authors and publisher do not diagnose, treat, or prescribe. If the reader uses the information to solve his/her own health problems, they are prescribing for themselves, which is their constitutional right, but neither the authors nor the publisher assume any responsibility.

Published by Shumei America Publications
2430 East Colorado Boulevard
Pasadena, California 91107 USA

Second Edition, 2007

Library of Congress Control Number: 2006933179
ISBN-13: 978-0-9772860-1-0

Cover design and diagrams by Tokiko Jinta
Text design by Hiroyuki (Max) Kondo
Illustrations by Yasushi Fujimoto

Printed and bound by Hignell Book Printing in Manitoba, Canada

Your ears are useless if you ignore words spoken on the meaning of Light.

— Meishusama *(Poems of Inspiration. Miakarishu)*

Contents

Chapter

PREFACE

This book is for people, especially Westerners, who wish for a deeper understanding of the teachings of Mokichi Okada. Known as Meishusama, Mokichi Okada was a spiritual teacher who was active in Japan during the first half of the twentieth century. His life was dedicated to serving humanity through spiritual healing, the arts, and spiritually-based food cultivation.

Quotes from his writings are used liberally throughout this text as we believe they allow his spirit to become more alive for the reader. Because of the abundance of these quotes, this book easily could have been subtitled: Commentaries on the Teachings of Meishusama.

Some readers might already be familiar with the spiritual benefits of Jyorei, and it is natural for them to want to learn more about Meishusama and his teachings after first receiving this blessing. We hope that this book satisfies them. We also hope that members of Shumei currently practicing Jyorei will find this publication revealing.

While writing *An Offering of Light*, we found that a reappraisal of Meishusama's teachings in light of Western culture was needed. So rather than routinely summarizing his teachings, we attempted to clarify and elaborate them using concepts familiar to Westerners, while still remaining true to his message. Therefore, some of his ideas have been paraphrased in terminology more familiar to those in the West.

The scope of Meishusama's writings and transcribed lectures is vast and diverse. He was not a systematic writer and a comprehensive overview of his thoughts does not yet exist. While it is not our intention to present a conclusive study of his ideas, we hope that this publication will offer a glimpse of the underlying unity and integrity of his thoughts. While it focuses on his most relevant thoughts, some ideas that he only lightly touched upon were thought important enough to explain further. Consequently, the organization of Meishusama's teachings found here is unique to this publication. Meishusama wrote and spoke to people in a variety of ways, depending on his audience and their circumstances, preferring to adapt his ideas to the situation at hand. This is understandable as his purpose was to give spiritual guidance rather than set forth a complete philosophical or theological system. For a deeper perception of his ideas, we encourage readers to study his writings directly.

The best way to validate Meishusama's teachings is through the practice of them. This cannot be done solely by gaining an intellectual grasp of his concepts or by reading this book. His advice must be acted upon. Meishusama felt that to realize his teachings fully, one must live the spiritual practices that he prescribed. As Mokichi Okada affirms about the truth of his own words:

> Those who appreciate the truth of this must give and receive Jyorei for a few years in succession. If they do this, they will be able to grasp the profound reality at which these words merely hint.
>
> — Meishusama. *(Natural Power. A Hundred Teachings of Meishusama)*

Our hope is that this book sparks a deeper awareness of Meishusama's teachings and thereby will benefit all.

ACKNOWLEDGEMENTS

The creation of this book was a collaborative effort involving many people. Its inspiration grew out of a leadership-brainstorming session held at the National Center of Shinji Shumeikai of America in Pasadena, California in November of 2001. The project coordinator was Atsushi Fujimaki. The main authors were Roy Gibbon and Atsushi Fujimaki. Gerard Rohlfing wrote the brief biography of Meishusama, and Sensei Koichi Deguchi provided valuable assistance with the chapter concerning Natural Agriculture.

We wish to thank Sensei Eugene Imai, Director of Shinji Shumeikai's International Department and Shumei America, and Sensei Alan Imai, Director of Shumei International Institute, for their guiding vision and assistance. The following people helped us with comments, critiques, and suggestions: Kenji Ban, Rod Barker, George Bedell, William Blake, Carole Buchannon, Bibi Chapman, Adrian Chatman, Robbie Christianson, Alice Cunningham, Marion Deland, Chuck Easter, Sharon Franquemont, Sensei Chisako Fukushima, Stephanie Gudeman, Akira Hashiguchi, Ron Helgesen, Michwel Heril, William Howell, Dr. Diana Jerkins, Olya Keeny, François Kuwata, Steven McCord, The Very Rev. James Parks Morton, Cathy Oida, Jody Pappas, Lothar Rapior, Don Riedel, Renee Ronnie, Mary Ann Scott, Sheila Shaw, Marty Shimomura, Sandra Snyder-Traverso, Linda Tan, Elizabeth Torres, Jan Totten, Linda Whitaker, and Shigeyuki Yamakata. We also received suggestions, encouragement, and support from numerous other friends, members of Shinji Shumeikai, and the staff of the National Center in Pasadena. For all their kind help we are deeply grateful.

Our special thanks go to Tokiko Jinta for her wonderful diagrams, to Yasushi Fujimoto for his beautiful illustrations, to Hiroyuki (Max) Kondo for his assistance with the layout, and to Nova Brown and Chuck Surface for their excellent editorial assistance.

Finally, we express our appreciation to Kaicho-Sensei (Ms Hiroko Koyama), President of Shinji Shumeikai, for her continuous support and encouragement. It is because of her recognition of the need for this publication, that we were able to finish this book.

Most importantly, it is with gratitude and joy that we dedicate this book to Meishusama, our source of inspiration, wisdom, and Light.

ABBREVIATIONS

Most of the quotes in this book are taken from two publications by Shumei America Publications: *A Hundred Teachings of Meishusama* and *Miakarishu (A Collection of Light)*. Also two other publications by Shinji Shumeikai, whose English titles are *Kannon's Way* and *Natural Agriculture Teachings of Meishusama*, are also frequently used as sources of quotes. (These two books are currently in the process of being translated into English.) These four titles are abbreviated as follows:

HT: A Hundred Teachings of Meishusama

MK: Miakarishu (A Collection of Light)

KW: Kannon's Way

NA: Natural Agriculture Teachings of Meishusama

1 MEISHUSAMA

Introduction

If we want to establish eternal peace on this earth of ours, we must first eliminate the feeling of discomfort from each individual and replace it with a feeling of ease and comfort. Everybody who has this feeling of comfort will loathe war and love peace. This is an indisputable and certain fact.
    – The Three Great Disasters and the Three Lesser Disasters. HT

A general sense of isolation, meaninglessness, and despair seems to pervade our times. For too many of us, life is full of tension and struggle. Despite all the modern conveniences and mass entertainment available, many of us are still left feeling empty and inwardly impoverished. There is an old saying that "money doesn't buy happiness," and this could also be said for many of the other luxuries of our post-industrial civilization.

Everybody wants happiness, but it is not always so easy to be so. People pursue happiness in many ways—including relationships, entertainment, health, wealth, and status, to name a few. Searching for happiness outwardly may distract us from our inner pain, but does not make us truly happy. Looking deeper into the subject, one might ask, "What exactly is true happiness, and how can we attain it in a meaningful, satisfying, and lasting way?"

Happiness is not a superficial mood or attitude, but is a state of being derived from our spiritual condition and the quality of our soul. It is a sense of joy, satisfaction, and well-being that permeates our life independently of changing circumstances and events. After we have found such happiness, it is quite natural for it to spill over into the various activities and relationships in our lives. Now, instead of looking for happiness, we begin to radiate it wherever we go.

The promotion of this true happiness was the fundamental concern of a man called "Meishusama," an honorary title that means "Master of Light," and by extension is the purpose of this book, as it introduces his teachings and prescribed activities.

Meishusama was born with the name Mokichi Okada in the late nineteenth-century Japan, and rose up from abject poverty to help millions of people attain greater health, happiness, and fulfillment in their lives. After enduring numerous painful illnesses and personal tragedies, as well as unjustified governmental persecution, he eventually emerged as one of the most dynamic spiritual leaders in modern times. Not only did Meishusama receive an invaluable spiritual blessing from God that allowed him to attain personal health and happiness, but he also found ways to share this blessing with people around the world. How was this done? What was his secret, and how is it relevant today, half a century after his passing?

Meishusama was one of the most prolific writers of twentieth century Japan. Beginning in the 1930's, he wrote extensively—creating books as well as magazine and newspaper articles. Many of his lectures were also transcribed into print. He created thousands of Japanese traditional-style poems and also left writings on various subjects estimated to comprise over nine thousand pages. His works, which were abundantly produced mostly during the ten years from the end of World War II to his passing in 1955, relate to almost every field of human endeavor, and they exemplify his spiritual insight, compassion, knowledge, and down-to-earth pragmatism.

Meishusama's personal will was surrendered to a higher power, the very power that created the universe in all its beauty, variety, and splendor. People have given this power many names, such as God, Allah, the Great Spirit, Brahman, Divine Mother, the Tao, and many others. What is important here was Meishusama's relationship to this divine source and the effect it had on his character and behavior. He was a remarkable person who seemed to deeply affect everyone who came into contact with him. Like many of the great humanitarians of the last century, he worked tirelessly and at great personal sacrifice to serve the society around him. The more he relinquished personal gain, the more he became filled with a profound, luminous energy that he was able to use to alleviate the suffering of others. By simply raising his hand toward someone, he could help that individual feel energized and healed.

Meishusama called this energy "Jyorei," which means "purification of the spirit." Not only was it powerful and profound, but this ability to heal could also be transferred to others. An increasingly large number of people have now dedicated themselves to assisting Meishusama in his mission to heal and transform the world. Through this miraculous power, numerous people from diverse backgrounds have been healed of painful ailments and incurable diseases. These miracles served to awaken many people to the power of God and were instrumental in inspiring them to redirect their lives towards serving others.

Many of Meishusama's followers considered him to be a divine manifestation of God in this world. Some saw him as the prophet of an approaching new age of universal salvation. He was graced with highly developed psychic perception and spiritual awareness which allowed him to see into the spiritual world and then describe what he saw there. He was also able to discern the inner principles and structures of the universe, the spiritual conditions of individuals, and the nature of divinity itself. Miracles followed wherever he went. He was continuously engaged in curing people and inspiring them to awaken to the spiritual dimension in life. Amidst all of this, he remained a man of easy humor and gentle kindness. Despite great persecution and endless demands on his time, he still managed to enjoy the simple things in life. It was not unusual to find him arranging flowers in his room, gazing at the clouds in the sky, laughing with friends, or catching the latest movie or concert.

His followers included people from all walks of life. Some were shopkeepers, students, farmers, office-workers, and ordinary housewives whom he helped to find a new purpose in life—to work for the betterment of humanity.

More and more I give my life to serving people and the world. – God's Love. MK

Biography

Early Life

The man who in later years would bear the honorary title "Meishusama" (Master of Light) was born Mokichi Okada in a crowded slum area of old Tokyo in 1882. It was during the time of Japan's most drastic modernization, following a long period of feudalism.

As a boy, Mokichi was always lymphatic and sickly, forever coming down with some new ailment. In spite of this, he persevered in his studies and graduated from middle school with an outstanding record and a passion for artistic creation. At age 14, with the dream of becoming an artist, he began a preparatory course at what is now the Tokyo National University of Fine Arts and Music. Amidst the ongoing storm of Westernization, this school was the first to place a special emphasis on the traditional expanse of Japanese and Eastern arts in which he had a strong interest.

Illness

But his dream was not to be. Barely six months into his new life, he encountered sudden eye pains and bleary vision. The famous eye specialists he consulted tried everything they knew, scratched their heads, and threw up their hands. Nothing worked; the infection would have its way. Young Okada—Meishusama—would have to face the future with the vision of his right eye greatly impaired. It was a crushing blow. In the context of the times, no one in the fine arts field could conceive of an artist with such a handicap. This meant he would no longer be acceptable at the university. With heavy heart, Meishusama abandoned forever his dream of becoming an artist.

There was more to follow. First came stabbing pains in his side—the onset of pleurisy. "At the university hospital sanatorium," he wrote, "my lungs became a wellspring, yielding nearly seven ounces of water!" He suffered with the illness for six months, and in spite of every known medication, it made a nasty comeback a year later. The final prognosis was dire. He was just 18 when a famous medical expert confirmed that he now had advanced pulmonary tuberculosis. This was a death sentence; the disease was then considered incurable.

Meishusama was despondent, but he refused to give up. After several years of searching for the right medication, he finally decided to try natural means, a strict natural diet. The result exceeded all expectations. "I had learned a certain tenacity," he later noted, "and this, combined with a change to a vegetarian diet, enabled me to throw off the TB."

Still fired by the love of beautiful things, he took up the study of fine Japanese lacquerworks and developed skill in the art of lacquer inlay. It was his hope to enter the antique and curio business in partnership with his father, but in May of 1905 fate intervened with the elder Okada's untimely death.

Business

Later that same year, Meishusama at age 22 overcame his deep sorrow and took an important step, entering the world of business on his own. With his mother's guidance and a modest inheritance from his father, he acquired a small sundry-goods store in Tokyo, naming it "Korin-do" in honor of a great artist he admired. Early in his business career he faced another test of fortitude—a permanent injury to his right index finger, the one he needed to apply fine gold-dust veneers to his artistic inlays. From that time on, he was forced to rely on others for the needed handwork to bring his lacquerware designs into being.

Nonetheless, his success was such that by 1907 he was inspired to enter the wholesale field. To gain more space for the venture, he remodeled the house in which his family was then living, just behind Tokyo Station. In February of that year, his new Okada Enterprises store, specializing in traditional artistic handicrafts for women, threw open its doors to the wholesale trade. Here Meishusama's feeling for beauty and his background in painting and lacquer inlay began to pay rich dividends. His original designs won many prizes in exhibitions, and word began to get around. In June of the same year, he took a wife named Taka. Their glow of happiness may have helped to promote business; at any rate, Okada Enterprises quickly became a leader in the world of fashion.

Meishusama's life now seemed complete, but in terms of health, he paid a high price. With all the work, he was seized by a chronic cerebral anemia so severe that even the noise of a passing streetcar made him faint and dizzy. At last he found relief in moxibustion treatments combined with exercise and long daily walks through the city streets.

Following his mother's death in 1912, Meishusama continued to push ahead in the wholesale field and soon reached the pinnacle of success. By this time he was hiring numerous employees, and he was known for treating them well, earning their loyalty and inspiring them to give excellent service.

More Sickness and Pain

Still sickness never ceased to dog him. Tonsillitis, stomach problems, rheumatism, neurasthenia, intestinal catarrh, valvular heart disease, scabies . . . it seemed he was going through the entire Medical Encyclopedia. Once he came down with severe typhoid, spent three months in the hospital, and at one point actually made out his will. Throughout his career, he was hospitalized three times and twice heard the doctors say he would die. Yet somehow his natural optimism always pulled him through.

Compared to everything else, a toothache might seem hardly worth mention, but when Meishusama faced this problem beginning in 1914, it almost drove him mad. Four teeth at once were screaming in agony. He tried all kinds of medicines, but all through the next year and into 1916, the pain just got worse. At times he even thought of suicide. When an acquaintance suggested a religious healer, he desperately stopped all his medications and consulted the man, though without much faith in the outcome. In a few days he began to feel better and was struck by a realization: the medications he'd been taking for pain were the actual cause of much worse pain. This gave him his initial insight into the possible side effects of modern medicine.

Despite his painful affliction, during this same period he created the beautiful *Asahi Daiya* (Morning-Sun diamond)—the sparkling artificial gemstone that earned patents in many countries and became one of the most fashionable jewelry items of the day in Japan.

Personal Tragedies

All through his youth, Meishusama's passions had flared when he heard of wrongdoing by politicians and others in responsible positions. His soul still burned with the desire to rid society of evil. At length he decided to start his own newspaper and use the power of the press to rectify injustices. Emboldened by his business success, he founded a finance company to raise the funds he would need. It was terrible timing. In the spring of 1919, following World War I, a floundering economy and the failure of his main bank left him deeply in debt, at the mercy of creditors. He tried desperately to save his wholesale business by incorporating it, but his efforts crumbled in the great market panic of March, 1920. About nine months earlier, he had also met with extreme personal tragedy. Taka, his wife of nearly twelve years, died of typhoid fever contracted during pregnancy. Their prematurely born baby could not be saved.

Spiritual Quest

At one time religion had appealed to Meishusama. "When I was young," he wrote, "I was so afire with love for the human race that I just wanted to become a man of religion and help the world." But as he got older, though his love for humanity never changed, he had come to consider religion pretty much a waste of time, and even thought of himself as an atheist. Now, however, at age 37, he was suddenly no longer sure of anything. Racked by the pain of his losses, he reached out for the only help that remained. There was nothing to captivate him in the established religions, but he was curious about Oomoto, a Shinto-related faith that was then growing in popularity. Often in those days he would stop by the Oomoto Tokyo center, taking time for meditation and learning to pray. Gradually he found solace and the courage to continue.

Early in this time of seeking, Meishusama also found consolation in a new marriage. For the next few years, buoyed by his natural optimism, he managed to keep his store afloat, eking out a daily existence for himself and his new bride. Then came a stunning shock—the giant Kanto earthquake of 1923, the most massive quake in Japanese history. Perhaps 100,000 people died, and much of the city was destroyed. To the small Okada store behind Tokyo Station, it was a near fatal blow.

By this time, distracted by all the pressures of business, Meishusama had entirely lost touch with Oomoto. But now he could no longer ignore what Life was telling him. As he noted later, "There was nothing left to do but return to God."

Setting his misfortunes behind him, he rejoined Oomoto and began devoting long hours each day to an ancient form of meditation, seeking to refine his soul, explore the spiritual world, and to obtain oneness with a great force that he began to sense all around him. His dream of reforming things by starting a newspaper had been a delusion, he realized. The only way to build a more perfect society was through universal spiritual awakening.

Over the next three years, his personal warmth and dedication to helping others won him many friends, and he rose rapidly in esteem at Oomoto. With joy, he realized that just through the power of prayer he could be a genuine help to those suffering from illness. Then came an event that was to put his entire life in a new perspective.

Words from Above

It happened one night when he was at home. As he later wrote, "It was about midnight on a night in December of 1926 that I cannot forget. The strangest feeling I have ever experienced rose in my heart. It was a most peaceful feeling, yet it urged me to speak something out loud. I couldn't stop the words from coming. I was taken over by an irresistible force. The first words out of my mouth were, 'Get paper and brush ready.' I asked my wife for her help. From then on there came unbelievable words."

Yoshi, his wife, hurried to get writing implements and began taking down his expositions, which continued page after page, and then day after day, week after week.

For three months the flood of words went on, laying bare the history of Japan and the entire world, and foretelling a great transition from the Age of Darkness to the Age of Light. The purpose of all Creation and mankind's divine mission were clearly set forth. God and man were to work as a team in building Paradise on Earth, creating a world of truth, virtue and beauty. But first would come worldwide catastrophe unless humanity could reform its ways, disperse negative clouds, and clear the way for higher spiritual vibrations in every field of endeavor.

Kannon

Meishusama had grown up respecting but not really accepting the traditional Japanese concept of Kannon, the Buddhist deity of compassion who could manifest in human form. Lately, though, in his meditations he had begun to sense Kannon becoming one with him; and now, as he spoke his prophecies, he could actually feel this deity directing what he said. But the words transmitted were not those of Kannon. The Buddhist deity was only serving as a messenger—a messenger who would at least be familiar to Meishusama. The words were clearly those of one single, universal God—the God of All.

At the time, the concept of such a single, universal God—the One Supreme Source and Creator of All, omnipotent and everywhere present—was still not entirely real to Meishusama. This idea played no great role in either of the two main religions he'd known from childhood, Shinto and Buddhism, and even in Oomoto there were several other prominent gods said to be aspects of the whole. Moreover, though he had made generous contributions to the Japanese Salvation Army, he didn't do it because of Christianity, but only because the organization did good things for humanity. Now, however, staggering as it was, he could not deny the truth of what he had experienced. Later he would write, "That was the beginning of many spontaneous revelations that were beyond my normal perception. It seemed that whatever I wanted to know would be revealed to me. Yes, for sure God exists. He is very close. No, He must be within me. This was extraordinary!"

Gradually over time he came to understand that God was indeed real and was present inside his very being. The force he had felt in operation was the God-force, and God had given him an overwhelming mission—to inform the entire world of the truth, help disperse all humanity's negative clouds, and to demonstrate God's love by healing the sick. On February 4, 1928, having resolved to devote himself entirely to spiritual work, he gave all that remained of his business into the hands of his loyal employees.

Healing

In Meishusama's heart, the joy of healing others was now strongly reinforced. He had been depending on prayer alone, but from this point on, he worked to develop and refine his own original method of healing. From his untiring spiritual research and his own history of suffering came the realization that what we call sickness is really purification, the body's way of eliminating toxins. The key to healing, he perceived, is not medicine, but Light—clear spiritual Light, brought in to cleanse the human spirit of negative clouds, helping the body rid itself of its toxins.

Increasingly, his family members, friends, acquaintances, and everyone who came to him for help began witnessing cures that could only be described as miraculous. Even people who were seriously ill got well, even those diagnosed as incurable. At the same time, he became aware of a mysterious sphere of light that had come to dwell inside him: a sphere of divine light in his abdomen, able to control his very thoughts and words and actions.

Before long, the sheer effectiveness of his healings, together with his growing body of followers, made him an influential figure in Oomoto. Everyone agreed he was a wonderful person to be around, a man who had fun doing things, enjoyed life to the fullest, and who always spread happiness even in trying times. His laugh was infectious, the kind that makes everything seem funnier to others. He was always fair, never judgmental—a man of action who could give firm reprimands when deserved, but always with the aim of helping, always with consideration of the other's feelings. In short, he was loved and respected by all. It is not surprising that in 1929 Oomoto advanced him to executive status, making him a regular member of the standing committee at their Tokyo headquarters and putting him in charge of his own Tokyo center, where he began conducting regular healing services.

In those days, Meishusama's personal life was still haunted by the past. His meals at home were meager, at best, and he was hounded by creditors, his possessions constantly impounded. Still he faced the future with his usual optimistic good cheer. "Don't worry," he told one visitor, "My finances will be abundantly blessed."

After work, he especially enjoyed going to the movies and other entertainments. He was fond of Western-made films, and would often take time off from his busy schedule to see them. It was then considered daring for husband and wife to go out together, but to Meishusama, it was simply the way things should be. He loved to enjoy music, drama, and the whole atmosphere of the theater with his wife by his side. Meanwhile, his spiritual studies were going well, and there were small but helpful donations from his healing work. Often he went out to give treatments to those who couldn't travel, and when the need was extreme, he would take people into his own home.

Divine Revelation

Then it was 1931, and momentous events were in the air. It was the year Japan began its campaign of aggression by invading Manchuria. On June 15, guided by some inner calling, Meishusama led about thirty of his followers to the top of Mt. Nokogiri, across the Bay from Tokyo, to conduct a sunrise prayer ceremony. As the morning mists parted, he was overwhelmed by a great vision. The events previously foretold in his spoken revelation now appeared before his eyes. He witnessed the great transformation of the world as part of an ongoing universal cycle. It was shown to him that the conversion from Night to Day had already occurred in the spiritual world, and would inevitably follow in the physical. But first would come a time of earthly cataclysm and great tribulation.

Meishusama came down from the mountain that day with the realization that his divine mission had now become imperative. The time was coming when he must extend his Divine Light healings to the general public, inform the world of God's Plan, and bring spiritual cleansing to all humanity.

For the next several years, he engaged in intensive spiritual studies, seeking to enhance his method of healing and map out plans for the future. Finally he felt ready. On May 1, 1934, in Tokyo's Kojimachi Ward, he opened a small clinic named "Ojindo." This marked the first official public appearance of the Divine Light treatment later known as Jyorei. The high number of recipients who returned to express their gratitude testifies to the effectiveness of these healings.

Initially, to fend off suspicions by the wartime government, he presented the new treatment as "Okada-style Spiritual Acupressure Therapy," with Light being directed into toxified areas of the body through touch. He would later refine the method several times.

Time of Decision

The police in those days had thought-control as one of their official functions. Unfortunately, they also despised religions, and Oomoto's popularity made it their likely number-one target. But equally disturbing to Meishusama was an inflexible atmosphere growing within Oomoto itself, arising partly in reaction to the militaristic regime of the time. In this environment, the more independence Meishusama showed in following his inner guidance, the more he faced extremist opposition from within the organization. By 1934, the chaotic yet rigid mood in Oomoto, the instability within the leadership, and the surrounding social turmoil had all reached a peak. Meishusama felt this was a sign for him to move on. In the fall of that year he sent a letter resigning his executive membership and withdrawing completely from the organization. The following year, all those in Oomoto leadership positions were arrested for "violations of the Public Order Act" and "contempt of the Emperor," and it was ordered that the organization be dissolved. All the accused would later be found innocent, but until the impending Pacific War had almost run its course, most remained in prison, and some faced torture, were executed, or died from debilitation.

Kannon Society

Meanwhile, treatments at the new Ojindo clinic attracted so many people that within eight months, Meishusama had to seek larger quarters. As a temporary measure, on the first day of January, 1935, he moved his practice to the now-unoccupied Oomoto center that he had headed a few months earlier. Here he founded a spiritual organization of his own, naming it the Kannon Society of Japan (Dai-nihon Kannon Kai). Most of its original members had been followers of his at Oomoto. Within the first year, their numbers had grown to 600, and eleven branch offices were flourishing throughout Japan.

At first, Meishusama's public resignation from Oomoto was enough to satisfy Japanese officialdom. He was allowed to go on mixing spiritual healing and religion under the watchful eyes of the police. Inevitably, though, as his new organization grew, it encountered increasing police harassment. All its publications were eventually banned, and there was pressure from opponents to have it dissolved.

The storm signals were ominous, but Meishusama held firm to his purpose, the construction of Paradise on Earth. The wheels of progress he set in motion at the Kannon Society were basically two. First were his own presentations, which centered on the "Kannon Lectures" dealing with his many revelations.

Ohikari

His other wheel of progress at the Kannon Society was something entirely new—the ohikari (then called omamori), a small parchment bearing his calligraphy and worn about the neck. In his personal healings, dating back to 1929, Meishusama had been using a white fan or *mite-shiro* on which his calligraphy or hand prints were inscribed. Now, in his continuing revelations, it had come to him that this new invention, the ohikari, would enable others to heal by Divine Light, much as he did.

At first Meishusama gave ohikaris only to thirteen of his close disciples. Then, at the Spring Grand Sampai in 1935, he made a far-reaching announcement: from that time on, anyone would be able to receive an ohikari and give Divine Light healings. He knew that, despite the efforts of other great religious teachers, the world was still in dire need of being saved. By teaching his followers the joy of spreading Divine Light to make others happy, he aimed to set in motion an exponential wave that would progressively rise to envelop and transform the entire world.

Meanwhile his organization continued to grow, making it essential to find a good permanent meeting place. With help from his followers, he was able to acquire a mansion with spacious grounds above the Tamagawa River on Tokyo's west side. The official opening at the Tamagawa Grounds was held on October 10, 1935. Near the mansion, which was later named Hozan-so, Meishusama built a dwelling place for himself and his family, now including six children.

Farming

Often at his new location, Meishusama could be seen directing work in the spacious garden area, showing his young helpers how to plant tea bushes, fruit trees, vegetables, and flowers, or how to channel water to the rice paddy. He was seldom at rest, and he didn't mind getting himself all muddy wielding a shovel, wanting always to set a good example instead of just issuing orders.

The poor farm villagers of that era had been weighing heavily on his mind, the tenant farmers who were suffering so terribly. The weather for several years had been abnormally cold, causing many crop failures. When he first realized this, he wasted no time in educating himself and beginning his own experiments. Chemical methods were then new, and at first they looked like the answer, but experience taught him that chemicals only ruined the soil, and pesticides just bred stronger insects. He tried to point this out in his publications, but most of the public just jeered, few would listen.

After many trials and many failures, Meishusama found he got the best results by using natural methods exclusively. No chemicals whatsoever, no pesticides, no fertilizers of any kind—nothing except natural compost to keep the soil loose and warm and moist. The soil itself was the key; along with nature's supply of nitrogen, it was the only fertilizer needed. There had to be love and respect for its spiritual nature, and understanding of its biochemical balance. Fresh soil, if needed, could be mixed in to restore the vitality.

One evening when his produce appeared on the family dinner table, Meishusama announced with pride, "I grew this with Natural Agriculture. What do you think? It's tasty, no?" He had to be pleased with the results of his labor. Crops grown using his Natural Agriculture method were tastier and of better quality, with more reliable harvests under varying weather conditions. And meanwhile the soil itself did not get depleted. Today Meishusama's Natural Agriculture techniques have silenced early critics and are winning increased recognition as the wave of the future.

Persecution

Nineteen Thirty-six, the year after his move to Tamagawa, saw the beginning of a long persecution. In August of that year, Meishusama underwent a police "questioning" that involved threats and torture. Shortly thereafter he was jailed for eleven days and his practice banned. At length, thanks to various public petitions, he was given a choice: he could operate either a religion or a treatment center, but not both. In 1937, just before his 55th birthday, Meishusama made his decision known: from then on, he would confine himself solely to giving treatments.

Despite his acquiescence, three years later he was charged with a minor violation of medical law and again thrown into jail. Enough was enough. Worn out, anyway, from treating scores of people every day, Meishusama announced his retirement. He returned to Hozan-so, where he limited himself to training "therapists" who were actually spiritual leaders, disciples. "I am stepping up," he told his followers. "From now on, the healing work is up to you."

But the very next year, fate played a hand. A number of prominent cabinet ministers, generals, admirals, and businessmen who had heard of his healings began visiting Meishusama, asking for his help. The police were stymied; all they could do was relax their restrictions. Meishusama was again free to give healings.

He had won a limited victory, but the climate of oppression in Japan still remained. Until the war ended in 1945, his organization had little chance to grow. In the meantime, he led a quiet life at Hozan-so, painting, doing calligraphy, writing, and conducting a poetry club with his followers. He still took daily walks, never complained, and always talked cheerfully of his projects and plans for the future.

War and Peace

From the start of the Pacific War in 1941, Meishusama had known that Japan was morally wrong and had no chance of winning. Looking ahead, he saw that after the war he would need a larger home for his organization, a place where it could grow and fulfill its promise. Meanwhile, the threat of bombing raids on Tokyo meant that Hozan-so was no longer a safe place for his family and his followers. He conducted a search and managed in 1944 to acquire two attractive properties. One was at Hakone, a mountain resort about sixty miles west of Tokyo. The other was a scenic villa at Atami, a small bayside city seventy miles southwest. He visualized these properties transformed into miniature paradises, one for summer residency, the other for winter. In May of that year he took his family to safety at Hakone and commenced his project to create twin models for Paradise on Earth.

Following his move, Meishusama took on the monumental task of supervising the entire construction process at both new locations. Each day he made an extensive tour of the site where he was staying. To the workmen, both volunteer and professional, he gave instructions that took in every building site, every garden, every tree, plant and rock on the grounds. He also designed a number of the buildings himself, including the new Hakone Hall of Worship, as well as Sunshine Hall at Atami, and the beautiful Crystal House.

In the wake of Japan's surrender in 1945, Meishusama faced a climate of fear in which he sought to be a stabilizing influence. He saw himself and everyone as citizens of the world, and viewed Japan's defeat as a rightful return for its treatment of other countries. True victory for anyone, he believed, could only come about with the realization of an ideal world for everyone. Toward that end he worked with renewed vigor. Along with all his other postwar responsibilities, he found time to write voluminously. Today his works fill over thirty volumes embracing every major field—religion, civilization, natural agriculture, healing, and the arts—including several thousand of his own hymns and poetry. He also wrote hundreds upon hundreds of articles for newsletters and other periodicals.

In 1947, Japan finally ratified a new national constitution that guaranteed freedom of religion and speech. Able at last to expand, within a few years Meishusama's organization grew to become one of Japan's most important cultural and spiritual groups.

Art

Shortly before his move to Hakone in 1944, stirred by an old love, Meishusama had begun a serious endeavor to collect objects of art. The times were particularly favorable; the market was blessed with a profusion of lofty art treasures at down-to-earth prices. Over time, his purchases would become the foundation of a collection such as the Japanese art world had never seen.

At first he bought fine arts just for his own enjoyment. But whenever he found a wonderful art object, he could not fully enjoy it all by himself. Instead, he wanted to share the pleasure with as many people as possible, so they could be happy, too. This had always been true of him. As he once wrote, "I am constantly thinking of how others can be made happy and more fortunate . . . . This way of thinking constitutes one underlying reason that I am a man of happiness and good fortune. And it is because of this that I say, 'If you do not make others happy, you can never be happy yourself.' "

In addition to this, he was now convinced that the love of beautiful things was a necessary touchstone for changing the human heart. Education, religion, and morals were all fine, but not in themselves sufficient. What was needed to create a beautiful society was more love of beauty in the lives of everyone.

To expand his already prolific studies in fine arts, Meishusama kept busy from dawn to the wee hours scanning textbooks and design manuals, going to exhibitions, and quizzing the leading experts. Year by year, he absorbed fields of art that would normally require decades to master. In an amazingly short time, he had become one of the recognized authorities, with a true sixth sense for telling genuine masterpieces from secondary works and forgeries.

In those days, besides Art, Jyorei, and Natural Agriculture, Meishusama was also promoting efforts to "turn society into a paradise through flowers." Since his youth, he had always enjoyed cultivating and arranging flowers, and planting them wherever he could. Now he grew and distributed them widely, encouraging their display in homes and public places, in stores, offices, and plazas. His aim was to uplift and refresh all classes of people, creating a society based on beauty.

Oneness

In May of 1950, recurring troubles with the authorities brought Meishusama to an incredible spiritual climax. The police in Atami, suspicious of his growing success, first ransacked his home and then, though they found nothing, decided to throw him into prison anyway. At age 67, he found himself subjected to torturous daily questionings that left him exhausted and debilitated. After sixteen days of this, he developed a severe pain in his stomach that would not go away. The next morning he woke from a wonderful dream in which he found himself entering a beautiful palatial building high atop Mt. Fuji. Knowing that dreams of Fuji are traditionally good omens, he felt a sense of joyful anticipation. That pain in his stomach—could it not be a purification to advance God's work?

The following day was June 15, the anniversary of his revelation on Mt. Nokogiri. He recognized then that his stomach pain was in fact related to the divine sphere of light in his solar plexus. The purification he was undergoing was nothing less than the final stage of his unification with God.

Some time later, after his innocence was established by the courts, he wrote that ever since his dream of Mt. Fuji, he no longer had to ask God for answers when people sought help; he simply knew the answers even before he was asked. He was entirely One with the sphere of divine light that was within him.

Museum

As that memorable year of 1950 drew to a close, Meishusama was taken by a new idea springing from his passion for beauty. Why not enhance society by making great works of art more accessible to the public? A corner site at the Hakone miniature paradise project was about to be vacated. He wanted to build something special there, to cap the project in an ideal way. Why not a museum?

It was the perfect solution—a place where everyone, of whatever social class, could come to experience beauty and find spiritual refreshment. The cost did seem prohibitive, but after discussing the matter with a loyal fund-raiser, Meishusama moved ahead, trusting in God. Work on his dream museum began in October of 1951. The necessary funds flowed in precisely as they were needed, and the work proceeded with record speed. On June 15, 1952—barely eight and a half months after construction began—members gathered for the dedication of the new Hakone Art Museum and also the rest of the Hakone miniature paradise.

Meishusama had designed the museum himself, playing the role of architect and supervising every part of the project: the unique modern building with its stately Oriental roof, the innovative interior, all the facilities, even the placement of the art objects and every rock, tree, and flower outside in the beautiful Japanese garden. It was the first museum in Japan to be open to the general public at all times. "I keenly believe," Meishusama wrote, "that wonderful art works should not be secluded, but should instead be shown to as many people as possible . . . . In this way, fine arts contribute greatly to the development of culture, and this is the true purpose of art."

Although now past 70, Meishusama continued to oversee the daily efforts of his organization. Often he directed work in the garden at Atami or showed guests through the Hakone Museum. His habits had not changed with the years. Even when tired, he kept up a full schedule, seldom wasting a moment and often getting two things done at once. When out walking, he was apt to be followed by an attendant with a portable radio so he could keep up with world affairs. In the evening, he had the daily news read to him while he studied art books, wrote letters, or did calligraphy.

In those days he also made some seven tours of western Japan, inspecting construction of yet another of his earthly paradises, the villa *Heian-kyo* in Kyoto, while also visiting certain other religious sites, giving a few public speeches, and steadfastly searching out fine arts for the Hakone collection. To the end of his life, he remained devoted to gathering masterworks for public enjoyment and the betterment of society. Shortly before his passing, he acquired the Wisteria Vase, one of Japan's national treasures, even at the cost of giving up Hozan-so, his beloved home and former headquarters in Tokyo.

Taking Leave

In mid-April of 1954, on his final tour, Meishusama made an unpublicized personal visit to a group of his followers headed by Kaishusama (see page 262) at their new sanctuary in Kyoto. This was a rare event; such personal visits were not at all his custom. In previous times, he had given the group its name *Shumei*, and had specified for them the method of directing Jyorei light to two key locations on the recipient's head: the forehead and the crown.

A short time after his visit to the Kyoto sanctuary, he fell ill. But still he remained in charge of things, directing activities from his bed and rising for important occasions. Few among his followers thought to be concerned.

June 15 was the day of the Revelation Ceremony, commemorating his ascent of Mt. Nokogiri. This marked the beginning of a mysterious change in Meishusama. To everyone's surprise, he appeared at the ceremony in formal attire, his kimono, robe, and cloak all in white. This was totally unlike him; he disliked formality and usually dressed in the casual mode. Again at his birthday celebration in December and at the 1955 New Year's service he appeared dressed formally, all in white. And just ahead lay more surprises.

As a rule, the spring celebration on February 4 was attended only by Senseis. But in 1955, invitations went out to everyone. The members assembled not knowing what to expect. They were amazed to see Meishusama garbed all in golden yellow. It was the divine color of the spiritual realm—the color traditionally reserved for royalty. Normally, no one else in Japan would ever dream of wearing it. In his brief speech that day, Meishusama gave no explanation, nothing to link his attire with what was to come. All he said was that everyone should be prepared for something unusual.

A few days later—at 3:33 in the afternoon of February 10, at Atami—Meishusama, age 72, departed from this physical world.

Firm and compassionate as always, he had given his mission into the keeping of his followers.

In his reminiscences of Meishusama, Shuten Oishi, director of an interfaith organization to help new religions, wrote: "Of all the religious founders that I met . . . he is the one who had a truly special way with people . . . . You never felt that he was trying to *show* his sensitivity and be considerate, but his considerateness nonetheless extended to the smallest particulars . . . . When I think about him now, I feel that his personality was a true manifestation of universal love."

Three Prescribed Activities

Most significant of Meishusama's many contributions were the three main practices he advocated. Foremost is the practice of Jyorei, a form of spiritual healing that promotes inner purification and spiritual growth. Through his empowerments and blessings, great numbers of people were helped to improve their lives and to find a deeper sense of happiness.

Secondly, he developed Natural Agriculture, a spiritually based form of farming that does not use any chemicals or fertilizer. For people to stay healthy, he stressed, it is important to eat healthy food that is brimming with life force and that is free of toxic chemicals. He also felt that a return to a sacred relationship with the land and the natural world had a rejuvenating effect on the spirit.

Lastly, he promoted appreciation of the arts and encouraged people to incorporate beauty into their daily lives. According to Meishusama, beauty is a doorway into Spirit. Beauty inspires happiness and helps to balance and refine one's character. He saw beauty not as a self-indulgent luxury, as some people do, but as a natural expression of spirituality.

Key Principles

Fundamental Spiritual Laws

All of Meishusama's teachings on sickness, healing, spiritual growth, transforming the world, and the attainment of overall happiness, rest on the foundation of two spiritual laws.

The Law of Spiritual Precedence – The first principle is that the spiritual always precedes the physical in both form and events. Events originate both directly from God's will and from the conditions we have created in the spiritual world by our thoughts, words, and deeds.

The Law of Purification – The second principle is the idea that all suffering is a form of purification, the by-product of a cleansing process instigated for the purpose of eliminating unhealthy mental tendencies as well as physical toxins accumulated in the body.

Essential Inner Qualities

We can also point to various inner qualities and attitudes promoted consistently in Meishusama's teachings, all of which reflect the vantage point of a larger, more impersonal consciousness. The cultivation of any of these personal traits supports spiritual growth and is the outcome of spiritual awareness.

Gratitude – By our responding to life's experiences, both pleasant and difficult, with gratitude, our life is transformed for the better.

Love for Others – Love is an expression of Spirit, and when we recognize this Spirit within ourselves and within others, it is expressed as generosity and compassion.

Makoto – Acting with sincerity, honesty, and integrity always generates the best results, even when outer appearances may seem to indicate the contrary.

Basic Perspectives for Living

In addition to the above spiritual laws and inner qualities, one can also discern a number of general perspectives from Meishusama's teachings. The following is a brief listing of some of the more important ones:

Respect for Nature – Recognizing nature as a gift from God and responding with reverence and respect promotes unity and harmony with all of life.

Aesthetic Appreciation – Creating beauty in our environment and in our hearts uplifts our spirit, promotes social refinement, and deepens our appreciation of life.

Global View – Cultivating a broadminded point of view that appreciates variety, values each country's unique contribution, and realizes that humanity is one large family, promotes peace and harmony. This includes an awareness and concern for the global effects of our actions.

Long–term View – Anticipating the long-term effects of our actions, rather than blindly rushing towards immediate, short-term gratification, prevents unexpected problems from arising in the future.

Holistic Perspective – Recognizing that nothing exists independently, and that everything is interconnected and is part of a larger pattern, helps us to value the whole as much as the individual parts.

Pragmatic Approach – Using common sense to determine whether our preconceived ideals need changing for the sake of helping others in practical, tangible ways.

Kannon's[1] **Way** – Adapting to circumstances based on a flexible, moderate, and balanced approach to life that includes patience and tolerance, and that brings harmony to one's life.

These inner qualities and approaches to life (covered in greater detail in later chapters) are sprinkled throughout Meishusama's work, sometimes overtly, and at other times implied as a general background attitude. To understand them is important for gaining a comprehensive grasp of his teachings. They are not abstract principles within a speculative philosophy, but are spiritual qualities that can be cultivated and embodied by sincere individuals. These qualities and approaches were critical for Meishusama to realize his vision of creating Paradise on Earth, an ideal world free from poverty, sickness, and conflict.

Creating Paradise on Earth was not just an imaginary vision, but also an urgent mission for him to fulfill. Being a pragmatic realist who underwent a number of severe hardships, he did not naively believe that earthly paradise would be brought into existence by the mere passing of time. Instead, he encouraged and led people to walk a path towards achieving heavenly conditions in a practical manner. He cared about action, not words. Meishusama was a man of tireless industry who expressed his basic teachings in a variety of ways so that they could be easily understood by different kinds of readers. This is evident in all of his published works.

Philosophy only has value when it is expressed as action.

– Religious Pragmatism. HT

---

[1] Kannon is the well-known Buddhist deity of compassion popular in the East. She is known by other names in other countries, such as Kwan Yin, Chenrezig, and Avalokitesvara. Sometimes she appears as female, and at other times as male. She maintains order and harmony in the world through her wonderful ability of uniquely responding to the needs of each person and circumstance. Kannon bestows upon people the ability to live in balance and harmony. Meishusama had his own conception of this deity, whom he felt preceded and transcended Buddhism. In this book, Kannon is described as female for simplicity's sake.

Style of Communication

Although Meishusama wrote prolifically, his writings and lectures were seldom intellectual or scholastic. The qualities of adaptability, flexibility, and simplicity of Meishusama's writings and speeches can be viewed as outer expressions of his spiritual insight. Nonetheless, because of his casual and spontaneous style of communication, and the way that it varied depending on the audience or context, it can be difficult for many readers to gain a comprehensive overview of the key principles of his teachings.

Another factor influencing the understanding of Meishusama is the recognition that, in Japan, communication is usually indirect, symbolic, and suggestive, and not necessarily requiring order and structure, in contrast to the more direct, overt, and logically consistent style familiar to Westerners.

It is helpful to be aware of two important factors. First, Meishusama varied his teachings depending on his audience. He could talk philosophically to an intellectual, simply and plainly to a child, in a very down-to-earth, practical manner to an ordinary worker, or softly and gently to an elderly woman. His primary concern was how well the person in front of him understood and could benefit from his discourse. He was pragmatic by nature, and was not overly interested in devoting his time to systemizing his teachings. Truth was expressed in living, not in words. Secondly, it is important to remember that he comes out of the unfamiliar context (to Westerners) of Japanese cultural references and historical influences.

There seems to be two basic approaches to the writings of Meishusama, based on the mindset and character of the reader. One approach analyzes the teachings and looks for methodically presented explanations and well-defined terminology, oftentimes becoming confused by apparent inconsistencies and ambiguities. The other approaches the teachings sympathetically, looking for what is useful or inspiring, and tends not to be overly concerned with categorical understanding.

Japanese Cultural Background

Meishusama spoke and wrote in Japan during the first half of the twentieth century, a time of enormous social, cultural, and economic turmoil. Japan went through rapid industrialization and social dislocation, suffered great economic depression, endured a militarist government, and experienced the ravages of World War II, along with the aftermath of total defeat.

Japan itself is also quite different from Western societies, with their Judeo-Christian heritage, rational empiricism, and individuality. Japan's cultural background is strongly influenced by the religions of Shinto and Buddhism. Shinto is an ancient folk religion without any known founder, no commonly accepted holy book, and no systematically formulated doctrines. Shinto idealizes a return to simplicity and harmony with the natural world—a world imbued with spiritual presence and mystical beauty. This return to simplicity is accomplished through purification of body and spirit by participation in ritual, cleansing with water, and immersion in the silence and beauty of nature. Shinto's ideal is the principle of mutually cooperative, peaceful coexistence.

Two different forms of Buddhism have also exerted a strong influence on Japanese culture. The first depends on "self-power," whereas the second relies on "other-power." Zen Buddhism seeks deliverance from Samsara, the world of suffering, through the pursuit of silent meditation, and by utilizing the power of one's own efforts. Pure Land Buddhism and Nichiren Buddhism, on the other hand, both seek salvation through faith and divine grace, or "other-power." Pure Land differs from Nichiren in that it seeks salvation in the Pure Land to the West through devotion and prayers to Amitabha Buddha, whereas Nichiren puts its faith in the saving grace of the Lotus Sutra and also requires its followers to undergo strict moral discipline.

Shinto is concerned with achieving harmony with community, nature, and the universe, whereas Buddhism tends to be more otherworldly. Neither puts a strong emphasis on the significance of the individual, and both are concerned with achieving an immediate, direct experience for their followers that will help them in a tangible way. Eastern traditions conceive of the ultimate reality in more abstract terms than the traditional Western concept of God, which tends to be more personalized. Curiously, Meishusama would alternate between both concepts of divinity, sometimes referring to a human-like God, while at other times using more impersonal terminology such as the "spiritual world." Overall, he could easily embrace a divinity that is both the One and the many, both personal and impersonal, and that can be found equally within and without all of creation. Meishusama made great efforts to live as a "Citizen of the World," incorporating ideas and values from both the East and the West.

The emphasis on purity, healing, and nature in Meishusama's teachings can clearly be found in the Shinto tradition, while his stress on the importance of spiritual growth and salvation parallels the teachings of Buddhism. Likewise, this dream of a "Paradise on Earth" can also be found in one form or another in the Western ideals of utopian civilizations. This is not to say that Meishusama superficially borrowed from all these various traditions. Rather, the union of these principles arose naturally from the universality of his revelation.

His synthesis and expression of these and other ideals were unique and very practical. The eclectic nature of his writings was natural for a thinker born in a country with a long history of incorporating foreign elements into its culture and society.

To be effective, a teacher must speak the language of the people he is attempting to reach. What is common sense in one culture might be considered superstition in another. Our environment affects all of us, and this was true of Meishusama as well. Wanting to appeal to the people in his immediate environment, he would incorporate their familiar customs and ideas in his communication. Yet, despite the many Japanese cultural and religious influences apparent in his teachings, beneath all of these can be found universal and timeless truths.

Meishusama was a divinely inspired teacher with a mission to help suffering humanity. Although he did not hesitate to borrow certain ideas from other sources, his teachings primarily originated from his own unique mystical insights. Not only could he directly perceive the spiritual influences operating behind external events, but also where others saw division, he saw unity.

The Achievements of Meishusama

- Founder of a new kind of spiritual movement, an "umbrella" organization open to all faiths.

- Master of positive thinking, triumphant over personal illness, poverty, and persecution.

- Effective spiritual teacher and guide to many.

- Originator of Jyorei healing Light treatments; successful healer of countless recipients.

- Leader in promoting gratitude, the happiness of others, and the oneness of all humanity.

- Innovative thinker in the field of health: identified sickness as purification, and advocated natural healing instead of drugs.

- Successful business entrepreneur; inventor of the *Asahi Daiya* artificial gemstone.

- Pioneer of Natural Agriculture.

- Promoter of natural beauty and art as ways to create a beautiful society.

- A foremost art expert and prominent collector.

- Architect and builder of a major art museum.

- Author of extensive volumes of spiritual teachings, and an excellent poet.

- A man of constant high character, integrity, and wisdom—ideal candidate for Divine Revelation.

- Designer/builder of miniature earthly paradises.

- Inspired prophet of Global Transformation and Paradise on Earth.

2 FUNDAMENTAL PRINCIPLES

My writings and speeches are all attempts to explain the Truth to all mankind in the most easily understandable manner. If you read them seriously, with an open and appreciative mind, an image of the Truth will come unbidden into your heart. – The Embodiment of Truth. HT

Is there an ultimate purpose of life, or are we just idly passing time until we eventually die? Too often the explanations in response to this vital question sound like children's fables. In his teachings, Meishusama gives us a simple answer to this question. He says that the ultimate purpose of life is the spiritual growth and perfection of all of creation. Although there is divine assistance, nonetheless, each of us is responsible for our own spiritual growth and development, and all of us are encouraged to assist in perfecting the world around us. Meishusama also offers practical guidelines for realizing this universal growth and perfection.

We will first expound upon Meishusama's key ideas and principles so that you have a sufficient background to fully appreciate his more practical recommendations. What may appear linear and categorical at first will eventually emerge as part of an organic whole when we later cover the topics of Jyorei, Natural Agriculture, and Art.

Of course, as we stated earlier, Meishusama was not normally inclined to write in this structured manner. Rather, he preferred to discuss current problems affecting humankind, and in the process, interject his various suggestions, values, and ideas. In his teachings, Meishusama was always looking to encourage the best in people, and to promote spiritual awareness in them, which is the foundation of real happiness.

Spiritual Principles

Universal Flux

Everything in the universe is constantly and ceaselessly moving. This year is different from last year in all respects. . . . Everything is in flux; nothing is at rest for even an instant. – Henri Bergson. HT

Everything is constantly changing and evolving from one state or condition to another. Night changes to day, and day changes to night. Flowers germinate, grow, blossom, wilt, and then decay back into soil. The seasons change from winter to spring, summer, and fall. Even giant mountains change their shape, although at an imperceptibly slow rate. We can also see this principle of change operating in our own lives, whether by looking back at the changing circumstances of the past, or by witnessing the continuously altering thoughts occurring in our minds right now.

Looking back on our lives, what were the circumstances and conditions that we found ourselves in ten years ago? What were our relationships like then, and how are they different now? Because everything changes, the things that bring us comfort today may cause us suffering tomorrow. Family, job, home, and health—all are subject to disruption or loss. And the more we value and cling to them, the more likely we are to suffer at their loss. We do not know what will happen one year from now, let alone in ten years, but one thing is for certain, and that is that everything will change.

If we pause to observe our mind, we will notice how our thoughts are constantly moving and changing from one image or idea to another. Throughout the day, our moods may vary from contentment to anxiety, anger, grief, boredom, joy, or humor depending upon the people and circumstances that we encounter. Sometimes we may receive praise from others, and at other times criticism. Each person we encounter will tend to have a different opinion about us and will also treat us differently. The roles we play with people can range from parent to employee, sibling, spouse, enemy, or friend. Everything depends on its relationship to everything else for definition and identity, and nothing is solid, fixed, or enduring.

All things, whether mental, emotional, or physical, are subject to change.

The only thing that does not change is the process of change itself. When we come to accept this fact and learn to embrace the constancy of change, then life embraces us.

Interconnectivity

There is absolutely nothing that spiritual cords are not connected with, be it the fundamental principles of relativity, the radiations that move through space, human society, or the individual. – The Spiritual Cord. HT

Nothing exists separately from everything else in the universe. A windstorm in the Sahara Desert can dump tons of sand on Mexico, and an ice shelf dropping off the continent of Antarctica can cause a hurricane to hit Japan. Crop failure in the United States can cause famine in Africa, and a rise in the price of oil can make some rich, while making others poor. From the largest galaxies to the smallest atoms, everything is linked in numerous invisible ways. At the level of Quantum Mechanics, according to Bell's theorem, pairs of photons or electrons (two of the tiniest known particles in existence), demonstrate immediate awareness of each other despite their separation by vast distances of space. The natural sciences recognize the mutual interdependency of plants, insects, birds, and animals within a larger ecosystem. The food we eat links us to the farmers who grow the crops, with the plant kingdom from which they come, and to the earth that supports us.

Each part of our body communicates with all the other parts, from bones and organs down to nerves and cells. No part is independent of the rest, as all parts depend on each other for proper functioning. Thus, anything that affects one part affects all the rest. If one of our legs is wounded, our whole body gets sick. Similarly, when we have the flu, the fever is not located in only one organ or limb, but in our whole body, because each part is intimately connected with every other part.

We are all interconnected like pieces of an elaborate, three-dimensional jigsaw puzzle. The convex curve of one piece is the concave curve of another piece, each shape complementing the other. On a spiritual level, we are all connected to God, people, places, and things by invisible spiritual cords. These cords bind us through thoughts, feelings, and sensation, and therefore, every thought and intention we hold affects others in some manner, either subtly or strongly. If we hold positive or loving thoughts, the people around us become cheerful, whereas if we become angry or judgmental, they feel badly. Each situation and environment has innumerable influences affecting it. Nothing occurs independently of the larger context within which it exists. Concurrently, everything we do is also reflected in the greater whole. These patterns of connectivity reflect a deeper underlying Oneness that unites all of existence.

Reincarnation

Repeatedly reborn and repeatedly dying, man's spirit travels towards eternal happiness. – Life and Death. MK

Our existence does not end with the death of our physical body. After we die, our soul returns to the spiritual world where it undergoes extensive purification until finally it is ready to incarnate once again in the physical world. About this purification, Meishusama writes, "Once the soul has returned to the spiritual world, the process of purifying it begins. The amount of sin that stains the soul determines the position of the soul in the spiritual world and also the length of time it must stay there to be purified. At the shortest, the period would be a matter of years or decades, and it sometimes extends to centuries. After being purified to some extent, a spirit is again incarnated into the material world, according to the will of God, and charged with a task from Him." – *Life and Death. HT*

The human soul continues to be reborn again and again, lifetime after lifetime, each time accumulating more experience, knowledge, and wisdom along the way. In addition to this knowledge, we also carry our limited conditioning, tendencies, and habits with us into each new lifetime, creating new circumstances based on old patterns of action. Each lifetime builds upon the previous one, as the soul continues to learn valuable lessons. Oftentimes, the reason for a person behaving in a strange or compulsive way can be traced to a past life experience that left a strong impression on their soul. Physical deformities or health problems can also have their origins in past life experiences. Deep emotional bonds between people can be carried over from previous lives, often drawing these same people together again in successive incarnations.

Life is always providing us with opportunities to learn and grow. In particular, we will often end up receiving the very same type of treatment by people in this life that we gave to others in a previous life. For instance, if in previous lifetimes we helped others, were generous to the poor, or were kind to those around us, in this life we might receive assistance from others, inherit money, or attract kind friends. Conversely, if we steal from others, slander or abuse people, or betray those who trust us, these same things may later happen to us. Such reciprocity of experience helps the soul to understand what it feels like to be treated in these ways, thereby encouraging empathy and compassion for others. Over time, such experiences help the soul to grow and evolve spiritually.

To find true happiness, the soul needs to let go of self-centered attitudes and behavior, and develop greater wisdom and compassion. As the soul matures, it begins to recognize its essential Oneness with all things and all beings, and comes to discover the underlying spiritual identity that we all share in common.

Spiritual Laws

The Law of Order

Materialism says, "Body first, spirit second," spiritualism says, "Spirit first, body second." – Methods and Results. HT

Underlying the diverse sensory phenomena of the natural world are fundamental laws of order and structure that are fixed and immutable. These patterns and structures can be found in physics, biology, mathematics, the cosmos, human society, and in our ordinary day-to-day affairs. Some examples are the ten fingers and toes of humans, the hexagonal shapes within beehives, and the spiral patterns of galaxies. Others, such as higher mathematics, are invisible to the human eye.

Order is present everywhere in nature. The seasons—spring, summer, autumn, winter—follow a fixed order. Day and night follow a fixed and unvarying order. Trees and plants, without exception, grow following the same natural order. Cherry never blossoms before plum. And there are many more examples of the same kind. – *Order. HT*

Because of natural order, things fall down, rather than up; water freezes when cold, not when hot; round things roll better than square things; trees bend with the wind, not against it; and we eat when hungry, rather than when full. Each of these common sense examples points to laws of nature that rule our day-to-day lives.

As well as the above physical laws, there are also subtler laws governing human nature and society at large, although the application of these laws will vary from culture to culture. For instance, all societies need some sort of leadership, however well defined or vague, to give them structure and direction. Different countries uphold different role models for the individuals living within them. All cultures are defined by their collective customs, protocols, etiquettes, and values. And underlying these structures are universal human needs for respect, affection, and social bonding. Although customs and behavior may vary from place to place, most people can recognize genuine courtesy and politeness when they encounter it. Even social rebels who refuse to conform to a culture's norms are actually adhering to their own set of values or principles. Order exists everywhere.

To every thing there is a season, and a time to every purpose under Heaven.
– *Ecclesiastes*

There is a correct time, place, and position for everything. Sometimes these are obvious and sometimes not. Recognizing these principles and then aligning oneself with them is the key to success in the world. Such understanding also helps bring us into better harmony with the people and circumstances in our lives.

To put it precisely, the fundamental cause of failure is a lack of under-standing of proper timing. Timing is critical for deciding whether things go well or not. For instance, flowers, fruit trees, and crops have their own natural sequence to follow. If the timing is not right, even if given favorable support, they will never grow well. The bulbs buried in soil in autumn come to bloom in spring, and likewise, the seeds sown in spring grow to beautiful flowers in summer and fall. The same can be said of fruit, which we cannot eat if it is not yet ripe. By picking it at the right time, we enjoy its best flavor. As for agricultural plants, there is a proper timing for sowing and transplanting seedlings, which of course needs to accord with weather and climate.[1] – *KW*

God arranges everything with perfect timing, and we cannot do anything about this divine arrangement but just go along with it.[2]– *Meishusama*

Only an unwise person will disregard the law of gravity, and only a foolish person will ignore the fundamental principles of social order or propriety. It takes a very high level of intelligence to successfully discover new laws of physics or to invent new technologies for harnessing these laws. So, too, does it require a greater than average intelligence and maturity to successfully alter social norms. Only if a person's attempt to change things fosters greater freedom, harmony, and respect for the people affected, can it be considered successful, otherwise not. Although to some, such limitations may feel constrictive, for most of us, freedom lies in creatively adapting to the natural order, rather than in fighting it or ignoring it, and in helping to improve conditions rather than trying to escape them.

If things do not go smoothly, the underlying cause can be found in the fact that the proper order has been disturbed. This is especially true of human affairs. – *Order. HT*

Life entails a hierarchy of values, and the highest of these values is reserved for Spirit. In a descending sequence, Spirit comes first, then mind,

---

[1] Meishusama, "Wait for the Right Moment," *Shumei Magazine*, vol. 268 (March /April 2007).

[2] Meishusama, "Lecture from a Trip to the Kansai Region," *Japanese Shumei Newsletter*, no. 185 (August 1985).

and then body. In our daily lives, following this simple but essential order is a sign of wisdom, because it aligns us with the divine structure of the cosmos. That which has spiritual value is usually placed higher rather than lower, first instead of last, or to the left instead of to the right. This is because high is more exalted than low, first is more honored than last, and left is more receptive than right.

The left side is spiritual and superior; the right side is physical and inferior.
– Order. HT

It is best to give spiritual matters your top priority. In Shumei, many of us begin each day with spiritual practices (such as prayer, contemplation, chanting, or Jyorei), as this will elevate the rest of the day to a higher level. We usually begin meetings with spiritual practices (such as chanting, Jyorei, and expressing gratitude) before attending to the business at hand. Also, we place sacred objects (such as spiritual books, photos, or items that have been blessed) in elevated places of honor, as this helps us to value the inner reality that they outwardly represent.

When we honor God, we reinforce the divinity within us.

The Law of Spiritual Precedence

The basic and underlying principle of the universe is that everything that exists in the material world has the origin of its existence and activity in the spiritual world. – Natural Power. HT

The spiritual world, like the world of the mind, is a realm invisible to the senses. It is all around us, yet we cannot touch, taste, smell, see, or hear it. The spiritual world is where subtle energies coalesce into powerful forces that directly impact our lives. Although it lacks material substance, it is no less real than wood, stone, or flesh. Everything originates within the spiritual world.

Max Planck, the Nobel Prize-winning father of quantum theory, expressed similar thoughts when he said, "All matter originates and exists only by virtue of a force . . . We must assume behind this force the existence of a conscious and intelligent Mind. This Mind is the matrix of all matter."

Meishusama clarifies this truth with the following statement: "As to the nature of the spiritual world, I would sum it up in the following way: it is the world of the fusion of idea and will. That is, freedom in that world is wonderfully unhampered by the limitations of the physical body." *(Are There Ghosts? HT)*

Spirit itself is eternal and unchanging, whereas the physical is temporary and subject to change. The closer something is to pure Spirit, the greater its power to affect the physical and to create long-lasting effects in the world.

We can gauge the general proximity of something to Spirit by its corresponding distance from the physical. In other words, the more formless and insubstantial something is, the closer its association with Spirit. Therefore, conscious attention, which cannot be seen, touched, tasted, smelled, or heard, is intimately related to Spirit. This is followed by thought, which has form but lacks physical substance. Next come emotions, which, although invisible, strongly affect the body. Following this comes physical vitality, which affects the breath and overall health of the body. Finally, most distant from Spirit is the physical body, which has both physical form and material substance. Although the physical world is the aspect of our experience that is most distant from the realm of Spirit, nonetheless, along with everything else in creation, it is contained within Spirit's all pervading presence, and is thus always capable of being infused with the Light of Spirit.

> When power takes on a particular form, the more concrete and visible it becomes, the weaker that power is. Conversely, the less visible it is to the human eye, the stronger the power. This is a fundamental truth. The former kind of power can be measured in horsepower or kilograms, but the latter kind is immeasurable and infinite. – *Power. HT*

All things originate in the spiritual world. External objects do not cause things to appear but only affect what occurs in the outer world. The things of this world merely provide the necessary conditions for something to objectively manifest. Circumstances and conditions in the physical world are like the soil in which a plant grows; they provide the necessary environment for growth but are not the source of life itself. That source is Spirit. It provides the invisible spark of life that germinates the seed and causes it to grow into a fully matured plant.

What is conventionally viewed as cause and effect is, from a higher perspective, understood to be only a series of outer effects. The wind does not cause the tree to bend, nor does a bent tree cause the wind to blow. Rather, that which causes the wind to blow is also what causes the tree to bend. The wind is just a much a secondary effect of this prime mover as is the bending tree. Both phenomena arise simultaneously just as mountains appear with valleys and beaches appear with oceans. Like chickens and eggs, which came first and which came second? Although we cannot see it, the spiritual world is the source and cause of all things.

For example, someone will first have the inspiration and intention to build a house before asking a draftsman to create a blueprint. After this, if everyone is satisfied with the blueprint and drawings, the craftsmen will put physical effort into building the house, which eventually gets completed as an actual material structure within the realm of time and space. The objective world is therefore a delayed outcome of the earlier conditions that existed in the spiritual world. First comes inspiration (which we receive from Spirit); then intention; then a mental plan; then an evaluation; then action; and finally the physical result. Similarly, if a child throws a rock through a window, did the window break because of the rock, or because of the thought or emotion that motivated the act? What was the real cause of the event? What physical, mental, emotional, psychic and spiritual patterns and conditions lead to outer events? According to Meishusama, the primary cause lies in the spiritual dimension, and everything else is, at best, a secondary cause. In summary, all things are born within and then find their way into the outer world. Or, as the American transcendentalist Ralph Waldo Emerson stated, "The universe is the externalization of the soul."

Character creates destiny because it predisposes us to certain actions. Our character is made up of our thoughts, feelings, and desires, which spontaneously arise in our consciousness, largely beyond our personal control. How we interpret the conditions around us is especially significant because this determines how we respond. When we judge a situation as bad, we usually want to change it, or if we judge it as good, then we usually want to sustain it. So much of our attitudes and actions depend on our highly subjective interpretations of fairness, rights, and obligations, not to mention our personal evaluations of other people's motives and intentions.

It is surprising how many of us go through life mechanically, almost completely unaware of our true intentions. Dr. Sigmund Freud, the originator of psychoanalysis, was correct when he stated that most of us are dominated and controlled by subconscious impulses. But these impulses reach much further back in time than he realized. We are molded by our childhood conditioning as well as by tendencies carried over from previous incarnations in the distant past, and this conditioning is then stimulated by circumstances in our present day-to-day world. We may like to think that we are the captains of our own ships, but really we are controlled by numerous hidden influences. What we hold in our hearts determines our fate, and a heart corrupted by hurts, resentments, anxieties, compulsive needs, and selfish ambitions creates a world of conflict and suffering, whereas a pure heart creates a world of peace and joy. This place, from where our tendencies and thoughts emerge, is the spiritual world. Although invisible to our senses, it is actually more real than the world we see around us.

If a person thinks good thoughts and performs good deeds, he feels good inside himself because his conscience is satisfied and the pleasant thoughts from this become radiant Light. This Light goes to increase and strengthen the radiance emitted from the spiritual body. This Light is also increased from the outside, for when someone performs a good deed the gratitude and appreciation of the person he has helped become radiant Light that is transmitted to him through the spiritual cords, thus brightening his aura.
– *Spiritual Radiation and the Aura. HT*

According to Meishusama, all living things are surrounded by an aura, an ethereal substance lighter and thinner than air. It is an invisible body of Light unique to each individual. Only through special cameras using Kirilian Photography or through exceptional psychic awareness can this aura be detected. Meishusama writes, "It is a basic and true rule of the universe that auras cannot be seen by the eyes of ordinary men, but there are very occasionally people who have this ability. If, however, a normal person stills his mind and gazes intently at another person, he can perceive this person's aura to a limited extent." *(Spiritual Radiation and the Aura. HT)* The aura is an outward expression of our soul—and its brightness, thickness, and size are important factors determining levels of personal happiness.

Our thoughts, words, and deeds also leave imprints in the spiritual world. They either generate spiritual Light and awareness or produce spiritual clouds that darken our aura and cover our spirit. Negative thoughts such as anger, jealousy, and greed are the chief causes of disease and suffering. Thoughts of love, appreciation, and goodwill, on the other hand, bring Light to the aura, dispel spiritual clouds and create good fortune and happiness. When we understand this, the conditions in the spiritual world take on greater importance to us.

> Conditions in the spiritual world directly affect the spiritual body and are in turn reflected in the physical body. Thus the fate of men is fundamentally decided by the spiritual world. – *Jyorei and Happiness. HT*

On a practical level, what this means is that our spiritual life is generally more important than the outer, physical things in life. Although cars, schools, jobs, and houses are important for comfort and survival, even more important are our thoughts and behavior in relation to these things. They are what determine our happiness. The same is true about the people in our lives. Everything physical comes and goes. Compared to the life of the soul, these outer things are somewhat trivial.

What good is a promotion at work if it is obtained by manipulation, aggression, or deceit? Hurting the feelings of our friends or family members comes back to haunt us later, especially through the effects such behavior has in the invisible realms. When we take advantage of the people around us, the potential benefit occurs only in the physical world, whereas a corresponding level of impoverishment occurs within the spiritual world. Lying, cheating, stealing, abusing, and other such selfish and unkind behavior immediately create disturbances in the spiritual world and directly impact the spiritual body. This is especially significant because the environment is a mirror of what is going on inside us; one cannot separate the higher from the lower, nor the inner from the outer. So we need to evaluate how our actions affect the invisible realms because the level of our ultimate happiness primarily depends upon the purity of our spiritual condition.

It is surprising how many of us go through life mechanically, almost completely unaware of our true intentions. Dr. Sigmund Freud, the originator of psychoanalysis, was correct when he stated that most of us are dominated and controlled by subconscious impulses. But these impulses reach much further back in time than he realized. We are molded by our childhood conditioning as well as by tendencies carried over from previous incarnations in the distant past, and this conditioning is then stimulated by circumstances in our present day-to-day world. We may like to think that we are the captains of our own ships, but really we are controlled by numerous hidden influences. What we hold in our hearts determines our fate, and a heart corrupted by hurts, resentments, anxieties, compulsive needs, and selfish ambitions creates a world of conflict and suffering, whereas a pure heart creates a world of peace and joy. This place, from where our tendencies and thoughts emerge, is the

> If a person thinks good thoughts and performs good deeds, he feels good inside himself because his conscience is satisfied and the pleasant thoughts from this become radiant Light. This Light goes to increase and strengthen the radiance emitted from the spiritual body. This Light is also increased from the outside, for when someone performs a good deed the gratitude and appreciation of the person he has helped become radiant Light that is transmitted to him through the spiritual cords, thus brightening his aura.
> – *Spiritual Radiation and the Aura. HT*

According to Meishusama, all living things are surrounded by an aura, an ethereal substance lighter and thinner than air. It is an invisible body of Light unique to each individual. Only through special cameras using Kirilian Photography or through exceptional psychic awareness can this aura be detected. Meishusama writes, "It is a basic and true rule of the universe that auras cannot be seen by the eyes of ordinary men, but there are very occasionally people who have this ability. If, however, a normal person stills his mind and gazes intently at another person, he can perceive this person's aura to a limited extent." (*Spiritual Radiation and the Aura. HT*) The aura is an outward expression of our soul—and its brightness, thickness, and size are important factors determining levels of personal happiness.

Our thoughts, words, and deeds also leave imprints in the spiritual world. They either generate spiritual Light and awareness or produce spiritual clouds that darken our aura and cover our spirit. Negative thoughts such as anger, jealousy, and greed are the chief causes of disease and suffering. Thoughts of love, appreciation, and goodwill, on the other hand, bring Light to the aura, dispel spiritual clouds and create good fortune and happiness. When we understand this, the conditions in the spiritual world take on greater importance to us.

> Conditions in the spiritual world directly affect the spiritual body and are in turn reflected in the physical body. Thus the fate of men is fundamentally decided by the spiritual world. – *Jyorei and Happiness. HT*

On a practical level, what this means is that our spiritual life is generally more important than the outer, physical things in life. Although cars, schools, jobs, and houses are important for comfort and survival, even more important are our thoughts and behavior in relation to these things. They are what determine our happiness. The same is true about the people in our lives. Everything physical comes and goes. Compared to the life of the soul, these outer things are somewhat trivial.

What good is a promotion at work if it is obtained by manipulation, aggression, or deceit? Hurting the feelings of our friends or family members comes back to haunt us later, especially through the effects such behavior has in the invisible realms. When we take advantage of the people around us, the potential benefit occurs only in the physical world, whereas a corresponding level of impoverishment occurs within the spiritual world. Lying, cheating, stealing, abusing, and other such selfish and unkind behavior immediately create disturbances in the spiritual world and directly impact the spiritual body. This is especially significant because the environment is a mirror of what is going on inside us; one cannot separate the higher from the lower, nor the inner from the outer. So we need to evaluate how our actions affect the invisible realms because the level of our ultimate happiness primarily depends upon the purity of our spiritual condition.

The Law of Purification

It is a universal law of Nature that if pollution gathers in any spot, then it will be cleared away and that spot will be purified.
– A Third World War Can Be Avoided. HT

Our souls were created pure, but over time, during the soul's journey through many lifetimes, this original purity became covered and obscured by spiritual toxins. These toxins came from exposure to psychic pollution, physical poisons, and most significantly, as a result of negative behavior on our part. What we do and what we experience leaves psychic residue in our souls, either positive or negative. Toxins create a clouding of the spirit that dulls our awareness and contributes to ill health, emotional unhappiness, and mental suffering.

If we have the misfortune of being poisoned by fumes from a chemical factory or radiation from a nuclear power plant, these poisons will leave a negative imprint on our auras, thereby affecting our spiritual condition. After we die, although the physical poisons will remain with the physical body, which is discarded by the soul, the damage to the spiritual body can sometimes continue. The soul will then need to undergo a purification process in the spiritual world and then eventually return to the earth in a new physical incarnation. To the extent that the spiritual body has not been sufficiently purified, the effect of the poisons will be carried over to the new life, resulting in still more suffering. Sometimes infants born with physical deformities are a repercussion of these toxins. For example, if the toxins in our body make us feel irritable, and because of this we take it out on our family over a period of many years by being mean to them, the resulting spiritual clouds generated by this behavior will lower our consciousness considerably. This lowered consciousness will then continue over into the next lifetime.

Although physical toxins have an indisputably harmful effect on the body, the underlying reason for the poisoning is always spiritual. Why did we happen to get exposed to these chemicals or radiation? Were we "accidentally" passing by the wrong place at the wrong time, or was it fated? Although we may have had various reasons for passing by these places at that time, the true reason for our behavior came from a higher level, from unseen factors and influences in the spiritual world. Nothing is an accident in this universe. The hidden laws governing all things and all events determine when and where something will happen. Possibly our soul may have needed to experience this poisoning in order to learn important lessons to further our spiritual growth.

Meishusama teaches that all suffering is a form of purification. Nature initiates a cleansing process within the physical body through sickness and pain, and in the outer world through the occurrence of natural catastrophes such as violent storms, floods, earthquakes, and fires, as well as social calamities such as epidemics, wars, and financial crisis. The body uses sickness as a way to discharge internal toxins through fevers, sweating, diarrhea, vomiting, runny nose, skin rashes, and other such symptoms. These unpleasant symptoms are all forms of physical purification. Personal conflicts with people, financial difficulties, and traumatic events are examples of types of external suffering that also help to purify our souls.

> The thing that we term, all too simply, "sickness" is in fact a process of physical purification caused ultimately by the need to dispel the clouds accumulated on the human soul. And not only sickness, but all kinds of human suffering, stem from the same underlying cause. Thus poverty and war too are signs that a process of purification is taking place and so it is obvious that there is no essential difference between sickness, poverty, and war. – *Jyorei and Happiness. HT*

This does not suggest that suffering in itself is justified or good. Only the cleansing and educational effects of purification have value. Suffering is the unfortunate and inevitable result of erroneous behavior, either individually or collectively. Great tragedies such as the Jewish, Armenian, Cambodian, and Rwandan genocides in the twentieth century, for example, are to be mourned and avoided at all costs. The need for humanity to grow up, and for individuals to learn to treat each other with kindness and respect, has never been greater. If we can begin to learn from the ongoing lessons of life and then finally create a world of true health, prosperity, and peace, then there will be little need for such mass purifications as have repeatedly happened in the past. Until that time, we can expect to see more wars, economic turmoil, political injustice, crime, and disease in the future. These events and conditions serve as inevitable outlets for mass purification of collectively accumulated negativity. In order to grow, we need to take responsibility, both individually and collectively, for these tragic occurrences rather than just blaming others for them.

Words and explanations can feel painfully inadequate following the death of a loved one or in the aftermath of horrible tragedies such as wars, plagues, and giant earthquakes. At such times, the best one can do is give emotional and spiritual support to those who suffer and also provide physical help when possible. But eventually, most people will begin searching for reasons and explanations for these events because it is human nature to seek meaning in life. This is the time when wise counsel can be valuable.

Purification usually reveals its true value in the future, not the present. To appreciate the idea that suffering can be an expression of purification requires one to temporarily suspend doubt, and instead become open to the possibility that there is an intelligent pattern underlying life's events. Not only is this pattern intelligent, but also it is benevolent and compassionate.

In general, when purification occurs on a personal level, it is better to learn from it rather than actively resisting the discomfort. We can benefit greatly by humbly asking ourselves, "How have I contributed to generating this purification? Have I been eating junk food? Have I been smoking or drinking too much? Have I been accumulating excessive financial debts? Or have I been behaving unkindly towards others?"

Those with the most spiritual clouds are not always the ones who suffer the most, nor are those with the least spiritual clouds the ones who suffer the least. For example, gangsters who live extravagant lives based on manipulation, deceit, and violence, though they accumulate many dark clouds through these actions, may not experience the negative effects of these clouds until much later in life. On the other hand, even great saints, prophets, and humanitarians may incarnate with unresolved spiritual clouds from former lifetimes that necessitate purification in this life. Or their souls may decide to burn off large amounts of clouds very rapidly despite the intense suffering that accompanies such purification. Thus, even in the midst of lives dedicated to good works for humanity, they may suffer from many hardships or diseases.

We, with our limited understanding, cannot know why innocent people so often suffer. There are always hidden spiritual reasons for the unexpected death of a young child, the horrible illness of a generous person, or the terrible financial problems of a great artist. Fortunately, from the long-term vantage point of the soul, even a lifetime of pain and suffering might seem like only a moment's brief disturbance because it is only one lifetime out of many.

That which is dying, as well as that which is birthing: each has its own reasons for following its fate. There are no accidents here, and everything is determined with exact certainty.[3] – KW

Although no one wants to suffer, we can all appreciate the general benefit to our health and happiness that results from a detoxified body and a purified spirit. As the clouding of our spiritual body dissipates, health and happiness increasingly begin to return, and our influence on others becomes more positive.

Temporary suffering can lead to greater happiness in the future, especially when we try to learn from our past mistakes. But it's important to remember that there is no need to actively seek suffering, for the goal of life is happiness, not sorrow. Life is basically positive (in other words, it has educational value to the soul), and purification can also be viewed as positive in this context. Appreciating the positive value of purification can cause deep and profound changes in our overall approach to life. We may find that our negative resistance to life's inevitable problems and hardships begins to be replaced by attitudes of acceptance and even gratitude. This leads to an affirmative attitude towards life and to greater peace of mind.

Fortunately, suffering is not the only way to attain spiritual purification and expanded awareness. There are other, more positive ways, such as the cultivation of virtue and the appreciation of beauty. One can cultivate virtue by doing good deeds for others and for society at large. By helping others we also help ourselves on a spiritual level. This is often a gentler and more effective way to purify our spiritual body than through suffering.

Among the various ways available to help others, the act of giving Jyorei is one of the easiest and most powerful. It is virtue of the highest kind. Jyorei is the art of focusing Divine Light for the sake of healing and spiritual growth. This Light purifies obscurations in people's energy fields, resulting in increased health, awareness, and happiness. Jyorei affects people physically, emotionally, mentally, and spiritually by clearing up negativity and toxicity at very deep levels. There are no limits to the benefits of Divine Light because its power is not limited to the physical world of time and space.

---

[3] Meishusama, "The Daijo Way," *Shumei Magazine*, vol. 267 (January /February 2007).

The other positive way to purify is through experiencing beauty, either from contact with nature or from experiencing aesthetically pleasing works of art. Objects and places of beauty, whether natural or manmade, emit high spiritual vibrations that benefit all who approach them with an appreciative heart. These higher vibrations purify us and help raise us to higher spiritual levels.

Each and every one of us, despite our age, gender, race, creed, or social status, is seeking happiness. This underlying drive is at the core of human nature. Through purification of body, mind, and spirit, the obstructions blocking our sense of happiness are removed. Eventually, it will be discovered by us that happiness is not something to be gained, but is actually our innate condition. When this is truly realized, we begin to radiate happiness toward others rather than seek it for ourselves. This selfless attitude is happiness of the truest kind.

The Law of Divine Justice

In the spiritual world, there are laws made by God, and men are judged according to these laws. – A Sense of Justice. HT

Actions have consequences, and what we do to others soon comes back to us. When we treat others with gentleness, kindness, and honesty our relationships improve and our sense of well-being increases. On the other hand, behavior that harms others—including lying, cheating, stealing, slander, or abuse—clouds our spirits and draws misfortune into our lives. The universe is like a mirror reflecting our actions directly back to us. In this sense, it can be said that we create our own reality through the energy that we send out onto the world. This principle is often referred to as karma, or "as you sow, so shall you reap."

A man's fate, his good luck and bad luck, depend on his thoughts and attitudes, and to understand this basic fact is fundamental to a perception of reality. – *A Sense of Justice. HT*

The quality of our lives is more often determined by our state of consciousness than by outer events and circumstances. All of our past thoughts, emotions, and sensory impressions accumulate within us and gradually become the internal tendencies that drive our actions. Many of these tendencies carry over from one lifetime to another and become entrenched within our character. The more dark and suppressed these emotions and tendencies are, the more power they have to disrupt our lives. For instance, aggressive action tends not to improve situations, but instead often makes things worse by provoking equally aggressive counteraction by others, and the tendency to judge others also prompts them to judge us.

Fortunately, though, when our spiritual condition rises to a higher level, everything else seems to improve as well. This is because the way we interpret our lives, and the feelings that result from these interpretations, are dependent on the clarity of our perceptions. When the mirror of our soul becomes cleansed of these dark, suppressed thoughts, emotions, and impressions, then everything becomes brighter and more positive. Our ability to perceive reality accurately improves, and we are then able to act more intelligently and effectively. All of the darkness needs to be wiped from the mirror by either releasing it from our being or by embracing it with love. When releasing our inner darkness, it is important not to act out these tendencies through negative behavior, but instead to allow them to arise and dissipate naturally. Then events and circumstances will miraculously improve as a result of this inner cleansing and healing process. Remember, we can offer all our negativity up to God, knowing that he will never judge us.

A foolish person sows seeds of destruction, not realizing they will be his to reap.
– Good and Evil. MK

3 ESSENTIAL INNER QUALITIES

Spiritual growth affects all areas of our lives, including our thoughts, emotions, and desires. The cultivation of the following three inner qualities helps transform our behavior into that which supports greater happiness and fulfillment.

Gratitude

The source of human nobility is deep and abiding gratitude for all of God's gifts.
– Gratitude. MK

Normally, the only time we pay attention to our body is when we are in pain. At this time, when our comfort is disturbed, we cannot help but take notice. Our immediate impulse is to resist the pain by tightening up the body, although this usually only makes things worse. As the pain lingers, our attitude may sink into self-pity, resentment, or anger. Finally, when the pain goes away, we usually go back to ignoring our body again.

Nobody likes to suffer, and the general human tendency is to get angry or depressed when we have to endure pain. This may actually become a permanent attitude if the pain continues for a long period of time. When the pain finally does go away, there may be some initial gratitude, but soon afterwards, that fades away, too. One might expect this gratitude to last longer because a pain-free body is such a significant gift; but that is not usually the case. Most of us take our physical and emotional comfort for granted instead of appreciating our good fortune.

The mind is much like a navigating device. It is always looking for problems to solve, and thinking of ways to fix them. This causes it to focus on what is negative, missing, or wrong rather than on what is positive, present, or right. Therefore, it does not notice when things are going well, only when they are not. This tendency for problems to grab our attention appears to be a biologically inherited survival response. The mind was created to help guide us through the world and to keep us alive. So it is always alert for potential danger. Yet this same fixation on problems can easily lead one to anger or self-pity when too many things seem to go wrong.

We also have a tendency to complain about what we do not have instead of being grateful for what we do have. We might have a perfectly good house, car, job, or romantic partner, yet still feel envy towards those who have something better. Instead of feeling grateful for the blessings that we already have, we may succumb to envy, resentment, or self-pity caused by comparison with others. Such cravings are never satisfied, though, even if we do manage to get the thing we want. There will always be people with better things than we have, and thus more temptations to feel envious. And no matter how rich a person becomes, there is never enough money to satisfy their greed. When we hold greed or envy in our hearts, we end up producing misery rather than gladness.

If we focus on the shortcomings of the people around us, our relationships will tend to get worse, not better. On the other hand, when we learn to appreciate people's good qualities, not only do our relationships with them improve, but often their behavior improves as well. This reciprocal principle is summarized in the Biblical saying, "As you sow, so shall you reap." Everyone appreciates compliments and expressions of gratitude, and it is wonderful to observe how often appreciation brings out the best in people. Learn to thank people for the little things they do and see how quickly they respond to your kind words.

As well as all the practical advantages that arise from thanking others, the feeling of gratitude is in itself a satisfying reward. Gratitude does not ask for anything in the future, but instead gives thanks for what currently exists here and now. It arises when we actively look for things to appreciate in our current circumstances. A person can view a glass of water as being either half empty or half full; the choice is up to us. It is possible to feel grateful in even horrible conditions because—who knows?—things could always be worse. We are lucky they are not; and if nothing else, we can be grateful for the simple fact of being alive. Not surprisingly, when we feel gratitude, life often reciprocates by improving. Meishusama adds, "Imagine that the value of life is the number ten. If one's gratitude for life also is ten, then one has achieved a kind of balance, and if it is above this, it is a plus that God will reward many times over with His blessings." *(The Rationality of Faith and Repurification. HT)*

We create our own destiny, to a large extent, by the results of our actions in either this lifetime or previous lifetimes. These actions either pollute our souls with subtle negative impurities or draw greater spiritual light into our being. The cumulative effects of these unseen influences in the spiritual world are what determine our future. As Meishusama puts it: "The amount of suffering that affects a person corresponds to the degree of clouding of the soul." *(An Evil Person Is a Sick Person. HT)* Instead of complaining about our misfortune, it is better to take responsibility for having earlier created this need for purification. This advice applies to even the worst of circumstances. The more grateful we are for the purification we receive, the higher our consciousness will rise, which then translates into a higher quality of life. The way we do something is more important than what we do, and it is the intentions behind our actions that have the greatest impact on our spiritual body.

Meishusama recommends the deliberate cultivation of gratitude for not only the things in our lives that we like, but also for the things that we do not like. Although this latter recommendation may seem strange or unnatural, on closer inspection, we can discover the profound wisdom in this advice. When Meishusama suggests that we feel grateful for our hardships and difficulties, he does not mean that we should deliberately pursue suffering. It is not the pain itself, but rather the process of eliminating spiritual impurities that has value. This process is what we can learn to appreciate. From a long-term perspective, the suffering caused by these bad experiences is just a temporary hardship we must endure while moving towards greater health and happiness. Purification opens the possibility for spiritual growth. Although it is good to appreciate the present, it is also good to consider the future because it can arrive sooner than we expect.

Meishusama writes, "Gratitude breeds gratitude; discontent spawns discontent. These are true and honest words. For a grateful heart rises straight to God, while a discontented heart finds only the evil spirits of Hell." *(You Are What You Think. HT)* This expression is not meant to warn us that if we grumble and complain we will be sent to hell by some wrathful, punishing

God, but, rather, points out that we create our own heaven and hell right here and now by our thoughts and attitudes. Just as gratitude arises spontaneously in moments of happiness, it's also true that gratitude gives rise to happiness. It silences the mind and dissolves feelings of lack and of neediness. About the significance of gratitude, the fourteenth century German Christian mystic, Meister Eckhart, stated, "If the only prayer you say in your whole life is 'thank you,' it would suffice."

Gratitude is both a feeling and an attitude. It is a positive affirmation about life and everything in it. Anger, jealousy, and resentment quickly melt when we hold appreciation in our hearts. Fear and defensiveness also shrink away and are replaced by peace and love. Within gratitude are the seeds of joy. It has the magical effect of transforming our minds and hearts in ways that all the effort in the world cannot duplicate. We may rush to self-improvement seminars and "instant therapy" workshops, but if our hearts are closed, what good will they do us?

A grateful heart draws spiritual Light into our being, and this Light is then reflected outwardly to the world around us. Gratitude is more than just a shallow attitude, because at its core, it is an expression of God's Spirit as revealed through the human soul. It is like a doorway allowing divine presence to enter into our hearts. When we take one step towards God, God takes ten steps towards us.

The universe is not our creation, nor is our nose, mouth, ears, or eyes. Everything was given to us. Even our first breath did not depend upon our own efforts; the body in which our soul found itself spontaneously drew in the air. Our parents nurtured and supported us—providing food, clothing, and shelter for our young bodies. These, and many more things, are still being provided to us by society. Also, without bicycles, cars, buses, trains, and subways, we would not be able to travel daily to work, school, church, or retail stores. It is easy to take all these things for granted because we use them so often, but we are actually very fortunate to have them. In some developing countries these things are quite scarce, and the people are often required to walk long distances. The more we contemplate this, the more things we can find for which to be grateful.

Start focusing on what you have, rather than what you lack. Even if you can find only one thing to be grateful for, by focusing on it your perception expands, as does your capacity for feeling even more gratitude. Be grateful for whatever has nourished, blessed, or benefited your life, be it a person, place, or thing. The more gratitude we feel, the more that is given to us for which to be grateful.

A simple, good exercise is to say "thank you" throughout the day. Actively look for opportunities to express sincere gratitude to people. By doing so, we bring forth the unique beauty in others. Looking for reasons to be grateful increases our appreciation of life and helps us enjoy each moment more fully.

Happiness comes mostly from our own inner perception—from how we interpret things and the value judgments we place on them. By changing our attitude towards what we experience, we can learn to want what we get rather than get what we want. In this way, we can feel grateful irrespective of what comes our way.

Trust in the divine order of things. Know that God does everything perfectly, giving each of us exactly what we need to further the spiritual growth of our soul. Expressing gratitude to God for all that arises, both the pleasant and the unpleasant, sanctifies everything and brings deep peace and joy to our hearts.

Our general attitude contributes more to our overall happiness than do the specific circumstances in our lives. Thankfulness, in particular, can improve the worst of circumstances, oftentimes revealing hidden gems that are immensely rewarding. Gratitude gives us wings to soar above our daily problems, and guides our arms to embrace the many gifts that come our way.

Love for Others

If you love the world and help people, God will protect you wherever you go.
– Love for Others. MK

Everyone, deep down, craves love. And unfortunately, the human need for love appears to be the source of much pain and confusion. Children who do not receive enough love and approval from their parents often become angry and bitter adults. And when these love-starved individuals form close relationships, they often end up struggling to control or dominate the other person rather than express and receive mutual affection. Society, as a whole, tends to reflect this tragic condition by creating institutions such as workplaces, schools, government agencies, and hospitals that are also based on control rather than love. These impersonal environments are almost devoid of human warmth and caring.

People whose hearts are closed tend to feel disconnected from others, including their own wives, husbands, children, parents, and friends. They also feel estranged from society and from nature. Often they lead solitary lives of quiet desperation, enduring painful feelings of alienation and loneliness even when surrounded by people whom they have known for many years. Plus, most of their efforts to improve their relationships fail because they do not know how to express personal warmth or affection.

One of the biggest challenges in life is that of cultivating and maintaining loving relationships with all the various people in our lives. It seems that success in this endeavor depends as much on our ability to avoid interpersonal conflicts as it does on our efforts to be friendly and likable. And although making such positive efforts is essential for harmonious relationships, one's outer behavior, no matter how pleasant and considerate, cannot in itself guarantee a return of genuine love. Rather, such love must be inspired in others, and we can only do that if we ourselves have love within our own hearts, because the outer reflects the inner, not the other way around.

The most essential things in life are difficult to define, because words tend to describe the outer surface of things rather than their inner reality. Love is like that. It is essential to who we are, but is hard to grasp by the mind. In our personal relationships, we experience love as a sense of affection for and affinity with another person. At a deeper level, love is a response to our perception of the spiritual presence within people, as well as within animals and plants. Love reveals to us their uniqueness and inner beauty. The greater the purity of an individual's soul, the more capable this individual is of perceiving the spiritual essence within others. Love reveals our common humanity beneath our superficial differences. This is why love fosters unity instead of separation. Love brings us closer together. The French theologian-biologist-paleontologist Pierre Teilhard de Chardin wrote, "Love alone is capable of uniting living beings in such a way as to complete and fulfill them, for it alone takes them and joins them by what is deepest in themselves."

The more we connect with someone's inner essence, the more we are able to love the many facets of their character, such as their attitudes, personality, and mannerisms. Love inclines us to accept the whole person; not just the admirable qualities, but also the negative and undeveloped aspects. People know when they are truly loved because they feel acknowledged and accepted on all levels. They feel safe in revealing more of themselves to the person who does not judge, but accepts them just as they are. When we shine the light of love on our inner darkness, it gets transformed into something beautiful. The same thing happens when we shine love on others. All of us yearn for this kind of unconditional love.

Love is one of the most healing forces in all of life. As psychologist Karl Menninger said, "Love cures people—both the ones who give it and the ones who receive it." In the Harvard University Mastery of Stress Study, which began in the 1950s with 126 healthy male undergraduate students, the most accurate predictor of future health was the perception that these men had of their parents' love and caring. This factor far superseded other factors, such as family and genetic history of disease or lifestyle conditions. Further, it turns out that those men who rated their parents high in love and caring not only proved to be more open to receiving love, but also more capable of communicating love to others.

The closer a person moves towards God, the more their heart will naturally fill with love. Although it might be easy to feel love in some abstract fantasy when we are sitting in solitude, the true test of love is in the way we treat others, especially the people we do not like or who cause us problems. It is possible to communicate effectively to those who mistreat us without expressing anger or hostility. Love is demonstrated by acts of gentleness and kindness. It thinks of others and seeks to serve. When we love someone, we give this person our energy and attention, which makes him or her feel recognized, valued, and cared for as an individual. As adults, we are easily impressed by outer appearances and social status, confusing this with inner worth—but children, in their innocence, could hardly care less about these things. Both children and animals respond naturally to love. They are not easily fooled by falseness.

A life lived only for one's own self is a life of isolation. At the end of our lives, everything will fall away, and at that time, if we ask ourselves, "What was my life all about?" the only satisfying answer would be to evaluate how much of a positive effect we had on the lives of others. Meishusama says, "If you do not make others happy, you can never be happy yourself." *(About Myself. HT)* Our life has greater meaning and value when we are able to help others. The extent that we are able to contribute to humanity, and especially to the people we encounter daily, is the extent to which we are able to feel good about ourselves. Helping others is a natural expression of the love we feel in our hearts. As the modern saint, Mother Teresa, stated, "We can do no great things; only small things with great love." In the final analysis, it is love that counts.

The ability to see ourselves in others is the basis for the experience of love. It is as simple as seeing through another's eyes and knowing that deep down we are fundamentally the same. This is the recognition of Spirit within form, and of God's grace touching each of us. God radiates love, and this love is at the foundation of all existence. The closer we are to God, the more we, too, radiate love. And when God resides securely in our heart, our love partakes of divinity. This love is both impersonal and all-encompassing. Like the sun, it radiates outwardly on both the good and the bad, while simultaneously exerting a magnetic attraction on those that it touches. God's love is unconditional, whereas human love tends to be limited by personal needs and affinities. About this, Meishusama writes, "While looking at the vastness of the sky, the extent of God's great love is brought to mind." *(Infinite Compassion. MK)* We all have the essence of God within us, and thus we partake of God's essential goodness. To love others is to connect with God through that love.

Love is an expression of the Oneness of all life. It removes all divisions and allows us to feel our essential unity with people, nature, and God. "Faces may vary in shape and color, but in God's eyes all are of the same land," writes Meishusama. *(Peace on Earth. MK)* At the level of Spirit, we are one and the same.

When we truly love others, there is no room for judgmentalism or animosity. These feelings separate us from love by projecting negative motives onto others. When we judge others, we are focusing mostly on their outward behavior, whereas when we empathize with them, we are identifying with their feelings and underlying needs. Empathy prompts us to sympathize with people's pain and to celebrate their joy. Possessiveness, on the other hand, by trying to own or control people, inadvertently pushes them away. We cannot make people love or like us, it must come naturally. To be genuine, love must be spontaneous, not coerced. So we need to set people free to be themselves. And selfishness, by making our needs more important than others, creates division and blocks the flow of love. A selfish heart tends to use others for personal gain, thereby fostering resentment rather than appreciation. Love flowers best in an atmosphere of selflessness, kindness, and generosity. As psychiatrist and physician David R. Hawkins writes in his book Power vs. Force, "love change(s) the world each time it replace(s) 'unlove.'"

Loving others does not require us to accept their negative attitudes or behavior. We need to be able to discern right from wrong. Sometimes people can be selfish, destructive, or cruel, and this must be dealt with appropriately, but always with as much kindness as possible. There is a difference between a person's outer behavior and their inner essence. Outer behavior can vary from good to neutral to bad, but our inner essence is always fundamentally good because it partakes of God's Spirit. And it is people's inner essence that we can learn to recognize and love, regardless of their actions or beliefs. This unconditional love is what will finally heal the world and bring peace and harmony to all.

The psychoanalyst and social psychologist Erich Fromm, in his book *The Art of Loving*, describes love as being not so much a relationship to one particular person, but instead a general attitude and orientation of character. It is a forgiving, nurturing, and supportive way of relating to people. This loving orientation determines how we relate to the world as a whole, and not just toward one individual. If this love is directed exclusively towards one individual, rather than universally towards everyone, then it is really a dependent attachment, and this other person is more likely an extension of one's own ego.

"To be loved, be lovable," wrote the ancient Greek poet Ovid. If we desire to feel the unifying oneness of love in our relations with others, then the first step is to take on the discipline of acting with gentleness, kindness, and forgiveness at all times and to all beings, including ourselves. This requires that we put aside any selfish desires, personal agendas, and self-serving justifications that might interfere with this love. Especially, we need to let go of judgmentalism, and learn to relate with compassion, both towards others and especially towards our own self. This inner discipline by itself does not cause love to appear, but it does open up a space within ourselves to allow love to spontaneously emerge.

Although we need self-love in order to feel love for others, it is the quality of our love that is the measure of its authenticity. Love is its own reward, and it is an end in itself. Its blessings flow like waves through water, soothing and nourishing all that it encounters. Love lightens the soul and creates happiness for no particular reason. Happiness is a spontaneous byproduct of love because the very nature of love is pure joy.

In its highest expression, love is unconditional and impartial, and is not dependent on people's actions. It is a universal attitude that is not restricted or constrained by anything that happens in the outer world. Such love excludes nothing; it applies to all things, whether sentient or not.

Love is the reason and motivation for being of service to others. It is both the means and the end, because love begets love. The true goal of love is to draw us into a larger version of itself, which is the all-embracing unity of divine love.

Go with God's love and extend this unconditional love to others, and then you can be a person whom everybody feels comfortable to talk to and to be around.[1]

– KW

Makoto

A person who has Makoto will keep his promises whatever happens.
– How to Find Makoto, True Sincerity, a True Heart. HT

The way we live our life is a reflection of the quality of our soul. The old saying, "Actions speak louder than words," expresses the importance of having our personal will in direct alignment with our thoughts, feelings, and behavior. While it is easy enough to think idealistic thoughts or feel nice sentiments, it is through our deeds that we truly reveal our inner character. Most of us would be upset if our car stopped on the highway because our automobile mechanic neglected to attach a wheel or a fan belt properly. Despite our mechanic's promises to do a good job, if he did a bad job, we would end up suffering the consequences of his carelessness. Like the mechanic, what we do matters because there are good and bad consequences for everything.

One who does not neglect small things is capable of achieving great things.
– Spiritual Cultivation. MK

---

[1] Meishusama, "Being Daijo," *Shumei Magazine*, vol. 267 (January /February 2007).

Our lives are an overall expression of how we live day-to-day. All the little things that we do throughout the day add up to a larger picture which reflects our general character. If we leave the faucet dripping in the kitchen, our bills unpaid, the oil unchanged in our car, and our shoes untied, then there is a good chance that we are just as negligent with our thoughts, as well. It is easy to rationalize and justify our laziness or procrastination, but it is not so easy to deal with the consequences. This is especially true when we neglect the people around us, and then our relationships deteriorate because of it. How can we focus our mind to accomplish anything important when our life is in chaos? If this is the case, then most likely the best we can do is dream and talk about big things rather than take decisive action.

When what we think matches what we say, and what we say matches what we do, then Meishusama would say that we display 'makoto,' a Japanese word for sincerity, honesty and integrity. It denotes a fundamental unity in a person's thoughts, words, and deeds. A person with great makoto tends to live according to a high code of ethics, and never wavers from it.

How often have we said or done something wrong which we later deeply regretted? This often happens because of unconscious divisions between our thoughts and feelings, and between our selfish tendencies and our altruistic intentions. Most people have mixed motives for what they do. They may halfheartedly attempt to serve others while simultaneously pursuing self-gain. Consequently, sometimes their actions are helpful and sometimes not. If a person volunteers to do charity work, but then starts bragging to everyone about his good deeds, then most likely he is operating under false pretenses. Eventually people will notice that he has been putting more time and energy into promoting a positive social image than into truly helping others, and questions will arise about the sincerity of his motives. Such behavior tends to reflect a self-centered desire for admiration and respect rather than an altruistic desire to help others. If he continues like this for too long, he might start to attract scorn and contempt because of his obvious inauthenticity.

People who do not attempt to impress others seem modest and courteous, and are viewed with heartfelt respect.[2] *– KW*

---

[2] Meishusama, "The Spirit of Izunome," Shumei Magazine, vol. 243 (Nov. /Dec. 2002).

Makoto is founded on the inner qualities of purity and wholeness. It is only possible to become inwardly whole to the extent that our desires are sufficiently purified and brought into alignment with our conscious intentions. The more we dedicate our actions to a higher purpose or ideal, the more these actions will begin to demonstrate inner wholeness. To be whole is to be free from distraction by conflicting desires and purposes. This wholeness allows us to put our hearts more fully into our actions, which not only improves the quality of our work, but brings greater enjoyment of it as well.

Sincerity is also an expression of makoto because it depends on consistency. We cannot be truly sincere if our left hand acts contrary to our right one, or if our words do not match our actions. It is false to declare our love for animals, if an hour later we kick our cat or dog because it damaged our furniture. Some would call this hypocrisy. Similarly, if we proudly proclaim our love for humanity and grandly promise to dedicate our lives to serving world peace, and then in our next breath start condemning the homeless and the poor, we will probably fail to convince anyone. Most will doubt the sincerity of our convictions and will dismiss the things we say. Such discrepancies between a person's actions and their words reveal a divided self, full of inner contradictions and self-deception.

Be a genuine person: one who is always concerned for the truth, for the world, and for man. – Poems of Inspiration. MK

It requires maturity to keep one's commitments. Dr. Fritz Perls, the originator of Gestalt Therapy, defined maturity as "the transformation from environmental support to self-support." He says that mature people mobilize their own inner and outer resources rather than manipulating others to get what they want. They stand on their own two feet and take responsibility for their actions rather than blaming others for their personal mistakes. Maturity is another expression of makoto.

Living with makoto means that we have integrity and act in accordance with our convictions. We follow our conscience and are true to our word. If we promise to do something, we do it. People can rely on us because of the honesty of our character, which itself is an expression of our concern for others. If we have makoto, we truly care for others and are always considerate. Being grounded in our own experience, we do not find it threatening to see things from another person's perspective. We are not divided against ourselves, but speak with one voice. We are integrated and whole.

To develop makoto, we must continuously examine our attitudes and motives for any sign of falsehood or deceit. It is the lies that we tell ourselves that undermine our ability to attain makoto within ourselves. Self-deception leads to self-destruction. Therefore, to practice honesty and sincerity is the best way to cultivate makoto and to discover genuine peace and happiness. The importance of true sincerity is affirmed in an ancient Shinto saying, "Where you have sincerity, there is also virtue. Sincerity is a witness to truth. Sincerity is the mother of knowledge. Sincerity is a single virtue that binds divinity and man in one."

Only when we are free of self-deception are we capable of real sincerity in all the things we do and say. Sincerity is a beautiful personal quality in which the inner self and the outer self align together in perfect harmony. A truly sincere person has the inner purity of a polished mirror that can accurately reflect the outer world without obstruction or distortion. This purity derives from a state of selflessness and honesty. Such a person is trusted by others because they can sense that he really means what he says.

It can be said that love is an attribute of the heart, gratitude is an expression of both the heart and the mind in balance, and makoto is a product of the heart, mind, and will, all fused together in perfect harmony. The quality of our will is determined by our desires, motives, and intentions. Someone with impure motives and desires suffers from continual conflict with others, whereas a person of inner purity finds harmony and happiness in life. As self-centered motives give way to altruism and a genuine concern for others, a person will increasingly tend to do what is best for everyone, not just for their own self. When an individual soul reaches true inner purity, it can be said that their desires and intentions are then in correct alignment with God's Will. Such a person chooses to serve God in whatever way they can.

Makoto is an outer expression of our inner character. Only when we consistently keep our promises, always act in alignment with our highest values, and at all times communicate with honesty and sincerity, will we truly embody makoto. To have makoto is to behave maturely and to do things with uncompromising integrity.

Because everyone and everything is infinitely connected, our actions have enormous consequences. Knowing this, a person with makoto assumes responsibility for everything he or she thinks, says, and does, and increasingly begins to dedicate him or herself to betterment of the world and all its varied inhabitants.

Return to your heart of Makoto and let God's Light illumine your soul.

– Recreation of Integrity. MK

4 MYSTERIES OF THE SPIRITUAL WORLD

Miroku[1] Omikami

If you find a deep knowledge of the spiritual world, then life is joyful and even death itself is pleasant. – Preface. HT

Miroku Omikami is a Japanese word for God that Meishusama uses when referring to God as an all-pervasive spiritual presence. 'Omikami' means Great God or Great Spirit, the one universal, all encompassing spiritual reality at the heart of all existence. 'Miroku' can be interpreted as ultimate. 'Kami', in Japanese, means a god, spirit entity, or conscious energy localized in a particular place, object, or phenomenon. Shinto, the folk religion of Japan, holds that trees, rocks, mountains, lakes, and rivers each have a conscious spiritual presence, or kami, residing within them. Such a world is experienced as alive and full of divine power. On a deeper level, the totality of God exists, undivided, in each and every particle of existence. To the limited minds of humans, everything appears fragmented into discrete objects, and therefore they cannot possibly perceive the infinite nature of God, which is always whole and complete. Paradoxically, Miroku Omikami is also much greater than manifest creation, and can exist complete unto itself even in the total absence of all phenomena.

God, or 'Miroku Omikami', is formless and everywhere. He is infinite con-

---

[1] 'Miroku' is most commonly recognized as a Buddhist term that refers to Maitreya, the future Buddha of all-encompassing love. According to Meishusama, there is not merely one, but actually three Mirokus. These are the well-known figures of Kannon, Amitabha, and the Buddha, who respectively symbolize the elements of fire, water, and earth, or sun, moon, and earth. The Miroku explained in this book indicates the One that unites and surpasses the power of these different Mirokus, in other words, three ultimate spiritual elements. He also identified the spiritual nature of Miroku Omikami with that of Maitreya in Buddhism.

sciousness and eternal presence. God's Spirit is not separate from the natural world, but exists within each one of us, as well as within all things. "The Divine Power of God is present in the world in many forms," says Meishusama. *(True Faith. HT)* This divine presence reveals itself in the patterns of nature, and can be found in the flowing movement of a mountain stream, in the blossoming of a flower, and in the flight of a bird in the sky. There is nowhere in nature that it cannot be found.

God knows everything because God is everything. But God does not know things objectively because nothing exists as an object outside of Him. Instead, God knows things subjectively because everything exists within the vastness of His own infinite being. Everything that God sees is a manifest projection of Himself, like images in a mirror. God sees Himself in all things because there is nowhere that He is not found. This unitary perception is the basis of unconditional love. It is God loving Himself through the agency of others.

God is not limited to any particular time or place. Everything that we see, taken together, is an aspect of God. The Light of God is in everything and beyond. It is porous, and fills all space. All of creation is surrounded by and pervaded by divinity, like the water in the sea that both flows around the fish and infuses every cell within their bodies. Each of us is like these fish, which never for a minute lose contact with this life-giving water. But just as fish are oblivious to the water that surrounds them, so too are we oblivious to God's eternal presence. Both are invisible and all-pervasive realities to those who live in them.

Although God is constantly guiding and influencing everything, we need to raise our consciousness to a higher level before we can perceive this. We can do this through internal purification and also through contributing to the happiness of others. How we treat others affects how we relate to God, because God dwells within each of them. Everything we do affects our relationship with God one way or another.

To grow spiritually, we must first establish a loving relationship with God. To do this, it is helpful to feel that he is close, rather than distant, because intimacy depends upon close proximity. Not only is God's Spirit nearby, it is even closer than our nose, more intimate than our breath, and more constant than our heartbeat. God's divine presence accompanies us everywhere, whether we know it or not. So, in this sense, we do not need to create a relationship with God because it already exists. However, most of us may find that we have room to improve on the quality of it. If we think of God as our close companion, as our spiritual guide, and as our helper and protector, then the relationship will become closer and more personal. Over time, this relationship may become so intimate that we will find God's presence within us, as well as within all things. After this, we will never again feel alone, because now we feel continuously embraced by God's invisible loving hands.

The eyes of God see to the furthermost depths of the human heart.
– Good and Evil. MK

Each of the three primary ways of relating to Miroku Omikami produces different effects. Discovering God's presence as our indwelling spirit promotes inner serenity and joy; relating to God interpersonally as the Supreme Being in heaven encourages love and devotion; and perceiving God's Spirit in the world of nature fosters reverence and gratitude.

Miroku Omikami refers to the absolute unity of the Supreme Being, which encompasses all apparent contradictions and dualities within a larger, unifying whole. Not only does God contain everything, as water contains fish, but the essence of God also exists within all things, like the water within each fish. God is equally immanent, dwelling within the world of time and space, and transcendent, existing above and beyond that which we can perceive. We, and all of nature, are part of God's body, and are supported by God's divine presence. Although manifesting in diverse forms, Miroku Omikami never loses its wholeness.

Beyond the Mind

No human wisdom or knowledge can penetrate to the bottom of the depths of God's plan. – Meishusama IV. MK

Meishusama teaches that although divinity is immanent in the world of space and time, it is difficult to perceive this divinity because of the spiritual clouds that block our perception. So, for most of us, God is more transcendent than immanent, and more distant than near. Yet, there are still ways to connect with divine presence. It can be sensed in the beauty of nature, through the healing effects of Jyorei, and in the loving kindness of others. We can also discover divinity in simplicity, because this quality allows space for something greater to appear. For most of us, though, God will seem distant and unknowable until we can free ourselves from excessive attachments to worldly things that distract us and cause emotional distress.

At first, faith is helpful in our journey towards God. But eventually, faith must be transformed into direct experience because then God's presence will become immanent within our very own soul.

God is neither exclusively transcendent nor exclusively immanent. Either concept of God, by itself, is incomplete because it reduces God to a partiality. Each concept expresses only half of the truth and thereby limits that which is by nature unlimited. To single-mindedly embrace one point of view at the expense of the other would result in locating God either wholly inside or wholly outside of creation, but not both. Yet to conclude that both are true is logically contradictory, and therefore seemingly impossible. To resolve this apparent discrepancy, it must be realized that this contradiction exists only on the level of the rational mind, which thinks similarly to the binary logic of a computer chip that uses on and off switches to make calculations. In actuality, the essential nature of God is a profound mystery that is beyond words and cannot be understood with the limited capacities of our minds.

Paradoxical descriptions of God have been uttered since the dawn of time. An ancient axiom attributed to the legendary Hermes Trismegistus declares that, "God is a sphere whose center is everywhere and whose circumference is nowhere." Another way of saying this is that God is within everything and everything is within God. This double-sided description is an expression of Kannon's Way, which is an inclusive frame of mind that always sees both sides of an issue and, as a result, approaches life with flexibility and balance. (See chapter 9.)

Meishusama is flexible in matters of theology. He describes his teachings as both monotheistic and polytheistic in nature. Out of the One emerges the many, but the many never separate from the One. Meishusama claims that God can manifest in numerous forms, each an expression of a different spiritual quality, such as peace, love, truth, or harmony. This variety of forms might confuse people and lead them to think that there are many gods because they fail to perceive their underlying unity.

Even though you tie a hundred knots, the string remains one. – Rumi

God's presence can be found in the world as well as within each of us, as the Light at the center of our soul. In a similar sense, goodness and beauty can also be found everywhere if our eyes are sufficiently open. The mind needs to become free of obscurations so it can unite with the beauty and Light that is everywhere.

See things from a spiritual perspective—a God-centered viewpoint. [2] *– KW*

The more we progress spiritually, the more we tend to lovingly embrace the world rather than reject it. This is because one has love in one's heart. Spirituality does not remove us from life, although it does free us from binding attachment to it. By becoming detached and peaceful, we become increasingly "in the world but not of it."

Personal and Impersonal

In this body Kannon has taken up humble abode. – Meishusama I. MK

In contrast to the impersonal concept of Miroku Omikami, Meishusama often personified God as one who frowns on those who do bad, and smiles on those who do good. This is a God who takes a personal interest in people and who actively cares about their welfare and spiritual evolution. On a grander scale, God also oversees the spiritual progression of the entire Cosmos. In this matter, as with everything else, Meishusama was quite flexible, and his wording and description of God varied according to the subject matter and the person he was addressing.

When looking inwardly, one can discover God as the eternal Spirit ever present at the core of our being, whereas when looking outwardly, one can discover God as the ultimate power and intelligence that directs all things.

---

[2] Meishusama, "Seeing form a God-Centered Viewpoint," *Shumei Magazine*, vol. 165 (May 1994).

Of course, these are both the same God because there are not two Supreme Beings—only one. Again, this division between inward and outward is created in our own minds, not in God's, for God is beyond the limitations of inner and outer, or subject and object. These opposites are like the two sides of the same coin. Stated simply, God, or Miroku Omikami, is both everywhere and beyond.

According to Meishusama, Miroku Omikami is continually personifying itself as the deity Kannon, the compassionate power of God. Meishusama claimed that this deity merged with his inner being and thereafter began to move and speak through him. As a result of this, Meishusama became a living embodiment of God—a fusion of the human and the divine. Now that Meishusama is no longer physically alive, but instead dwells in the spiritual world, some feel that he continues to intercede on their behalf and so they extend their prayers and gratitude towards him.

Whether one views God in a personal or impersonal way, or both, is up to the individual. Both views can support one's faith and trust in divinity. In any case, God is not accessible through philosophical speculation, but only through spiritual perception. This is gained through inner transformation, not through ideas.

To be free, we should not create fixed images or frameworks.
– Kannon's Way. HT

The Three Spiritual Elements

Miroku Omikami is infinite, eternal, ever present, and changeless, and also finite, temporal, elusive, and changing. Change is a creative process that occurs within the realm of manifestation, whereas the changeless is a nonoccurrence within the unmanifest realm, the world of the ultimate mystery. Miroku Omikami creates the world from the metaphorical elements of fire, water, and earth, the three fundamental components of existence. Meishusama writes: "Everything in the universe is composed of three great elements. In other words, there is not a single thing that does not owe its creation to the power of these three elements. These three great elements are the sun, the moon, and the earth. The sun is the source of the spirit of fire; the moon is the source of the spirit of water; the earth is the source of the spirit of earth. These three elements flow and mingle inextricably together." (*The Spirit of Fire, The Spirit of Water, and The Spirit of Earth. HT*)

The spirit of earth is the gross, material dimension; the spirit of water is a subtle, semi-material dimension; and the spirit of fire is a luminous, immaterial dimension. The distribution and balance of these three elements determine the nature and condition of our world. Within human beings, they represent body, mind, and spirit. The body is dense and heavy—like earth; the mind flows forward—like water; and spirit radiates Light—like fire. Earth, water, and fire can also be interpreted as symbols for qualities and processes in the natural world, such as solid, liquid, or gas.

The Three Spiritual Elements

Fire	Water	Earth
Sun	Moon	Earth
Sunshine	Rain	Soil
God's Realm	Spiritual World	Physical World
Spirit	Mind	Matter
Perception	Feeling	Action
Oxygen	Hydrogen	Nitrogen
Subjective	Inter-subjective	Objective
Thoughts	Words	Deeds
Heart	Lungs	Stomach
Immaterial	Semi-material	Material
Gas	Liquid	Solid

Symbols are images that represent complex realities: a heart can symbolize love, a bird can symbolize Spirit, and a car can symbolize freedom. A symbol cannot be reduced to one single definition or a simple sign, but is open to multiple interpretations. Symbols are meant to evoke, not represent, and therefore, some symbols have many possible meanings.

Although the three spiritual elements are described symbolically, they are real things. They are the energetic qualities that underlie all of manifestation, similar to the way atoms and molecules underlie all forms of matter. How they manifest in the world depends on how they combine with each other, as well as the environment in which they appear.

The Inconceivability of God

Use the Light that is in you to recover your natural clearness of sight. – *Lao Tzu*

The human mind is constantly accumulating knowledge. While this might be useful for dealing with the complexity of the world, in spiritual matters it often creates confusion. This is because God is not an object, not even in the subtlest sense, and so cannot be understood through symbolic representation. When relying solely on thought, we disengage from Spirit, because the mind is only capable of thinking "about" things, and cannot know them directly. Once God is perceived as an idea, additional concepts inevitably get attached until entire religious systems and philosophical traditions arise, further binding Spirit to the conceptual realm.

If a person's spiritual understanding is based on concepts rather than a direct, living experience, they might easily delude themselves with problematic ideas and beliefs. Or worse, they might use religious doctrines to justify their own poor behavior while condemning that of others. Bound in the mind and lacking the living touch of God, they become susceptible to dogmatism, exclusivity, and self-righteousness, which give rise to intolerance, religious persecution, and violence.

One gains authentic spiritual insight from direct inner experience, not from facts and opinions. What people need most are experiences that open their hearts and purify their souls. They need love, kindness, and beauty. These gentle qualities are what will bring peace on earth and goodwill towards all.

The Spiritual World

The spiritual world is like the material world in being divided into a great number of ranks. It divides roughly into three major ranks, upper, middle and lower. At the top of the ranking is of course God and the other ranks, although they are divine to some extent, are inferior and subordinate to Him.

– Jyorei and Happiness. HT

Everything originates in the spiritual world, a realm that encompasses and surpasses the world of our physical senses. The spiritual world is subdivided into three main levels roughly corresponding to heaven, purgatory, and hell. Beyond this is the world of the ultimate mystery, which is the realm of pure Spirit, in contrast to the spiritual world, which contains images and forms. Spirit itself is formless. All forms arise out of the formless realm, like water out of steam. Spirit, the world of the ultimate mystery, can neither be thought about nor imagined, and thus remains a mystery to the mind.

The conditions in the spiritual world create events and circumstances in the physical world. What appears to be a chain of events, with a specific cause and effect, is actually a secondary effect resulting from its true cause, the conditions within the spiritual world. The spiritual world influences our ideas, which then form our values, which then determine our behavior on both an individual and collective scale. The civil rights activist Rev. Martin Luther King, Jr., put it this way: "Everything that we see is a shadow cast by that which we do not see."

One level of the spiritual world acts as a repository of the mind, and can be viewed as a reflection of the collective psyche of all humanity, which can be subdivided into specific cultures such as American, Arabic, Japanese, etc. This collective psyche can think and dream, much like individuals do. A dream is both subjective (because it is an expression of the mind), and also objective (because it contains people, places, things, and events, not to mention abstractions, memories, and moods). Some gifted individuals such as psychics and visionaries are believed to actually see into the spiritual world and report back to others what they have seen.

The spiritual world is inhabited by many disincarnate beings, including our departed friends and ancestors, various animal spirits, as well as other non-human beings. This is also the place where we ourselves go when we die.

The spiritual world is a world of concepts, of pure idea.
> – *The Marvels of the Spiritual World.* HT

The Three Worlds

The three worlds can be summarized in the following manner:

The physical world is *objective* in nature. – It can be perceived by the five senses, and can be experienced and validated by more than one person. It is subject to the laws of time and space.

The world of the ultimate mystery is *subjective* in nature. – It is silently aware of life's changing phenomena and is the impersonal backdrop of all experience. It is the causal source of all that arises and cannot be known objectively. Although unseen, it is the harmonizing, transformative agent within all that can be seen. It is the source of Light. The world of the ultimate mystery (which Meishusama sometimes referred to as "God's Realm" or as "the world of the third dimension of profundity") can also be defined as the highest aspect of the spiritual world, depending on how you divide it up.

The spiritual world is everything that lies *in-between* the subjective and objective poles of experience. – It is made up of thoughts, feelings, desires, and dreams, which can be simultaneously subjective and objective. They are subjective because they color our perceptions, and are objective because they are observable to the mind. The spiritual world is a dreamlike realm hovering between conscious awareness and deep sleep, between the manifest and the unmanifest realms of experience.

The three worlds operate simultaneously, and overlap in time and space. All three are components of day-to-day experience. The spiritual world and the physical world interact with each other in a dynamic, living process. Commenting on their relationship, Meishusama says, "The spiritual world is a continuation of the material world." *(Aspects of Death. HT)* The world of the ultimate mystery, on the other hand, resides above the world of time and space, illuminating all things, like sunshine on a spring day.

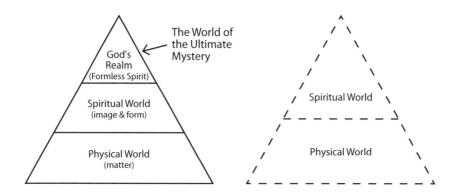

Levels of Reality – The Three Worlds

God is the creator, and material things are the creations made from denser vibrations of God's Spirit. Everything can be seen as a manifestation of divine energy, and the three elements are the three main levels of vibratory frequency. As Meishusama said, "To sum it up simply: earth is material, water is semi-material, and fire is immaterial." *(The Spirit of Fire, The Spirit of Water, and The Spirit of Earth. HT)*

We can compare the relationship between the spiritual world and the physical world to the difference between phenomena that we can touch, taste, smell, hear, or see, and phenomena such as radio waves, ultraviolet rays, and X-rays that are invisible and inaudible. One is a world of tangible experience, and the other is intangible (except though the agency of secondary devices such as radios or photographs). In this analogy, the world of the ultimate mystery would be the space in which these phenomena occur.

Much like the subatomic world, the spiritual world is imperceptible to our senses, yet no less real. It affects us just as significantly as the physical world, and even more profoundly.

I refer to the world that lies within man's immediate knowledge as "the material world" and the world unknown to exclusively scientific man as "the spiritual world." – Natural Power. HT

5   SOUL AND SPIRIT

The Soul and its Spiritual Influences

According to Meishusama, the human soul is primarily affected by three invisible spirits: the divine spirit, the animal spirit, and the guardian spirit. The divine spirit infuses the soul with awareness and sensitivity, the animal spirit activates its desires and instincts, and the guardian spirit affects its conscience and good fortune. How the soul responds to their combined influences determines the degree to which it evolves spiritually.

Soul

Man is not simply a material body; there is also a soul we cannot see. Men are made up of both elements, physical and spiritual, but the spirit is the chief of these. As the spirit moves, in other words, as the will dictates, so does the body move. – Methods and Results. HT

The soul is individuated Spirit. It is a condensation and crystallization of the inherent Oneness of God's essential nature. The soul is related at one end to God and at the other end to the sensorial world. The soul is subject to change, in contrast to the Spirit, which is unchanging. Located within the center of the soul is the divine spirit, which illuminates the soul's form with pure awareness. Just as the moon is but a dim reflection of the sun, so too, is the soul but a dim reflection of the inner spirit. Each borrows its light from a brighter source, one from outside, (the sun), and the other from inside (the spirit).

The soul acts like a container for accumulating memories, habits, emotions, and desires. We are not really separate from God, but we may think so because of the layers of impurities that cloud the soul's innate awareness. The more impurities we have, the more God's positive influence is blocked from affecting us. A pure soul is gifted with natural wisdom and is inclined towards good, whereas an impure soul is restrained by ignorance and is dominated by selfish desires and binding compulsions. The impure soul feels heavy and slow because it is impeded by negative impressions and attachments.

One can imagine the soul as being similar to a bubble with swirling transparent colors floating on its surface. These swirling colors represent the various memories and tendencies accumulated over time by the soul, and tend to create an illusion of separation between the space inside the bubble and the space outside the bubble. But despite appearances, it is always the same space on each side of the bubble's skin. The apparent division between inner and outer does not affect the space. Similarly, the spiritual awareness within the core of the soul is at one with the greater field of spiritual awareness that permeates all things. There is only one Spirit—not many. The soul, by its transparency, occupies an intermediate position between form and the formless, time and the timeless, and the personal and the impersonal.

The soul is the animating principle, that which makes living things alive. It is the carrier of the life force, which is synonymous with movement and breath. Although God's Spirit takes residence within all things, it lies dormant until the soul activates it. When the soul enters into an organism, the organism inhales a breath and comes to life, and when the soul leaves it, the organism exhales and dies. Breath is the difference between a lifeless rock and a living animal. Indeed, the quality of the breath reflects the mood and temperament of the soul. Not only do humans have souls, but so do animals, insects, and plants as well, although their souls are probably much less individuated than those of humans. Even soil, which is alive with billions of microorganisms, may have something resembling a group soul. Unlike the body, the soul is indestructible. It is the personal essence that survives beyond physical death, after which it moves on to other realms.

The soul is also the emotional or feeling aspect of our being. It is our inner character—that which makes us unique. We can sense this inner character in others by looking into their eyes, which are popularly referred to as "the windows of the soul."

After the soul has completely purified itself and surrendered all traces of egoic separativity, it becomes one with God. This is what Jesus Christ meant when he said, "I and the Father are One," and what Meishusama indicated when he stated, "As the saying goes, I have 'the Light of God in my heart.' This is the supreme God, and everything I do and say is guided by God. In other words, there is no distinction between God and man. I am God personified." *(God Personified. HT)*

Whereas Spirit is impersonal in nature, lacking individual characteristics, the soul, by contrast, is personal, containing many unique qualities and tendencies, all of which were slowly developed over the course of many lifetimes. At birth in the physical plane, these soul qualities and tendencies exist as dormant potentialities similar to the invisible plans for an oak tree that exist within an acorn. All that is required for the soul to grow and develop into a well-defined individual are the proper supportive conditions, such as a mother, father, food, shelter, school, etc. Similarly, the acorn needs fresh air, pure water, adequate sunlight, and proper soil to grow into a giant oak tree. As the soul grows toward adulthood, its past life tendencies, combined with genetics and the environment, determine what type of person it will become. The soul functions as an intelligent matrix for organizing and integrating its various internal qualities, memories, and tendencies.

The soul is an invisible field of energy and awareness, not an object with fixed dimensions. Not only does the soul reside within the body, but it also extends beyond it. In this sense, the soul is unlike a bird stuck in a cage because it is bigger than the cage. The body is like a little marble swallowed by a large bird. The bird carries the marble wherever it flies, but eventually eliminates the marble and then continues on its journey through the skies.

Each of us has a particular mission to accomplish in this life which will further the evolution of our soul in the spiritual world. To discover this mission we need to undergo extensive purification and spiritual renewal.

Divine Spirit

It is said that man is the child of God, and that God is enshrined in man. This means essentially that man is charged with a mission by God and born into this world; he is given a part of God's Spirit. This is his divine spirit.

– Guardian Spirits. HT

Our soul, as it travels through countless lifetimes, is subject to numerous influences and conditionings, both inner and outer. The highest and most important influence comes from our divine spirit (also referred to as the main spirit). "The divine spirit is the best part of one's personality, the conscience," writes Meishusama. *(Guardian Spirits. HT)* This is the core of who we are, and that part of us which partakes of divinity. The divine spirit is eternal and unchanging, and operates as the core awareness within our soul. It is the subtle spark which lights up a person's eyes, and the unmoving force that moves our breath. The divine spirit is our very essence.

God dwells within all things, from the natural world of animals, vegetables, and minerals to manmade inventions and creations. Life forms are capable of expressing this inner divinity through conscious action. The more evolved a biological organism is, the more consciously it can act. The paleontologist, theologian, and Jesuit priest Pierre Teilhard de Chardin writes, "Whatever we may think of, we can be sure that. . . a richer and better organized [physical] structure will correspond to the more developed consciousness."

Rocks do not contain sufficient organic complexity to sustain life, nor do they have any mechanism for consciously perceiving the outer environment. Living things are able to breathe, consume food, grow, respond to stimuli, and reproduce. And although animals are alive and conscious, in general, their souls are much less conscious and evolved than those of humans. As a species, humans have much greater capacity for self-awareness, intelligence, and moral conscience than do the lower creatures of the animal kingdom. The human range of experience extends much further up into the mental realm than does that of the lower creatures. Humans read, compose music, design buildings, create machines, and communicate in sophisticated languages. They also reflect upon the past and plan for the future. And most uniquely, humans have a reflexive capacity that allows them not only to be self-conscious (as an object observed by others), but also to be conscious of their own consciousness (as an object to themselves). They are aware that they are aware. Although God's Spirit can be found within each of us as our innermost essence, this spirit cannot fully express itself in the world until the soul has been thoroughly purified in the spiritual world. The purer the soul, the more it tends to exhibit various spiritual qualities in its thoughts, words, and deeds.

Unlike the soul, the divine spirit is essentially pure. Nothing can affect it because it is without form or substance. Nonetheless, it can become covered with spiritual clouds to the extent that its presence within us is obscured.

Again, unlike the soul, the divine spirit does not evolve. Instead, it acts like an impartial observer of the soul's changing fortunes. It is unmoved by our personal joys and sorrows, and is forever peaceful and serene. The divine spirit functions much like the spotlight at a theatre, illuminating the various scenes of the play but remaining unaffected by any of it.

The divine spirit, despite its intimate association with the body and soul of an individual, remains forever one with God, just as a wave, despite its surface level movement, always maintains an inseparable unity with the ocean. Our divine spirit, as an aspect of divinity, exists beyond time and space, patiently waiting for us to rediscover its eternal presence deep within our soul.

Animal Spirit (Instinct and Desire)

Everyone is possessed to some extent by an animal spirit in the form of his secondary guardian spirit. This is unavoidable because of the very nature of human existence in a world where fleshly desires are to some extent necessary, and God permits this kind of animality for that reason. An evil person, on the other hand, is possessed by yet another animal spirit, or finds that their secondary guardian spirit has degenerated into a purely bestial form. Both these conditions are brought about by the clouding of the person's soul.

– An Evil Person Is a Sick Person. HT

The spiritual world is inhabited by a variety of beings, both human and nonhuman. Among the nonhuman beings are those of animal spirits such as wolves, fish, hawks, bears, foxes, turtles, snakes, and so on. Similar beliefs about animal spirits can be found in the cultures of indigenous people throughout the world.

According to Meishusama, early in life each person is assigned an animal spirit (or secondary guardian spirit) that exerts a guiding influence over the physical body, activating its various physiological processes, instinctual drives, automatic reflexes, and sense perceptions. Similarly, we do not consciously control our respiratory, digestive, circulatory, or nervous systems, but rather depend on the body's own innate intelligence to regulate these internal functions for us. Although the divine spirit, through the vehicle of the soul, breathes life into the physical body, it is the animal spirit that actually animates the body by stimulating its desires and passions. This influence is quite appropriate because, physiologically, humans are a type of animal with an anatomy and a DNA code similar to many simian species, most notably the chimpanzee.

The animal spirit tends to be selfish and unconscious and has no sense of ethics or morality. Psychologically, it operates in a manner similar to the Freudian concept of the Id, which is driven by lust and aggression. The animal spirit's actions tend to be compulsive and automatic, rather than conscious and deliberate. It gravitates towards the lower emotions of hate, anger, resentment, jealousy, depression, sorrow, and fear, and can also be consumed by the lower appetites of lust, ambition, and greed. Despite its lower tendencies, the animal spirit performs a useful and needed function: the survival of the human body. The animal spirit's instinctual nature provides us with the aggressiveness necessary to defend ourselves from harm and to acquire what we need. Without these instincts, we would not have the drive to eat, procreate, or succeed in the world.

The animal spirit is not an enemy to be attacked or conquered, nor is it an evil to be annihilated. Rather, it needs to be tempered by our conscience, which (in its pure form) is an expression of our divine spirit. Sometimes the animal spirit will respond best to compassionate understanding rather than judgmental repression, but at other times, if it is too wild and impulsive, then it must be kept on a tight leash. While it is important to appreciate our body and to take care of it, it is also important to understand that the body sees things from the perspective of separateness, and is most concerned with sensual pleasure and physical survival. In a purified state, the body is a useful vehicle for manifesting awareness, intelligence, and love, but is not really the source of these higher qualities. That source is our divine spirit.

Within the spiritual world there also exist other animal spirits that can temporarily inhabit and possess the bodies of human beings, thus overpowering the beneficial influence of the divine spirit. Meishusama elaborates, "These spirits are, of course, of the bestial type, such as fox-spirits, raccoon-spirits, dragon-spirits, and so on, and their behavior when they take over a person is, accordingly, very much like that of an animal. They are capable of cruelties and pitilessness beyond the limits of what a human being could tolerate." (*An Evil Person Is a Sick Person. HT*) Spiritual possessions like this can occur when a weak soul becomes too clouded with impurities that accumulate as a result of wrong actions in the past. Spiritual clouds block the higher influences emanating from our divine spirit, leaving us in spiritual darkness. To remedy this unfortunate condition, a person needs to increase the Light within their soul through purification, positive action, and faith in a higher goodness. It is important to remember that darkness cannot exist where there is Light.

There is no one who is totally without any spiritual deficiencies, and therefore everybody is to some extent controlled by possessing spirits, and to that extent is suffering from some mental disorder. – *Mental Disorders, God's Way to Health. HT*

Individual animal spirits can function as secondary guardian spirits or as externally possessing spirits. The first is constructive and useful, and the second is destructive and harmful. It is not necessary to know what type of animal is operating behind either of these functions because excessive interest in them tends to strengthen their negative influence over us—which can be problematic. Animal spirits have necessary functions to play in our lives, but our main interest and concern should be the soul's spiritual development, which is the only thing that guarantees true happiness.

Guardian Spirit

Souls that have been purified to some extent in the spiritual world are chosen as guardian spirits and extend protection to people in this world through the spiritual cords. – The Spiritual Cords. HT

The guardian spirit (also known as the primary guardian spirit or as the ancestor spirit) is a discarnate being residing in the invisible spiritual world that is assigned to guide and protect a particular soul living in the physical world. In this regard, it is similar to the Western concept of a guardian angel. However, unlike guardian angels, which are selected from among the community of angels, the guardian spirit is usually selected from among an individual's ancestors in the spiritual world. It is their job to accompany and watch over the soul of a person until his or her physical death. On certain rare occasions this guardianship position has instead been assigned to a uniquely divine animal spirit. The guardian spirit has the responsibility of encouraging the soul to behave in a virtuous manner, and of pointing it in a higher direction. In this way it supports the soul's spiritual advancement. The guardian spirit often communicates to us through symbolic dreams, creative inspiration, and through the silent voice of our inner conscience.

> Spiritual dreams are caused by guardian spirits wanting to tell human beings something. Dreams created by guardian spirits are often allegorical or metaphorical, and frequently require specialized interpretation. As I have said before, the material world reflects the changes of the spiritual world, and therefore the guardian spirits who live in the spiritual world know of things that will inevitably come about in the material world in the future. They use dreams as a means of informing humanity about these. When you have a presentiment that something is sure to happen, this is due to the influence of a guardian spirit. – *Dreams. HT*

Because of their higher vantage point, the guardian spirits can see more clearly what the future holds, and can benefit us by providing protection and advice. They can also contribute to our good fortune by various magical means. The animal spirit within us, which is selfishly motivated towards survival at the expense of others, is tempered by the beneficial guidance of our guardian spirit. The effectiveness of this guidance depends on our inner purity as well as our receptivity to the higher influence. To this, Meishusama adds: "It is one's own animal spirit that urges one towards evil, and it is one's guardian spirit that urges one towards good. Above both of these, however, is the divine spirit, which directs the soul strongly towards absolute good. Therefore, the basic force necessary for the conquest of evil is to be found in an increase in the power of the divine spirit." *(Defeat the Evil in Yourself. HT)*

Lamp Analogy

Our divine spirit, which expresses itself through the agency of the soul, can be viewed as the essence or foundation of our personal identity, whereas the animal spirit and the guardian spirit can both be viewed as outer influences that support our existence. Although we each also possess a physical body and a conscious mind, these too are not part of our fundamental self. Rather, they are temporary structures inhabited by us in this lifetime that are eventually discarded at death.

The divine spirit is the impassive witness of all phenomena. Like clean lenses on a pair of eyeglasses, its transparency allows it to see clearly. Anything that can be perceived—including sensory phenomena and internal thoughts and feelings—is not the divine spirit, because these are objects whereas the divine spirit is not. It is pure subjectivity, and a subject is unperceivable as an object. The divine spirit is the observer, not the observed—the perceiver, not the perceived. It transcends death and is eternal. Although the divine spirit may identify with the various bodies and minds that it temporarily inhabits during its journey from one lifetime to another, it is also capable, through grace, of dropping this limited identification and awakening to itself as pure Spirit. When this happens to people, they become selfless.

One possible way to visualize the relationship of the soul to the three types of spirits is to use the analogy of a light bulb within a lamp. At the center of the light bulb is the bright light radiating from the metal filament. This light represents our divine spirit, which is pure awareness. Surrounding the brightly lit filament is the glass bulb, which is the soul. The soul is illumined by the spiritual Light radiating from deep within the center of its being. If the glass is clean and transparent, the light shines brightly, whereas if the glass is dirty or darkly tinted, then less light filters through. The amount of light that shines from the bulb indicates the purity of the individual soul. The physical body, which is under the control of the animal spirit, is the lamp itself. The lampshade represents the mind, which can also block the Light if it is too dense. The light bulb needs a lamp to hold it in place and to conduct electricity, just as the soul needs a physical body to function in the world. But the light is the most important factor to the user—not the lamp—just as Spirit is the most important factor to the soul—not the body. The electricity is God's Power, which brings life to that which is otherwise inanimate. The guardian spirit is the one who comes by regularly to dust off the light bulb and the lampshade, thereby allowing an increased amount of light to shine through.

Lamp Analogy – Spirit, Soul, Mind, and Body

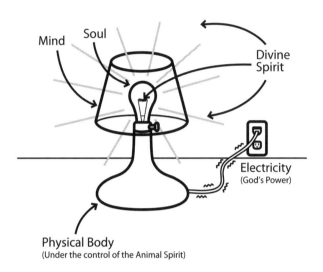

Throughout a person's lifetime the guardian spirit and the animal spirit compete for influence over the soul. For some people, the animal spirit may be more dominant, thereby influencing them towards negative action. Other individuals may find that the guardian spirit is more persuasive, thereby helping them to be better people and also bringing them good fortune.

An example of this might be if a person came upon a child drowning in a rushing river: the animal spirit, being selfish, would be primarily concerned with its own personal safety, whereas the guardian spirit, being altruistic, would be inclined to save the child despite the risk. The stronger influence of the two would determine the resulting behavior of the person.

The Soul in Relation to the Spiritual World

One must first heal the spirit by Divine Light in order to bring a cure to the body. The soul of a human being belongs, of course, to the spiritual world; the physical body belongs to the material world. – Natural Power. HT

Spirit within the Soul

What dwells behind us and what dwells before us are small matters compared to what dwells within us. – Ralph Waldo Emerson

Meishusama, demonstrating his typical flexibility, uses a variety of examples to explain certain concepts. An alternate way of viewing the inner structure of the soul and its relation to the spiritual world is to locate the divine spirit in the center of a circle that is surrounded by the mind, which, in turn, is surrounded by the soul at the outer circumference. This can be illustrated using a diagram consisting of a series of concentric circles with each succeeding circle more distant and removed from divinity, which is located in the middle.

The Soul in Relation to the Spiritual World

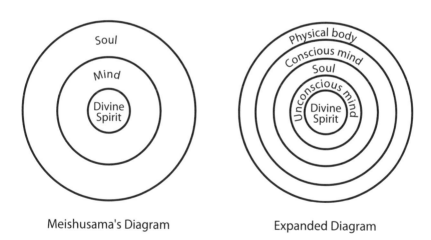

Meishusama's Diagram   Expanded Diagram

The reason for placing the divine spirit in the middle should be obvious, as it is the true center of our being. Spirit is that from which all else emerges. On the other hand, some might question the reason for placing the mind ahead of the soul in its proximity to the divine spirit, as the soul is often regarded as being of a subtler, more refined nature than the thinking process. For example, most people can experience their thoughts, but not their soul, and therefore have only a vague idea about the latter. To help clarify this confusion, a simple distinction can be made between the conscious mind, which is overt, and the unconscious mind, which is hidden.

Each soul is on a long journey through countless lifetimes during which it experiences a full range of possible conditions, including health and sickness, peace and conflict, and success and failure. Such a variety of conditions allows the soul to learn and grow spiritually. The essence of these experiences is accumulated and stored deep within the soul as unconscious memories and tendencies.

The universe is God's extended body, and thus a part of God evolves in conjunction with the evolution of that body. Just as our arms, legs, nose, and teeth are each a part of us, so too is each and every thing in all of creation a part of God. Humanity, as the highest life form on the planet, leads this evolution, like the crest of a wave, and so carries a great spiritual responsibility. Each of us, individually, as we continue to learn and grow, has a valuable role to play in the Creator's cosmic drama.

Outside the soul is the conscious mind, which is able to think, evaluate, and organize experience in a rational manner. In order to access memories from the past, the conscious mind must reach into the soul, which contains the unconscious mind. Most of our memories and conditioning are unavailable to the conscious mind except under unusual circumstances, such as through hypnosis or dream recollection. With this understanding, we could say that the mind is both within and outside the soul, depending on whether one is referring to the unconscious or conscious component. The mind is one entity, but is divided by function.

In addition to expanding Meishusama's model to include this distinction, with the unconscious mind contained within our soul, and the conscious mind outside its perimeter, we can also extend this model by displaying the relationship of the physical body to the mind. Our brain houses the conscious mind, as well as a large percentage of memory and emotions. In relation to our diagram, we can say that the outer ring of the conscious mind is surrounded by and enveloped by the physical body. Both conscious and unconscious thoughts are stored in it like software stored in a computer. Each outer ring of the circle is further removed from Spirit, manifesting a progressively denser and slower vibration. Physical matter is the most removed from Spirit.

Meishusama also sub-divides the mind into three main components: reason, emotions, and will (or desire). He writes, "To analyze people's thoughts, we can say that they consist of reason and emotions, and a desire to put them into motion. The organs of the forebrain are connected to reason, and the rear parts of the brain are the sources of emotion. Whichever it may be, reason or emotion, it must be rendered into action, and when this happens—indeed, every time it happens, however trifling—will or volition is necessary. This will is strengthened by an invisible energy center located in the middle of the stomach. This is what we may call the source of action. A combination of these three makes up the tripartite entity of human thought." *(Mental Disorders, God's Way to Health. HT)*

Arrangement of the Spiritual World

The spiritual world can also be arranged in a circular diagram. Meishu-sama writes, "The center of this configuration is God in Heaven. The further away from this center the circle is, the less divinity it partakes of and the more it differs from Heaven. In addition, every circle is different in some way from its neighbors." *(Jyorei and Happiness. HT)*

One's soul is on a journey from the outer material rings toward the spiritual center. With each progressive step inward, one experiences greater peace and joy. Meishusama adds, "Thus we can see that as a man's fate on earth is decided by his position in the hierarchy of the spiritual world, he should strive to rise as high as he possibly can, for the higher he rises the less suffering and abomination he must endure and the greater the happiness within his grasp. Or, to put it another way, the higher he goes the less impurity he has and the less purification he needs to undergo." *(Jyorei and Happiness. HT)*

In the center is God, or Spirit, and at the outer circumference is physical matter. Although God's Spirit exists in everything, in both the center and the circumference, the further away from the center one gets, the less consciousness there is of this divine presence. Physical matter is solidified energy vibrating at a slower frequency than more subtle forms of phenomena such as sound or light. Matter is neither good nor bad in itself. Its purpose is to function as a container for Spirit. The human body is a necessary vehicle for our soul to journey through this world, and as such it supports our spiritual growth.

From another perspective, this diagram can be reversed, with the physical body situated on the inside, surrounded by a much larger spiritual body (the aura), which, in turn, is surrounded by Spirit, which is infinitely larger. This configuration can be illustrated by a series of concentric circles with God, or Spirit, on the outside, the mind inside that outer ring, and the physical body located in the middle.

The spiritual world is less constricted by time and space than is the physical world. This non-dimensionality is also why there are so many possible ways to represent the spiritual world in a diagram. The higher up in the spiritual world, and the further away from the senses, the less everything can fit into any single form of symbolic representation. This is why spiritual experiences are so hard to describe. About this, Meishusama writes, "One problem is that spiritual matters are not approachable through the five senses, and so it follows that to gain a direct perception of their existence and reality is very difficult indeed. However, it is not a case of conjuring something out of nothing, but rather perceiving something that already exists, and this perception definitely lies within everybody's grasp." *(Preface. HT)*

Although Spirit is invisible, we can recognize its expression in others by how well they demonstrate love, truth, humility, patience, humor, generosity, purity, kindness, and wisdom. A person will automatically tend to exhibit these traits after having sufficiently purified both their spiritual and physical bodies. At this point, there is less of an effort on their part to be virtuous because their innate goodness manifests naturally.

Spiritual Cords

The term "spiritual cord" seems to be relatively new. It is primarily because these cords are much finer and more subtle than the atmosphere, and therefore invisible, that their importance has been neglected for so long. Their influence on all human affairs, however, is impossible to ignore. They are the cause of human happiness and misery; they shape history, in the widest sense. And so the human race must learn to recognize the nature and importance of spiritual cords.

– The Spiritual Cords. HT

Each of our lives is defined by relationships. These include relationships with parents, spouse, children, friends, co-workers, neighbors, as well as with possible rivals or enemies. Beyond this, we are each related to our community and our country and, beyond this, to the planet and the entire universe. We are also in relationship to the animals, plants, and inanimate things. All of these relationships affect our state of mind and behavior.

Beyond the outwardly visible forms of relationships, there are also invisible components to our relationships with people, places, and things. Meishusama labeled these components "spiritual cords."

Spiritual cords are invisible lines of energy that stretch between various people, places, and things. Like the aura, they are invisible to most people, yet exert powerful influences on everyone. There are literally thousands of spiritual cords attached to each person. The relative significance of a relationship can be measured by the thickness and strength of the spiritual cords connecting two people. The strongest cords are usually between husband and wife, then parent and child, next between brother and sister, and so on. There are also long-lasting spiritual cords connecting us with our deceased ancestors. Thoughts and feelings flow invisibly along these lines from one person to the other.

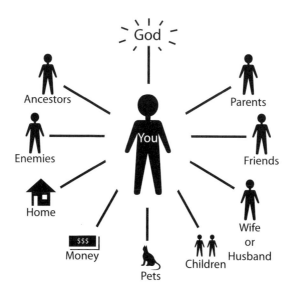

The Varieties of Spiritual Cords

There are tens, hundreds, thousands—uncountable numbers of spiritual cords attached to you. Some are thick, some thin; some are long, some short. And some of them are good, while others are bad. They all, to a varying degree, influence and change your life. It is no exaggeration to say that human beings stay alive because of these spiritual cords. – *The Spiritual Cords. HT*

In reality, all of life is interconnected and interrelated in innumerable ways beyond our imagination. Spiritual cords can affect us in both positive and negative ways, depending upon the type of thoughts that pass through them. Negative thoughts bring us down and positive thoughts uplift us. If we associate with people of noble character we tend to become good, but if we associate with people of poor character we tend to become bad. This is why we often become like the friends we keep. The effect is largely derived from the influence of the spiritual cords we share with them.

Not only are we affected by the thoughts of others, but our thoughts affect them as well. Therefore, it is important to hold kind thoughts of the people in our lives. When our relationships are based on mutual love and respect, beneficial energies are exchanged through the spiritual cords.

The spiritual cords from God are pure radiance. – The Spiritual Cords. HT

Of all our relationships, the one we share with God is the most significant. As the spiritual cords connecting us to God become thicker and stronger, our soul begins to glow with God's radiant peace and joy. These most significant of all cords extend deep into the heart of existence itself and also into our innermost core, where our divine spirit resides. It is here, in this silent inner core, that God's blessings can be found.

Evolution of the Soul

The greatest aim of the discipline undergone in the spiritual world is the removal of worldly attachments, and the height to which a spirit can rise depends on the degree to which it has been able to rid itself of these.

– Egotism and Worldly Attachment. HT

All of nature is subject to the cycles of birth and death. Only Spirit is unchanging and eternal. Death is not the end of existence, but only a transition to another realm. At death, the physical body is left behind, and the soul continues to accumulate experiences in the spiritual world. If a person is burdened with excessive attachment to the people or conditions in their earthly life, after death they risk becoming trapped in one of the lower dimensions. This can happen because they are obsessively looking backwards to their former life rather than letting go and moving forward towards something new.

The lower dimensions of the spiritual world are populated by many otherworldly beings, including ghosts and various other disincarnate spirits. Usually, depending on the individual's level of spiritual evolution and the amount of spiritual clouds he or she has managed to burn off, his or her soul will bypass this dimension and move on to the level of existence most appropriate to it. After it has been sufficiently purified, the soul will reincarnate again into another physical body.

In the spiritual world, human souls are purged to some degree of the many and various sins they have committed in the material world, and they are subsequently born again into this world. – *The Spiritual Cords. HT*

Our relatives and ancestors remain spiritually connected to us after they pass on to the other side. These connections are like invisible wires or cords through which psychic communication travels back and forth. Consequently, it is not just through our genetic heritage that our ancestors influence us, but also in subtler, nonphysical ways such as through their thoughts and feelings.

Many people in Asia pray for the happiness of their deceased ancestors. They believe that by honoring and appreciating their ancestors, it encourages the ancestors to provide valuable assistance from "the other side."

The view from the spiritual world is similar to the view from atop a tall mountain. It allows one to see the vast panorama down below. Living in this physical world, we may not see the traffic jam further down the road, but from the vantage point of the spiritual world, our ancestors can see it quite easily. They can also see what we need to do in order to avoid the traffic jam, and can also inspire us to take an alternate road to our destination. Or, they might draw outside help to the scene to quickly clear it up.

> When the body reaches a state of complete powerlessness through old age, illness, injury, or loss of blood, the soul and the body part company. This is death. In other words, death is when the soul breaks away from the material world. The spirit reverts completely to the spiritual world for a time and is subsequently born again into this world; the body rots and returns to the earth. This is what people know about the process. And one implication of this knowledge is that the soul is capable of unlimited life, while the body is limited and exists as a thing of secondary importance.
>
> – *Natural Power. HT*

After we die, we discard our physical body and lose most of our personal identity, along with its accumulated memories and habits. What remains afterwards is our soul, which was only temporarily visiting this world of density and form. Upon being reborn into a physical body, an infant appears to be empty of all past memories and thoughts; but just as an acorn has the invisible blueprint for the giant oak tree hidden within it, so too does the infant contain latent tendencies and memories from past lives. Although these are not usually conscious to the infant, nonetheless they begin to influence the soul as it gains experience in life. During the soul's interactions with people and events, the old tendencies begin to reassert themselves. The physical body, under the influence of the animal spirit, also conditions the soul through genetic, neurological, hormonal and other biochemical processes.

The relationship between reborn human beings and the spiritual world is as follows: Each person has a mission assigned to him by God. As he carries it out, he accumulates, knowingly or unknowingly, the stains of sin on his soul. At the same time his body becomes weak with illness or old age, and his task becomes harder and harder to carry out. Eventually he casts off his mortal body and returns to the spiritual world. The body is no more than "remains," as the expression has it. – *Life and Death. HT*

The soul learns and evolves by experiencing the various consequences of its actions. Ignorant or harmful behavior generates suffering either immediately, in the afterlife, or in the following incarnation, whereas actions that are wise and helpful create happier experiences in the future. This process of cause and effect is an immutable law that governs all things; it is the Law of Divine Justice.

When a human being dies—in other words, when the spirit leaves its physical shell—it leaves mainly from three parts of the body. These are the forehead, the navel, and the tips of the toes. The reasons for these three distinct exit points are that the purest kind of spirit leaves by the forehead, the more defiled through the navel, and the most muddied and corrupted through the toes. A pure spirit is one that has been purified by good works and virtue while the person was alive; the muddied and corrupt spirit is one that has been stained by a lifetime's sin. There are also spirits that fall between these two extremes. All actions on earth affect spirits, and all spirits are thus divided into these three. – *Life and Death. HT*

In this sense, nothing is really lost because we cannot escape the repercussions of our actions. Justice regulates the cosmos. Good deeds brighten our soul, and bad deeds diminish its luminosity. Sometimes we move forwards, and sometimes backwards, but always with the opportunity to learn from our actions. It is through the continual cycle of reincarnation that the soul grows and matures. Through the experiences of countless lifetimes, the soul eventually develops wisdom and spiritual maturity and thus rises higher up in the spiritual world.

Everything in the universe is constantly evolving, step-by-step, towards conscious union with God's Spirit, the divine presence that surrounds and per-meates all things. Meishusama refers to this Presence as, "The world of the ul-timate mystery, that is, the world of the third dimension of profundity." *(Repent, For the End of Night Is at Hand. HT)* This "world of the ultimate mystery" can be found within. It is the spiritual home that we've all been endlessly searching

6 SPIRITUAL CLOUDS AND PURIFICATION

Physical and Mental Toxins

In each and every man is a certain amount of polluting toxin. Some is inherent and some acquired after birth.
                                     – The Three Great Disasters and the Three Lesser Disasters. HT

Much of the sickness and suffering that we experience occurs as a result of toxins that have accumulated in our bodies throughout our lives. The food we eat is full of chemicals from pesticides, artificial flavorings, and preservatives. Meat and dairy products are often loaded with hormones and antibiotics. We are surrounded by air and water pollution, not to mention electromagnetic pollution and other types of harmful radiations. Fumes from cleaning fluids and chemical gasses released from new carpeting and furniture pollute indoor air. Personal hygiene products and cosmetics also contain poisonous chemicals that soak into our skin. Dental fillings contain mercury and other heavy metals that slowly seep into our body. In our modern world, it is hard to escape this constant onslaught of physical toxins. Most of these physical toxins fall into one of three main categories: heavy metals, molds and yeasts, and man made chemicals, although some can also come from radiation, plants, insects or parasites. In addition to this, some toxins can be inherited directly from our parents or from the genetic inheritance of our ancestors.

As well as environmental pollution, we can also suffer from autotoxemia, the self-poisoning that occurs as a result of poor digestion caused by systemic yeast or parasites or from the malfunctioning of the liver or kidneys, the two organs responsible for removing toxins from the blood stream. When toxins are not adequately filtered by the kidneys or broken down by the liver, they begin to accumulate in those organs, as well as in the blood, the lymph glands, the joints, around the nerves, and in other sensitive areas of the body.

Subtler than physical toxins are the mental toxins that cloud our judgment and cause stress and emotional suffering. We live in a virtual sea of negative thought forms generated by all of humanity. This combination of negative thoughts and feelings engulfs the environment, easily disturbing our peace of mind. When anger and hostility are directed towards us, they can sometimes be just as damaging to our health as the effects of physical toxins. More significantly, we also generate our own internal toxins from the negative thoughts and feelings that we hold within our hearts. Actions that hurt others, whether deliberate or through neglect, can generate some of the strongest and most enduring toxins by leaving negative impressions deep within our soul. All toxins leave their mark in the spiritual world, thus causing negative outcomes in the physical world.

Our physical body is a living canvas on which we paint our thoughts and emotions. Every thought we hold manifests as a chemical messenger, telling the body what to do, when to do it, and to what degree. Anxiety causes the heart to pump faster, the adrenal glands to work overtime, and the brainwaves to speed up. Anger causes the lungs to constrict, the muscles to tighten, and the blood to flow to the surface of the skin. Sorrow depletes vital energy, slows down the metabolism, and makes the breath heavy. These types of negative thoughts and feelings also disrupt the hormonal balance within the brain and the internal organs, which exacerbates the misery still further.

Negative thoughts are self-perpetuating. They paint a dark picture of the world, and then we respond to this dark picture by becoming even more negative. Each reinforces the other. That is why it is hard to change a bad mood once it has taken hold of us.

If a person thinks evil thoughts and performs evil actions, the clouding of his spiritual body increases accordingly. Resentment, hate, jealousy, and other such feelings form cloudiness, and when they are transmitted to a person they increase the clouding of his spirit. – *Spiritual Radiations and the Aura. HT*

According to Meishusama, all suffering ultimately originates in the spiritual world. To a large extent, our lives are the result of thoughts and feelings generated now or in the past, either by ourselves or by others. Selfishness, animosity, judgment, envy, despair, lust, greed—these all leave negative impressions in the spiritual world that eventually generate corresponding conditions in the outer world. These negative impressions Meishusama called "spiritual clouds." The collective thoughts and actions of large societies and entire countries generate spiritual clouds as well, which can result in such catastrophic incidents as earthquakes, floods, economic crisis, wars, and plagues.

> Sufferings of society such as the havoc of storms, natural calamities, earthquakes and riots are all methods of purification similar to individual sickness. The most considerable suffering is, of course, that brought about by war, and it must be obvious that the only way to prevent this kind of disaster is to clear away the clouds from the souls of mankind— all the individuals who make up society. – *A Third World War Can Be Avoided. HT*

All living things, including vegetables and insects, emit invisible energy fields called auras that, according to many experts, vibrate at various rates of speed. These fields of energy surround the human body and reflect both a person's spiritual and physical condition. The auras of human beings vibrate much faster than do those of less evolved creatures, and even amongst humans the range of vibration can vary tremendously from one person to the next. Although most people do not see auras, we can all sense them to some extent if we try, especially when in close proximity to others. Auras can vary in size, brightness, and color depending upon a person's internal condition. A small, cloudy aura reveals an unhappy or sick individual, whereas a large, bright aura reveals a happy or healthy individual. Someone who is spiritually advanced will have a huge, luminous aura. Meishusama writes, "A normal person's aura is one or two inches in thickness, a virtuous man's is two or three feet, and a saint's is infinite. In contrast, the aura around a sinful and clouded spirit is thin and feeble." *(An Examination of Miracles. HT)*

The more we can eliminate physical toxins from our bodies, and mental and emotional toxins from our minds, the quicker we can regain our health and happiness. The spiritual healing practice of Jyorei (see chapter 10) is very helpful for this purpose. Also, exhibiting kind and loving behavior towards others while maintaining a happy and positive disposition brightens the aura and also enhances the cellular activity within our physical body.

In fact, there is always a biochemical response within our body from every thought and emotion we hold. Recent discoveries in microbiology and mind/body medicine are beginning to confirm these and other psychosomatic connections.

Most noteworthy are the recent discoveries by cellular biologist Dr. Bruce Lipton, demonstrating that the cellular membrane is intelligent and aware, and is the active agent responsible for programming the DNA. According to Dr. Lipton, our genetic conditioning is not fixed but is constantly responding and adapting to our thoughts as well as to conditions in the outer environment. For instance, he points out that stress causes blood to leave the internal organs of the body and to rush to the outer muscles in a "fight or flight syndrome." Peaceful and loving thoughts, on the other hand, induce the blood to nourish the inner organs, allowing the body to regulate and repair itself.

Spiritual Clouds

The clouding of the soul that we talk about is in fact a deficiency of power, of Light, making it through from the divine spirit.
                                            – An Evil Person Is a Sick Person. HT

Our spiritual nature is like the sun in the sky. On sunny days, our spirit, the sun, shines brightly, but on cloudy days it is obscured and there is less brightness. According to Meishusama, these clouds superimposed over our spirit cause inner darkness, resulting in a dulling of awareness and a corresponding increase in suffering. The amount of spiritual clouding polluting the aura determines its overall size and thickness. Spiritual clouds are created by environmental toxins that have accumulated in our body, and also from impressions left in our aura as a result of our wrongful thoughts and actions.

Although all human souls were originally created innocent and pure, over time, as a result of errors and misdeeds in the world, we all became corrupted by negativity and spiritual pollution. Our thoughts and actions create immediate changes in our personal energy fields, which, by radiating outward, influence the world around us. The way that we view the people and circumstances in our lives determines the types of responses we make. Negative thoughts lead to negative actions, whereas positive thoughts lead to positive actions. Appreciation, empathy, gratitude, love, and humor magnify the aura and promote greater awareness and happiness, whereas resentment, worry, judgment, jealousy, and hate create spiritual clouds that weaken the aura and promote dullness and unhappiness.

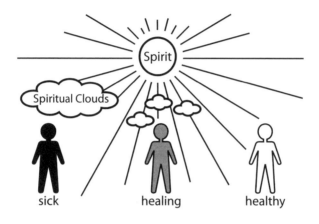

Three Stages of Purification

This same principle also applies to our actions. Everything we do either brightens or darkens our aura, depending on its overall effect on the world. We are literally a product of our past actions, which is summarized in the common expression, "character is destiny." Helping others with kindness and consideration is a powerful way of improving our own lives because of the effect it has upon our consciousness and character. By serving others we also serve the greater good.

As you enter into a faith and turn to God, Divine Light flows into your soul through the spiritual cords, increasing the radiance within and dispelling the clouds. – *An Evil Person Is a Sick Person. HT*

The spiritual clouds that we create continue to affect us until they are purified by either our actions or by painful external events. By covering and diminishing the radiance of our spirit, spiritual clouds can burden our thoughts and moods as well as attract unfortunate events into our lives. Based on this principle, we can say that the radiance of our soul is the primary determinant to the quality of our life.

People whose minds are heavily polluted by spiritual clouds fail to see the essential unity of all things, but instead see only division and separation. Coming from a place of lack, they are driven by compulsive desires and bound by personal attachments. They imagine the world to be a hostile place full of potential enemies and are quick to attack others or withdraw in fear. Some will compensate by striving to succeed in the world, hoping to demonstrate their superiority over their competitors. Others try to escape their pain by becoming addicted to alcohol or drugs, developing co-dependent relationships, or burying themselves in obsessive reading or compulsive work. All of these clouded people are easily subject to fear, anger, or depression based on deeply held insecurities, alienation, or low self-esteem.

> When we see things in this light, the reason for a person becoming evil is to be found in the clouding of his soul, and he is really a sick man. Of course, the violence with which he is purified depends on how evil he has become, and a very evil person can suffer greatly, even to the extent of becoming seriously ill. – *An Evil Person Is a Sick Person. HT*

This is not to equate being ill with being evil, but to make the connection between spiritual clouds and suffering in some, and spiritual clouds and evil reaction patterns in others. Most of this behavior is reactionary, and fails to bring a clouded mind any real sense of peace or happiness. These people tend to project all sorts of false images, fantasies, and motives onto others, instead of seeing them for who they really are. Additionally, because of their limited self-awareness, they are subject to delusions and self-deception. This condition is a breeding ground for neuroses, emotional instability, and mental confusion. These are all symptoms of the negative influence that spiritual clouds can have on the mind of an individual.

Not only do thoughts and actions have this influence, but toxins from the outer environment can also create spiritual clouds by polluting our physical bodies and poisoning our blood. Additionally, we inherit spiritual clouds from the genetic inheritance of our parents and ancestors, as well as from the social conditioning received from our childhood upbringing. Also, because we are not separate from our outer environment, the spiritual clouds generated by society affect us as well. The more repressive or dysfunctional a culture or society is, the greater the damage. (Countries that oppress women, minorities, and other nationalities are good examples of this.) Finally, we are subject to spiritual clouds carried over from our past lives. All of these factors influence our behavior to an enormous degree.

Toxins and spiritual clouds block the beneficial influences of our divine spirit and guardian spirit, allowing the animal spirit to drive us towards destructive behavior. This results in increased personal suffering. According to Meishusama, delinquents and criminals are spiritually sick people whose ability to distinguish between right and wrong is severely clouded. Individuals who are mentally ill also suffer from oppressive spiritual clouds that confuse their minds, disturb their emotions, and generate irrational cravings, leaving them vulnerable to domination by evil animal spirits.

Meishusama teaches that all suffering is caused by impurities existing in the spiritual world. Physical toxins contribute to impurities in the spiritual body, since the physical and the spiritual are related. However, the most important point to consider is that the primary cause is in the spiritual world, not the physical. Thus, if we trace it backwards to the fundamental reason for why we were exposed to toxins in the physical world, we find that the reason originated in the spiritual world. This is why it is always useful to look to the spiritual world to find the meaning and purpose behind outer events.

When impurities accumulate to a sufficient degree, a natural process of elimination occurs that can be unpleasant or painful to experience. *The essence of Meishusama's teaching focuses on removing spiritual clouds as gently and pleasantly as possible rather than through suffering.* We can avoid suffering by doing things that create more Light in the spiritual body, and by not indulging in activities that create more spiritual clouds. The healing energy of Jyorei is an especially powerful way to eliminate clouds and to infuse Light within the spiritual body. The overall movement of the universe is towards greater unity, harmony, and consciousness, and from this perspective, all forms of purification can be seen as necessary occurrences brought on to further this ongoing evolution.

Refine your spirit and soul to serve as a part of God's work of transforming the world. – Refining Body and Soul. MK

Purification and Health

To purify means to remove unnecessary elements corrupting the integrity of a substance or object. For individuals, it means to eliminate those things that are not essential to our original nature. Whatever pollutes the body, mind, or spirit must eventually be removed through a process of purification.

Suffering and Purification

By its very nature, the spiritual body rises and falls according to the amount of its clouding. A pure spirit is light, and rises; a clouded spirit is heavy, and sinks.
– The Strata in the Spiritual World. HT

We inevitably experience the effects of negativity or pollution as sickness, emotional disturbances, or external problems. The more these harmful influences accumulate, the more powerful the resulting purification will be. Purification serves the purpose of releasing the negativity or pollution so that we can return to health and internal harmony. From a larger perspective, *all suffering can be viewed as a process of purification.*

Meishusama gives an example of physical purification:

In each and every man is a certain amount of polluting toxin. Some is inherent and some acquired after birth. These toxins gather at the places of greatest nervous activity—that is, the nerve centers of the part of the body from the neck up; or the brain, eyes, nose, mouth, and ears that function all the time that a person is awake—unlike, for example, the limbs, which sometimes rest. It is therefore inevitable that the toxin should accumulate in this upper area, and this is why a great many people complain of stiff necks and shoulders, and so on. This toxin gathers and solidifies, as time passes, into a lump, and when this lump exceeds a certain limit, the process abruptly reverses itself. In other words, the lump is dissolved and expelled from the body. This is what we call the process of purification. This process is always accompanied by a fever, which is necessary to change the solidified lump into a form easily expelled by the body. That is, the lump is melted down into a liquid. This natural purification is what is called a cold, and the signs of its activity are phlegm, nasal mucous, perspiration, and other excretions. This kind of cold varies from quite serious to a semi-permanent type of purification that almost everyone is undergoing all the time. This latter is so slight as to be unnoticeable to the person, who considers himself to be healthy. – *The Three Great Disasters and the Three Lesser Disasters. HT*

Although all suffering can be viewed as forms of purification, it is important not to use this understanding as a convenient excuse to avoid dealing responsibly with a situation. Sometimes the universe presents us with a purifying event as a way to draw our attention to a circumstance that needs correcting. The best way to learn and grow from experience is to recognize our mistakes and to take responsibility for our actions. Although this may require some deep soul searching on our part, to do so promotes wisdom and maturity.

When confronted by the sickness or suffering of others, the best response is one that communicates empathy and compassion, not apathy or dismissal. Empathy is communicated when the recipient feels that we share in their misfortune and can identify with how they feel. And compassion, which is motivated by the desire to alleviate the suffering of others, is expressed by offering a helping hand. Sometimes just listening with a nonjudgmental attitude and an open heart is the most effective way to help others. There is no need to outwardly label someone's suffering as purification or to lecture the person on spiritual philosophy. Usually that will cause the suffering person to feel denigrated and dismissed rather than cared for or helped.

Generally speaking, understanding and accepting the theory of purification promotes detachment from pain, which can help us endure our own suffering more easily. But this detachment, if directed towards others, can appear as cold indifference. Therefore, it is important to remember, when confronted with another person's suffering, what it feels like to suffer ourselves. This allows us to sympathize with their pain and thereby offer genuine emotional support.

> Thus the underlying cause of this spiritual corruption is the clouding of the soul, and since this clouding directly results in an impurity of the blood, there is sure to be a time when this is purged and purified in a violent and dreadful way. At that time, the amount of suffering that affects a person corresponds to the degree of clouding of the soul. – *An Evil Person Is a Sick Person. HT*

Although clouding of our spirit leads to suffering, the resultant process of purification brings us eventually to increased health and happiness. But there is no need to deliberately seek out suffering in order to quicken this purification. That would be like "putting the cart before the horse." Suffering occurs when it is needed, and only the higher intelligence of the Creator knows when and how that should occur. For those individuals who want to speed up their quest for greater health and happiness, Meishusama recommends giving of oneself in loving service to others, engaging in the practice of Jyorei, striving to improve one's character, cultivating an appreciation of beauty, and adopting a healthy, natural diet. These are the most effective ways for us to actively promote positive purification and profound healing. The rest is left up to God.

Physical Health

Health is the state wherein all cells are functioning optimally. – Raymond Francis, D.Sc, M.Sc, R.N.C. (Chemist, Registered Nutritional Consultant and Naturopathic Physician)

To be healthy is to have abundant inner strength and power. It is to feel vital and alive, and be full of energy and enthusiasm. Good health is a condition in which all the various systems within the body, such as the respiratory system, nervous system, immune system, cardiovascular system, skeletal system, and digestive system, function optimally, and work in harmony with each other. On a psychological level, this means a state of mental peace and emotional balance. We exist on many levels: structural, chemical, electrical, emotional, mental, and spiritual. Health is a condition of the whole person, not just one level, part, or system of the body.

According to Meishusama, health is the result of a physical body that is free of toxicity and injury, and a spiritual body that is free of spiritual clouds and is full of spiritual Light.

Raymond Francis explains the practical effects of health on the cellular level:

When your cells are functioning as they should, you have ample adaptive capacity to thrive in our constantly changing environment without ill effects. With properly functioning cells, you have strong resilience to various kinds of stress—physical, chemical, biological, and emotional. You have the ability to make daily repairs to your cells, the ability to build healthy new ones, and the ability to efficiently remove pathogenic microorganisms and toxins from your body. You become an optimally balanced organism, with integrated mental and physical equilibrium. Perhaps most important is that achieving good cellular health gives our society the ability to produce healthy offspring. (*Never Be Sick Again*)

When we live in harmony with nature, including both the internal terrain of our bodies and the external terrain of the world, we enjoy abundant health and happiness. Unfortunately, the societies we live in are out of touch with nature, and hence create unbalanced lifestyles and toxic environments. Even the remedies that society promotes for its problems are unbalanced and toxic, which leads to still more problems. All of this poses great challenges for those of us who seek to avoid sickness and misery.

If we examine the way in which people enter the abnormal state of sickness, what do we find? The reason for them entering this state is, above all, that they go against nature. True medical treatment consists of perceiving this anti-natural condition, correcting it and restoring the person to his or her normal and natural state. – *The Truth about Health, God's Way to Health. HT*

Despite the industrial world's many advances in safety, sanitation, food productivity, and health care, statistics reveal that most of the population suffers from a variety of health problems. Obesity, diabetes, cancer, heart disease, arthritis, mental disorders, and many other health problems continue to rise towards epidemic proportions.

In fact, many primitive societies—those that have managed to avoid excess exposure to modern civilization—tend to enjoy far greater health and vitality than those living in technologically advanced countries. Their lives tend to be simple and free of inordinate stress. They live close to nature, and maintain strong ties with their fellow family members and local communities. Their food is fresh, organic, and locally grown, and their air, water, and land are clean and free of pollution. Most also get plenty of exercise and sunlight.

As we get further removed from nature, our health and vitality tend to decline.

The truth is that man is born to be sound and healthy.
– The Truth about Health. God's Way to Health. HT

Sickness and Modern Medicine

So-called "medicines" are all poisons, and it is precisely because they are poisonous that they have an effect. To be exact, the poisons we call medicines act in a toxic way to reduce the symptoms of disease, and thus give the superficial appearance of a cure. No real cure takes place.
– What is Illness?. God's Way to Health. HT

When people get sick, they usually want to eliminate their physical discomfort as soon as possible. Often they run to either their local pharmacy for a somewhat toxic over-the-counter drug or to their doctor for a prescription to a stronger, potentially more dangerous drug. Unfortunately, most pharmaceutical drugs do not cure disease, but only suppress its unpleasant symptoms. They do this by disrupting normal cellular functions. According to chemist and naturopathic physician Raymond Francis, abnormal cell function is the very definition of disease, and because drugs tend to cause our cells to malfunction, they actually promote disease rather than eliminate it. In the long run, they do more harm than good. In his book, "Never be Sick Again," he describes the effects of poor cellular health as follows: "For a more meaningful understanding of disease (cellular malfunction), we must consider the health of our cells. Remember that noticeable health problems begin when a large number of cells malfunction. As this happens, important cellular chemicals are not produced, cell-to-cell communications become garbled and the body ceases to regulate itself properly. Our tissues suffer and noticeable symptoms appear, e.g., allergies, fatigue, aches and pains, colds, flu, depression, anxiety, cancer, or any of thousands of other complaints." *(Never Be Sick Again)*

Modern medicine is usually quite toxic to the body, and despite the temporary benefits it may bring, one has to wonder what the long-term effects of these toxins might be. Drugs can be severely damaging to the liver, kidneys, or other vital organs in the body because poisons are designed to kill, not cure. We need to question why anyone would want to ingest more toxins into a body already suffering from toxic overload. Might not modern medicine, because of its toxicity, actually be contributing more to the problem than to the solution?

Not only do drugs harm the cells of the body, but so also do many other therapies offered by Western medicine such as chemotherapy and radiation therapy. The former poisons them, and the latter burns them. Both destroy health rather than improving it. Meishusama was equally critical of radiation therapy:

> Again, cancer is sometimes attacked and destroyed using radium. This would be fine if it were only the cancer that is destroyed, but in fact the entire cell organization of the body suffers, and the negative effects of the treatment far outweigh the positive ones. – *The Truth about Health, God's Way to Health. HT*

The article, *Doctors Are the Third Leading Cause of U.S. Deaths,*[1] listed these startling statistics:

> Medical errors constitute the third leading cause of death, after deaths from heart disease and cancer, according to a study by Barbara Starfield,

---

[1] *The Whole Life Times Magazine* (September 2000).

M.D., M.P.H., from the Johns Hopkins School of Hygiene and Public Health, in Baltimore, Md. Published in the July 26, 2000, *Journal of the American Medical Association*, the article lists 225,000 deaths per year in hospitals alone, broken down as follows:

- 12,000 deaths/year from unnecessary surgery
- 7,000 deaths/year from medication errors in hospitals
- 20,000 deaths/year from other errors in hospitals
- 80,000 deaths/year from infections in hospitals
- 106,000 deaths/year from non-error (adverse effects of medications)

The figures were even higher in the 1999 Institute of Medicine (IOM) report, *To Err is Human.* (Please note that these figures include, for the most part, deaths caused by doctors in hospitals, so deaths from medical errors outside hospitals would be another subject.)

Too often assembly line medical care fails to sufficiently educate patients in the proper use of medicines. Sadly, many deaths occur shortly after discharge from hospitals due to a patient inadvertently adding another medication to their current one without considering how the two might interact. Sometimes something as seemingly innocuous as Tylenol or Benedryl can cause severe sickness or death when combined with a prescription drug.

Poisoning from prescription drugs has risen to become the second-largest cause of unintentional deaths in the United States, according to the federal Centers for Disease Control and Prevention. In its Morbidity and Mortality Weekly Report, researchers found that deaths from prescription drugs rose from 4.4 per 100,000 people in 1999 to 7.1 per 100,000 in 2004. This increase represents a jump from 11,000 people to almost 20,000 in the span of five years. Among the 20,000 that died, more than 8,500— double the number from 1999—were from "other and unspecified drugs." Psychotherapeutic drugs, like antidepressants and sedatives, nearly doubled from 671 deaths to 1,300.[2]

---

[2] Adams, Mike. "Unintentional Poisoning Deaths – United States, 1999 -- 2004" (February 9, 2007). Centers for Disease Control and Prevention [On-line], Available at: http://www.cdc.gov/mmwr/preview/mmwrhtml/mm5605a1.htm

Most medicines are composed of toxic ingredients derived from petroleum or other synthetic chemicals. Although some drugs may be derived from various plants or herbs, these also tend to be toxic because they are made from isolated chemicals instead of whole plants. The human body was designed to consume either plants or animal products as food, not synthetic or isolated chemicals. Whereas food is composed of many nutrients (such as protein, fats, carbohydrates, vitamins, minerals, and various natural phytochemicals, all bound together at the molecular level), chemicals, on the other hand, are relatively simple substances. When one ingests these chemical formulas, they tend to create stress and imbalance within the organs, glands, and tissues of the body, rather than nourishing them. Some drugs, such as various forms used in chemotherapy, indiscriminately destroy cells throughout the body, ruining one's health in the process.

Taking a survey of the damage can be alarming. It is becoming increasingly obvious to many that antidepressant drugs can make you psychotic; cholesterol/lipid-lowering drugs can destroy your liver, hormones, and entire nervous system; diabetes drugs can destroy your liver and pancreas; chemotherapy can ruin your immune system; and anti-inflammatory drugs can cause gastric ulcers, GERD (gastric esophageal reflux disease), and liver and kidney disease. Meishusama adds: "Drugs and treatment by medical devices bring temporary good effects, but as time passes the effects reverse themselves and become harmful. But people are dazzled by the initial good results and pursue the same method of treatment, come what may. The resulting harmful effects grow greater and greater." *(It is Not True that "Honesty does not Pay." HT)*

I no longer believe in modern medicine. I believe that the greatest danger to your health is the doctor who practices modern medicine…. Don't trust your doctor. Assume that if he prescribed a drug, it's dangerous. There is no safe drug. – Robert Mendelsohn, MD *(Confessions of a Medical Heretic)*

Toxic residue from pharmaceutical drugs affects everyone, even those who do not personally consume them. "Apart from the vast number of drugs taken directly, people are also, unknowingly, consuming large amounts of drugs and other chemical substances indirectly from the food they eat. Most food industries rely on chemical substances from soil to supermarket, and the animal products industries are by far the most excessive users of these substances. The avalanche of drug and chemical usage by these industries occurred with the shift in production methods from free-range farming to factory and feedlot farming in the last 20 to 30 years." *(The Pharmaceutical Drug Racket Part-1[3])*

Modern medicine is based on the presumptions of Newtonian physics, which maintains that both the universe and the human body are like machines —entirely composed of collections of individual parts—and that by isolating the parts and studying them separately, we can understand the whole. Health writer Mike Adams writes, "M.D.s practicing today literally believe the body is divided into isolated compartments that have no effect on each other; hence the dividing up of doctor duties into roles like foot doctor, ear doctor, eye doctor, brain doctor, and heart doctor. What happened to the WHOLE patient?" (http://www.healthranger.org)

The mechanistic model promotes a fragmentary approach to health that treats only one or two malfunctioning organs in the body at a time rather than working to heal the entire body.

This leads practitioners of modern medicine to view the human body as a battleground on which wars are waged against malevolent invaders and tumors. Their main weapons in this war are synthetic chemicals, surgery, and radiation. What doctors and pharmacists fail to realize is that diseases are not separate from the person. In fact every disease can more accurately be called an expression of the patient's lifestyle, beliefs, and subtle energies, which in turn are strongly influenced by the culture and civilization that they live in. (Thus, a toxic society breeds toxic individuals.)

By attempting to attack and destroy disease, modern medicine invariably ends up damaging the greater person in the process. Such injuries to the overall health and functioning of the body are viewed as unavoidable causalities of war—the war against disease. If the patient ends up losing his or her kidneys, heart or liver, it is considered the lesser of two evils because at least they did not die (hopefully).

This is a shallow approach to healing that only attempts to treat the symptoms of an illness rather than its underlying cause. It is like dealing with

---

[3] John Leso, "The Pharmaceutical Drug Racket Part-1," *Nexus New Times Magazine*, vol. 2, no. 13 (April/ May 1993).

a fire by taking the batteries out of the fire alarm! Yes, the alarm has become quiet, but the flames are still smoldering, causing even more damage, and by the time you see the flames, it is too late, everything is already being destroyed.

Similarly, a tumor or malignant growth is only the symptom, seen or felt, of deeper, systemic disorders within the body, such as toxicity, malnutrition, or metabolic malfunction. Therefore, removing the tumor through surgery is not usually sufficient to overcome illness because it does not address these vital health issues. In addition, on a deeper level, the underlying negative energy connected to the tumor will continue to remain in the spiritual body and continue to cause damage. Usually, the best that surgery can do is to buy some extra time for the patient, although the price is high: the injury and disfigurement of the body. And how can the body function well if an essential part of it has been removed? Surely there must be another way—one that respects health rather than destroying it.

To overcome illness and attain true health, first the spiritual body must be purified of its clouds, and then the physical body must be cleansed of its internal toxins. Good nutrition is also important. Junk food should be avoided, including sugar filled desserts such as cookies, pastries, donuts, ice cream, and candy; and processed foods such as hotdogs, instant coffee creamer, corn and potato chips, margarine, artificial sweeteners, sugary breakfast cereals, sports drinks and soft drinks. A diet consisting of a wide variety of fresh, chemical-free fruits, vegetables, whole grains, beans, and nuts will help the body to recover and regain strength. Ideally, choose locally grown food, in season. In addition, fresh air, sunshine, pure water, moderate exercise, and a positive attitude should also be included in one's overall lifestyle.

The cure of an illness is a process of dispelling an accumulation of toxin or breaking up a mass of toxin in part of the body. When this process takes place in the soul, the accumulated toxin takes the form of clouds that dull the spiritual body, and the "dissolution" is the dispelling of these clouds. Medical treatment until now has been directed only towards dealing with physical symptoms, and this misdirection has not resulted in true cures.

– *Natural Power. HT*

Current medical technology has been quite successful in treating victims of car accidents, patients suffering from life-threatening infections, and those in danger of imminent organ failure. It offers much needed help during trauma and emergencies, but is not very useful for chronic, long-term health problems. This is because it assumes an adversarial approach to illness, rather than a supportive approach to wellness. Such practices will never cure anything, but only postpone recovery. The medical establishment needs to understand that health is not the absence of disease; it is a condition of optimum vitality. And in order to promote true health, they need to focus more on what is good for the body and less on what is bad for it.

These same problems of suppression and toxicity also hold true for psychiatric medications, as well: they do not cure mental illness, but only make people emotionally numb. Although the emotional pain may lessen by taking these psychiatric drugs, the underlying problems of guilt, depression, anxiety, confusion, and rage do not go away, but only get buried for a while. The patient soon becomes dependent on these drugs to maintain a tight lid on their troubles, because if they dare to stop taking them, their old problems resurface with increased energy. It is like using a pressure cooker with a clogged steam release valve; the pressure soon builds up to a dangerous level. Thus, the longer they suppress their problems, the worse they get. There are many stories of people, both young and old, exploding into violent behavior after having been on psychiatric medications for long periods of time. According to recent studies and stories, these drugs also increase the chances of suicide by those who use them. Plus, the toxicity of these drugs presents serious dangers to the patient's physical health, including potential damage to his or her brain, nerves, liver, and other vital organs. Although the use of psychiatric medications may sometimes be required to control extreme behavior, it is important to understand their limitations. True healing must go beyond chemical suppression. It must work to purify the underlying problem and to nurture the whole person, both emotionally and physically.

Viruses and Bacteria

Modern medicine considers viruses and bacteria to be the enemy, and sets out to destroy these harmful invaders. Meishusama viewed the occurrence of a cold or flu as the body's attempt to rid itself of accumulated toxins. Viruses and bacteria are instrumental in initiating a healing process by actually feeding on toxins in the body. A runny nose, sweat, diarrhea, vomiting, etc. are often healthy symptoms of the body purifying itself of toxicity. A similar condition occurs in nature, where toxic or decaying substances are quickly broken down and assimilated by various bacteria, worms, and insects. This is nature's way of maintaining balance and harmony.

Understanding this, Meishusama advocates that we appreciate the benefits of purification, despite how unpleasant it might feel at the moment. If we keep in view the possible benefits of a clean and purified body, we would not try to suppress the purification process, but would actually support it. The physical body must throw off its toxins, whether inherited, ingested, acquired, or generated in some particular manner, if it is to remain healthy and functional. Better to eliminate them now, while the body has sufficient strength to handle the effects, rather than to wait until a serious illness occurs. When the body is weak, the purification process is more difficult. Receiving and giving the healing energy of Jyorei will strengthen the body, ease the pain of purification, and bring illness to a speedier conclusion.

Dr. Antoine Bechamp—a medical doctor, pharmacist, chemist, microbiologist, and university professor who lived in the nineteenth and early twentieth century France—postulated that disease is usually the result of an unhealthy "terrain" within the body. He found that when the internal condition of the body was weakened from poor nutrition or environmental toxicity (such as smoking, over-consumption of alcohol, ingesting drugs, or exposure to harmful chemicals, heavy metals, or radiation) then the natural, healthy bacteria inside the system would change and evolve into harmful microorganisms. He called this phenomenon pleomorphism (having many forms). According to Dr. Bechamp, the most important approach to healing is to reverse this condition by cleansing the body and strengthening it with healthy food, fresh air, sunshine, and exercise.

One of his students, Louis Pasteur, advocated the opposite theory that disease was the result of hostile, invading germs and viruses. He claimed that bacteria do not change or evolve, and promoted the use of aggressive applications of synthetic medicine to kill them. This was a theoretical model resembling the violent tactics of open warfare, rather than the gentle art of promoting health and healing. Yet, despite his dismissal of the importance of strengthening the physical body—what many would consider to be common sense—his approach became more popular than Bechamp's because it was more in sync with the prevailing paradigms of the time, and also because it supported the financial interests of the medical establishment who wanted to promote profitable chemical drugs. Preventative medicine, on the other hand, was not profitable.

Of course, Pasteur was correct in his declaration that illness can occur from outside sources. Some viruses and bacteria can indeed be deadly, such as Anthrax or Ebola, and an open wound is easily susceptible to infection. Pasteur also deserves credit for championing the once-controversial practice of doctors washing their hands before performing surgery. This single procedure alone has probably saved millions of lives since it was accepted within the medical community a century ago. But Bechamp's point is that a healthy body, full of vitality, is much less susceptible to contracting a virus or bacteria, because its immune system is strong and its internal organs are functioning well. And Pasteur—despite his lifelong advocacy of the germ theory—on his deathbed seemed to have a change of heart, and was reported to have exclaimed, "The germ theory is nothing; the terrain (internal environment) is everything." Antoine Bechamp's theories are currently being rediscovered, and the fundamentals of these theories might well have been embraced by Meishusama had they been better known in Japan during his time.

Although the life expectancy of men and women in industrialized countries has risen during the past 100 years as infectious illnesses have been controlled, according to German nutritionist, M.O. Bruker, M.D., the primary reason is improved hygienic conditions, not better medicine or the use of antibiotics. "People live statistically longer, but they are not necessarily healthier," he explained. "Today we have sewage systems, water faucets, and better sanitary conditions that have helped eliminate mass epidemics, such as typhus, cholera and tuberculosis. But more people are becoming sick from heart disease, cancer, and intestinal illness than ever before. The idea that antibiotics and modern medicine deserve most of the credit for improving both the length and quality of people's lives is a fraud."

Accidents and Spiritual Clouds

Man is purged of his spiritual clouding by suffering.

– An Evil Person is a Sick Person. HT

Sickness can also be caused by injuries or from exposure to harmful chemicals in our environment. These externally caused illnesses are also forms of purification. Our spiritual clouds may have drawn these experiences to us in order to help facilitate a particular purification. Thus, from Meishusama's perspective, events are not interpreted as resulting from chance or coincidence, but rather, are understood to have their origins in the spiritual world. *Outer events are the secondary effects of pre-existing inner conditions that were generated in the past.*

To be cheated and suffer a loss, to suffer damage by fire, to be injured or robbed, to encounter family bereavement, to suffer business setbacks or failure, to lack money or fall deeply in debt, to argue with your wife or husband, to be alienated from your parents or children, to be on bad terms with relatives or friends—these are all without exception examples of this process of purification. As there is no way other than suffering to remove clouding from the soul, suffering cannot be avoided as long as such clouding exists. – *You Are Free to Make Your Own Destiny. HT*

Mental Purification

A small amount of mental disorder seems to be the common lot of mankind. The so-called "man in the street" is slightly mentally ill.
– Mental Disorders, God's Way to Health. HT

There are many types of purification, including physical, mental, relationship, financial, environmental, familial, and societal purification. Mental purification can involve depression, anxiety, insecurity, jealousy, guilt, resentment, and anger. The main cause of these emotions is usually our pre-existing attitudes and tendencies, not the outer circumstances in which we find ourselves. Financial problems, accidents, or rude and aggressive people merely act as triggers for unresolved mental and emotional patterns that already exist within us. This is why some people can explode in rage over an innocent remark made to them by a friend, family member, or stranger. When we hold unresolved emotions within us, they tend to distort our perceptions and judgments, causing us to misinterpret other people's feelings and motives.

Our emotional reactions based upon these misinterpretations only tend to provoke negative responses from others, resulting in further interpersonal conflict. Each person will, of course, mentally justify his or her actions, no matter how negative or irrational, while simultaneously criticizing other people's actions. These dysfunctional cycles are at the root of most relationship problems, and are a chief cause of much personal unhappiness.

Our emotional disposition tends to color everything we experience and can sometimes blind us as to what is really going on around us. Most interpersonal conflicts are the result of mutual misinterpretations and unconscious projections. We usually tend to take things too personally, frequently expect too much from people, and often fail to consider the needs of others. Until we purify our minds of the spiritual clouds that dull our awareness, interpersonal conflicts of one sort or another will continue to plague our lives, promoting misery for all concerned. One of the fundamental truths in life is that *the inner world of our thoughts and feelings actually determines what we experience in the outer world.*

If you suffer cruelly in this human world, the ultimate cause is lack of wisdom.
                                                        – *God's Writing. MK*

An especially significant cause of mental purification is the suppressed feelings we accumulate from the past. Feelings of inadequacy, low self-worth, neediness, anger, resentment, loneliness, anxiety and compulsiveness remain within us because we refuse to acknowledge and release them. Instead, we blame others. When we judge feelings such as anger, fear, or sorrow as bad, we inevitably try to avoid them both in ourselves and in others. This causes us to repress our feelings, and the more we repress them, the more deeply entrenched they become, thereby locking us into limiting behavior patterns that are exceedingly difficult to change.

But, like a pressure cooker, whatever gets suppressed has to eventually burst out because it is the nature of energy to move—not stand still. Often when we judge and blame others, we are actually reacting to qualities in them that secretly remind us of those same qualities within ourselves—although we refuse to admit this to ourselves. One of the main ways we tend to grow psychologically is by experiencing ourselves mirrored objectively in the outer environment. Consequently, we often attract people and circumstances to ourselves who can reflect disowned or projected parts of ourselves back to us. By triggering our repressed feelings, they provide us with opportunities to learn more about ourselves and to expand our consciousness to a larger extent. Furthermore, this is why we draw the same types of people and circumstances to ourselves, again and again. Until we learn and grow from our problems, we are destined to repeat them.

However much we refuse to see and acknowledge negative feelings within ourselves, to the same degree will we have difficulty dealing with those same negative feelings in others. This type of avoidance prevents meaningful communication because healthy relationships depend on openness and honesty, not secrecy and deception. How can people resolve interpersonal conflicts if they chronically avoid dealing with each other's feelings? Plus, people tend to get frustrated and angry when they feel they are being ignored or avoided, which then makes relationships deteriorate even more. The emotional suffering caused by these continual rounds of avoidance and reaction are good examples of mental purification.

Each time an emotional reaction occurs within us, it is a chance to learn and grow by acknowledging and releasing it. Through mental purification, life is giving us the chance to free ourselves from the old conditioning that has kept us bound and unhappy for so long. So this type of mental purification, although painful, is actually something to feel grateful for. It is a gift from the Creator for our own long-term benefit.

What joy that the dark side of my heart has cleared and shines with the brightness of noon. – My Salvation. MK

One might notice that good things often happen to bad people and also that bad things often happen to good people. But it would be a mistake to conclude that life is therefore unjust or cruel. In actuality, life is not so much concerned with our limited views of fairness as it is with giving us whatever experiences will most help us grow spiritually. Meishusama himself suffered enormously in his life, but that did not imply that he deserved to suffer or that he had a great deal of negativity he needed to burn off. On reviewing Meishusama's life, we discover that the tremendous suffering and adversity he experienced throughout his life actually furthered his purification and thus supported his dramatic spiritual growth. Because of this, he tended to look back on his suffering not with regret but with gratitude for all the blessings that he received from it.

Terrible tragedies in our lives that we cannot understand are often the result of accumulated spiritual clouds either in ourselves or in those around us. When a sufficient amount of negativity or darkness accumulates within the spiritual world, purification inevitably occurs. Not only can this take the form of sickness, strife, financial problems, natural disasters, or wars, but it can also present itself as moodiness, neurosis, or even extreme psychiatric problems such as schizophrenia or psychosis. Cultivating purity of mind and body is the best prevention against these terrible conditions.

The only good way of improving your fortune is to lessen your spiritual clouding. In other words, if you reduce the clouding to some extent there will be less need for purification and what would have been bad fortune will be transformed into good fortune. – *You Are Free to Make Your Own Destiny. HT*

Viewing hardship and suffering as forms of purification can encourage feelings of acceptance and trust rather than bitterness and resistance. This view also promotes a positive attitude toward life as well as greater hope for the future. When we understand that the true source of happiness is our internal spiritual condition, then our priorities begin to change. Instead of the transitory rewards of this world, we begin to value that which promotes spiritual growth, including purification and the challenges that accompany it. Step by step, purification draws us ever closer to eternal peace and happiness.

Luck comes not to he who waits, but to he who is purified.
                                    – You are Free to Make Your Own Destiny. HT

7 TOWARD A WORLD OF LIGHT

Paradise on Earth

If I were to express as simply as possible what is meant by the words 'Paradise on Earth' I would say it is the world of beauty. That is to say, people have beauty in their hearts, a beauty of the spirit. Words and deeds should embody this beauty. This is beauty at the individual level. And when beauty spreads, social beauty comes into being.[1] *– Meishusama*

The story of humanity in many ways is a tragic tale full of wars, poverty, disease, social oppression, and injustice. Past attempts to correct these problems seem to have made little meaningful difference in the overall picture. If things got better in one place, they inevitably got worse somewhere else. After much disillusionment and despair about the condition of humanity, Meishusama received a revelation—a vision of a rapidly approaching New Age, which he labeled "Paradise on Earth." This paradise would be a world of truth, virtue, and beauty: a world free of the three perennial afflictions of sickness, poverty, and strife.

Although things will improve dramatically after the arrival of this New Age, we do not need to wait until then to find individual freedom and happiness. We can establish our own personal "Paradise on Earth" right here and now, during this very lifetime, to the extent that we can purify our souls and also begin to live a life dedicated to the happiness of others. This world of ours was created to be a place of genuine happiness—not misery. But humanity, through the long-term effects of its ignorant and selfish behavior, has gradually corrupted and ruined it. Indeed, the world has been darkened to

---

[1] Meishusama, "An Invisioning Heaven on Earth," *Japanese Shumei Newsletter*, no. 262 (January 1992).

such an extent, that for universal happiness to finally arise, the human heart must first go through a dramatic transformation. This will require no less than a deep and thorough purification of the spirit. Mahatma Gandhi expressed a similar awareness when he said, "You must be the change you wish to see in the world."

Meishusama's vision of Paradise on Earth incorporates not only the higher ideals of spiritual growth, but also the lower ideals of ordinary worldly happiness as well. He was not a religious extremist like those who denigrate or dismiss the world. He was neither ascetic nor otherworldly. Instead, he valued this world for all the love, beauty, and joy it provides. Meishusama understood that for most people, their outer circumstances were at least as important to their happiness as was their inner state of consciousness. They need family, friends, jobs, homes, and food. No one is an island unto himself, despite how detached or inwardly free they might be. For example: how can one's body stay healthy and pure if the food and the surrounding environment are full of harmful chemicals and other poisons? How can one feel comfortable if one is living on the streets without food, clothing or shelter? And how can one maintain a peaceful and loving heart if one is in the midst of violent hostility

I am urging the human race towards a great awakening through the flowering of a spiritual culture. - Preface. HT

Not only is happiness important in its own right, but for many it is also the foundation for the cultivation of spiritual growth. The humanistic psychologist, Dr. Abraham Maslow, argued that people usually must have their basic needs met before they will begin to focus on higher matters. The following is a brief summary of Maslow's famous "Hierarchy of Needs":

1. Physiological: the need for food, water, and physical comfort.
2. Safety: the need for structure, order, security, and predictability.
3. Belongingness and love: The need for social acceptance and intimacy.
4. Esteem: The need for social recognition and status through personal achievement.

These first four are the most basic needs that must be satisfied before higher interests and drives can emerge within the individual. After this, people tend to demonstrate "higher needs" or interests as their chief motivating factors:

5. Cognitive: the need to know, understand and explore new things.
6. Aesthetic: the need to appreciate and express beauty, order and symmetry.
7. Self-actualization: the need to find self-fulfillment and realize one's potential.
8. Self-transcendence: the need to connect to something beyond the ego or to help others find self-fulfillment and realize their potential.

The more that each of these latter needs is fulfilled, the more the individual starts to exhibit a greater degree of wisdom, altruism, and awareness in his or her life. Meishusama and Maslow both agree that people's basic needs for safety, comfort, and good health must be satisfied before they can realistically hope to obtain greater happiness and authentic spiritual development. To these basic things, Maslow would add the needs for love, social acceptance and personal achievement. Meishusama writes, "There are the desires for wisdom, the sense of superiority, the competitive urge, and the desire for progress on one hand, while on the other there are the physical cravings for love and pleasure. They all find a place within the human mind." *(Atheism. HT)* Although everything has value, from the most basic physical need to the most abstract, real happiness depends upon attaining a higher level of consciousness. And it is a basic truth in life that what we value we become, according to our actual priorities.

Meishusama dreamed of a world of warm-hearted people who were naturally inclined towards treating each other with kindness and generosity. His primary objective was to create a world where everyone was free of physical sickness, had good food to eat, attractive clothes to wear, and beautiful homes to live in. He envisioned a society that would nurture the sick and feed the poor, not abandon or shun them. It would be a world free of war, conflict, and crime.

According to the contemporary American philosopher, Ken Wilber, life's activities can be divided into four general categories or quadrants:

1. Interior-Individual: Our subjective state (thoughts, feelings, and intentions).
2. Exterior-Individual: The outward actions and inner (biochemical) responses of our physical body.
3. Interior-Collective: The beliefs, attitudes, and values of each culture.
4. Exterior-Collective: The outward structures and collective behavior of societies.

The comprehensiveness of Meishusama's teachings is evident in the fact that he addressed each of these four areas in one way or another. To create a world free of disease, poverty, and strife, all facets of life need to be healed and spiritually transformed. Jyorei, Natural Agriculture, and beautiful art promote a healthy mind, body, society, and external environment. Each of these four facets is inseparably linked because if any one of them is unbalanced or toxic it will inevitably affect the others. The inner affects the outer, and the outer affects the inner. Similarly, the individual affects the collective, and the collective affects the individual. This is why a total revolution in human affairs is necessary if we are to create a significantly better world. Again, the basis for this revolution is a deep spiritual purification and transformation in all areas of life.

The great American civil rights crusader, Martin Luther King Jr., expressed similar sentiments when he stated, "On the one hand, I must attempt to change the soul of individuals so that their societies may be changed. On the other (hand) I must attempt to change the societies so that the individual souls will have a chance."

Spiritual Development

I myself am striving with all my heart for progress and elevation, from last year to this, from this month to next. – New Men. HT

In our busy lives, it is easy to become over-preoccupied with such worldly concerns as earning a living, recreational activities, and interpersonal relationships. We worry about such things as job security, our finances, and our health. We spend our time shopping for the latest fashions in clothes, the newest electronic gadgets, or the most recent computer game, compact disc or DVD. We compete with each other for the better job, the nicer car, and the bigger house. Food itself can become a major distraction, either for enjoyment or to avoid emotional pain.

In contrast to these worldly distractions, the soul has its own set of priorities relating to its spiritual growth and development. It can be said that although perfection resides within each of us because of our innate divinity, this perfection, to varying degrees, has been buried and obscured by the spiritual clouds we have accumulated over the course of many lifetimes. Therefore, to actually manifest our inner perfection in the outer world, a great amount of purification is usually required.

Selflessness and Expanded Awareness

In human life there can be nothing more terrible than self. This can be realized if we consider the fact that the most important part of the discipline in the spiritual world is directed towards the removal of egotism. – No Egotism. HT

In the process of spiritual growth, a person becomes increasingly empty of self, while simultaneously developing greater capacities for dealing effectively with the complexity of the world around them. On the other hand, a person whose awareness is clouded by excessive personal desires and fears cannot effectively deal with the numerous challenges that come up in his or her life. This is because desire and fear distract attention, cloud judgment, and weaken our mental, emotional, and physical stamina. As a result, the mind cannot stay focused, and thus makes bad decisions, often resulting in both inner and outer conflict. Those who are distracted by inner conflicts are unable to find lasting peace and happiness, even in the best of circumstances. Only spiritual purification and inner discipline can bring them what their soul deeply craves. For this to happen, the person needs a strong determination and commitment, which will restructure their mind and emotions according to a hierarchy of values, with spirituality at the top.

Just as a calm pool of water can reflect the nearby trees and sky without distortion, so too, can a person with a clear mind perceive and understand the world accurately. Meishusama writes, "As a person's aura becomes thinner, he becomes more liable to suffer misfortune and disaster. The reason for this is that clouding dulls the activities of the brain and decisions and judgment become inaccurate and lacking in point. The person becomes incapable of seeing things in their proper perspective." *(Spiritual Radiations and the Aura. HT)*

Gradually, step-by-step, it is possible to reach a level of spiritual development where suffering is not a foregone conclusion. The structure of human consciousness evolves and progresses gradually from simple-minded to intelligent, and from compulsive to inwardly free. Spiritual development is like climbing a progressive series of steps on a ladder until finally reaching the highest step, whereupon one merges with the totality of God. Huston Smith, one of the leading authorities on comparative religion, points out that models of spiritual ascent such as this have been found in all of the world's spiritual traditions throughout the ages.

Spiritual growth is based on a lessening of egotism and self-centeredness. The ego is our sense of personal identity. It is a mentally constructed self that takes everything personally, and thinks in terms of "me" and "mine." Our ego is reinforced by our various social roles, such as that of husband, wife, friend, student, or employee. This is further defined by our social status, based on job, wealth, education, car, house, and physical appearance. The more we identify with such things, the more we diminish our own innate sense of self-worth. The ego is always comparing itself with others, and then ranking itself accordingly. It feels superior to some, and inferior to others, resulting in either pride or shame. Such comparisons lead to feelings of alienation from society. The ego creates separation and promotes selfishness, whereas Spirit reveals unity and fosters selflessness.

On a relative level we each have a particular name and form, but on a higher level we are nameless and formless—we are pure Spirit. Like clothing, we temporarily put on a physical body, mind and social identity, but when we die, we discard these things and return to our true nature as invisible Spirit.

During the course of spiritual development old, selfish patterns of behavior that were based on limited levels of awareness gradually diminish. In place of egotism, an expanded state of consciousness that is selfless, unlimited, and highly aware begins to emerge. This state does not deny our own needs and desires, but instead seeks to fulfill them. Yet now the needs and desires of others often become more important than our own. We seek the happiness of not only our personal family and friends, but also the happiness of all beings everywhere. No one is left out, not even ourselves. The limited personality continues to function effectively, although at the core of our being there is only sublime peace and radiant awareness. About this state, Meishusama says, "This realization is what Buddhists call 'Empty of self, full of peace.'" *(Atheism. HT)*

Evolution of Spirit through Form

Grass and trees grow higher and higher, reaching for the sky. Not a single one grows downwards. All of nature progresses onward and upward in this way.
– New Men. HT

The driving purpose behind the creation and evolution of the universe is the transformation and expansion of consciousness, using physical matter as a vehicle for the emergence and manifestation of Spirit. All things are subject to a grand evolutionary impulse moving towards greater consciousness, intelligence, and love. On a physical level, there is a step-by-step evolution from simple structures towards those of greater organized complexity. The universe evolves sequentially from atoms to molecules, minerals, cells, bacteria, plants, insects, reptiles, mammals, and finally to humans—the most complex phenomena that we know of. Each depends on a previous level of structural development in order to evolve to the next step. Animals are composed of the trillions of cells which make up their bodies, and cells are made up of countless atoms and molecules. Humans would not have evolved such highly developed minds, capable of complex reasoning and understanding, without the evolutionary support of a physical brain with a large cerebral cortex located within an animal body that can stand erect on two feet and that has hands with opposable thumbs.

In short, life is an active process of making imperfect matter into perfect matter.
– The Comedy of Nutrition, God's Way to Health. HT

Each stage of development will have a greater structural and functional complexity than the previous stage. The higher a life form is, in terms of evolutionary development, the more sophisticated will be its brain, biochemistry, and nervous system. This evolutionary trend is mirrored by that life form's greater capacity for intelligent interaction with the environment. Protozoa are limited to simple stimulus and response behavior. Plants alter how they grow depending upon the weather, soil, and competitive life forms. Insects, fish, birds, and reptiles have an advantage over plants in their ability to crawl, swim, or fly in search of food, and in their ability to flee from danger. Mammals are still higher in their evolutionary development, as demonstrated by their innate capacity for maternal love, feeling, and social bonding. Humans have a greater ability than other mammals to learn from the past and to plan for the future. Evolutionary biologist Elisabet Sahtouris states, "Nature evolves by intelligent response to crisis (not by accidents, as we've been taught)." These evolutionary stages of development are mirrored in the human triune brain, containing the reptilian brain stem, with its "fight or flight" impulses; the limbic system, with its capacity for emotional bonding; and the neocortex, with its ability to reason and conceptualize. The French philosopher Henri Bergson also promoted the theory of the evolution of consciousness. He wrote: "The more complicated the brain becomes, thus giving the organism greater choice of possible actions, the more does consciousness outrun its physical concomitant."

Humans have greater intelligence, capacity for empathy, aesthetic awareness, and freedom of choice than do other life forms. Especially unique to humans is our strong sense of self-consciousness, which allows us to self-reflect, and to learn and grow as a result. Most importantly, we have the ability to consider how other people think and feel. This expanded consciousness gives us a highly developed social intelligence, which helps us to interact with each other harmoniously and effectively. Beyond this, not only can we observe others, but we can also interpret how they see us.

Consciousness underlies all of manifestation, and is the engine driving all things towards both greater awareness and higher functional capacities. Thus, trees are more conscious than rocks; animals are more conscious than trees; and humans are more conscious than animals. Each stage of development brings with it the capacity to interact on a more complex and sophisticated level than before. All of creation is gradually evolving from matter, to body, to mind, to soul, and finally to spirit. This upward ascension guarantees the eventual liberation and salvation of all life. Together, all of us are evolving into pure Light.

Man must constantly strive for progress and evolution. This is especially true for those who have faith in God. – New Men. HT

Growth and Maturity

Even the greatest tree that stretches to the sky was once but a tiny sprout.
– For Youth. MK

An infant is inwardly close to God because of its fundamental innocence and purity, but paradoxically, it also separates itself from God through its exclusive identification with its own needs. At that early age, it is unable to stand outside of itself or to see things from another person's perspective. Infants are self-absorbed and are only concerned with fulfilling their immediate desires. They have not yet developed the complex mental ability to understand the world around them, nor have they the maturity to respond to the needs of others. Similarly, two-year olds only want to do what they want to do and hate it when they do not get their way. They are incapable of detaching themselves from their immediate moods and desires. The Swiss biologist and psychologist, Jean Piaget, claimed that a child's cognitive structure gradually increases in sophistication as the child continues to grow and mature. As each year progresses, the child's ability to mentally stand outside of itself increases, along with an increased capacity for human relatedness and empathy for others.

Although a teenager may often appear to be insecure and rebellious, nonetheless, his level of growth and maturity tends to surpass that of a child. If all goes well, by the time he grows into adulthood he will have reached a level of maturity in which he is less self-centered and is more responsive to the feelings and needs of others. This progression of self-development often continues into parenthood, where the needs of his children often take on greater importance than his own.

Human development does not need to stop at ordinary adult maturity because each of us has the innate potential for greater spiritual growth. Each level or phase of development surpasses and includes the abilities of the levels that precede it. As spiritual growth continues, the mind develops a greater capacity for handling challenges that confront it in the world, while simultaneously expanding its self-awareness and creative abilities. Hope and optimism replace anxiety and despair. Stronger ethics and higher values emerge within the person's consciousness, followed by altruism and unconditional love. The emergent recognition of our common humanity fosters the desire to be of service to others and to the greater whole. Meishusama writes about one of the psychological benefits that people derive from spiritual growth: "Their view of their own future becomes bright and clear, and their worries and anxieties disappear." *(The Strata in the Spiritual World. HT)*

Heaven and Hell

The spiritual world extends in range from the lower worlds, to the middle worlds, up to the higher worlds. These are also known as the hell worlds, purgatory (Yachimata), and heaven. About this, Meishusama elaborates, "The difference between these levels is a matter of radiance and heat. On the highest level, the radiance and heat are both very intense, while on the lowest level everything is dark and frigid. Yachimata lies between these two extremes, approximating the material world in this respect." *(A Description of the Spiritual World. HT)* We create our own heaven and hell in the way we live our lives. People in constant conflict with others live in their own private hell world, while those who love to make others happy and delight in their joy live in heaven itself. As Jesus Christ said, "The Kingdom of Heaven is within." Most of us currently live in various levels of purgatory; sometimes happy, sometimes suffering.

The Path to Spiritual Growth

Perfection seems a distant hope in this imperfect world of ours, but the aim of nurturing the human mind and spirit so it can gradually, step-by-step, approach perfection, is the right attitude and reveals the aspirations of true faith.

– Common Sense. HT

There are many ways to progress in our upward reach for God. Meishusama suggests actively purifying our spiritual clouds through Jyorei, learning to always think of others first, helping people to be happy, and cultivating the appreciation of art and beauty. Studying spiritual teachings is also valuable for receiving wisdom and inspiration. In particular, Meishusama says that we can actually absorb Divine Light from his written words.

Along with these outwardly directed activities, there are inner practices as well. These consist of scrutinizing one's own fears, motives and desires; cultivating love, gratitude, and detachment; chanting sacred words of power, such as contained within the Amatsunorito; and sitting in prayer or in meditative silence. And when the dark mists of negative thoughts and emotions cloud one's view of the sky, it is helpful to remember that everything, both the good and the bad, is a gift from God, given to help us to purify and grow.

Dedicated commitment to all of these practices is guaranteed to positively transform our character and further our spiritual development. "We must improve and elevate our souls. That is, the elevation you must achieve is an elevation of character," writes Meishusama. *(New Men. HT)*

How can we tell if we are progressing in our spiritual development? About this Meishusama says, "There is a standard against which you can measure the extent of your progress in faith and the pureness of your spirit. It is not difficult. It is the degree to which you dislike strife, and the amount of courtesy and gentleness that you show." *(Gentleness and Courtesy. HT)*

This does not mean that one cannot take a stand against hatred and aggression. On the contrary, it can sometimes be quite appropriate to intervene if we see someone being physically attacked. But in these situations, one should not return hostility with more hostility, because that would only increase the violence. What is needed is for the cycles of violence and hatred to stop completely. It is important to remember that even cruel or hateful people deserve respect, even though they do not give it to others. Whenever possible, it is best to be the peacemaker, not the avenger, and to promote universal harmony, wherever we go.

It is not just our own personal happiness that we seek, but also the happiness of everyone. Dedicating our practice to the salvation and happiness of others purifies our desires by lifting us above our self-absorbed motives and intentions. Surprisingly, happiness comes as a gift when we do not seek it selfishly. By helping others to be happy, we find that happiness emerges spontaneously in our own heart.

Thousands of candles can be lit from a single candle, and the life of the candle will not be shortened. Happiness never decreases by being shared.

– Gautama Buddha

Transformation of the World

The change from Night to Day is taking place in the following sequence: It has already begun in the profoundest recesses of the world of the ultimate mystery, whence it has spread to the spiritual world and eventually it will to the material world. – Repent, for the End of Night Is at Hand. HT

As a species, the human race does not seem to have evolved very far in its consciousness. We still do terrible things to each other, as well as to our surrounding environment. During the past century, in particular, through the use of modern weapons technology, the level of death and destruction has increased. The collective effects of all this pain and negativity have accumulated in the spiritual world to such an extent that a great worldwide purification and transformation now seems all but inevitable.

Nature moves in cycles; some large, some small, some fast, and some slow. There are cycles of day and night, cycles of the moon, cycles of the four seasons, and cycles of fertilization, birth, growth, maturity, aging, death, and renewal. There are also much vaster cycles in God's plan, in which the heavenly bodies move in grand succession over eons of time. About this process, Meishusama writes, "Everything is in motion, perpetually following fixed criteria with absolute precision, never an instance of delay." (*Atheism. HT*)

According to Meishusama, a long cosmic cycle of comparative darkness is rapidly coming to an end, and history is now turning towards the dawning of a new Age of Light, a world of crystal clarity and universal harmony. This will be a time when the divine energy that permeates all things will begin to manifest throughout our physical world with increasing intensity and power. But before this age can come about, a great cleansing and purification must occur. All that has been hiding in the dark shadows must be exposed to the Light and brought into alignment with it.

Everything in manifestation, from the largest galaxies to the smallest atoms, is subject to the Law of Purification. This process of purification itself also seems to move in cycles, and this approaching time of enormous change is the culmination of one of these grand cycles.

The Law of Spiritual Precedence states that the conditions in the spiritual world determine the outcome in the physical world. At dawn, on June 15, 1931, on the summit of Mt. Nokogiri, near Tokyo, Meishusama received a divine revelation indicating that on that very day a New Age of Light and harmony had begun in the spiritual world, and that it was inevitable that this New Age would eventually manifest on the physical plane.

The spiritual world has its own timetable, and what may seem like a long time in the physical world may seem short when viewed from the spiritual world. Therefore, how soon the effects of this change in the inner worlds will materialize in our daily lives is unpredictable. As each day passes, the Divine Light becomes brighter within the spiritual realm, with a corresponding increase in its essence, the spirit of fire. Since 1931, the power of the Light has been steadily increasing in the outer world as well. The world's response to this increase has been, in part, massive purification through wars, revolutions and other social upheavals. The intensified purifying frequencies of Light are now affecting everything, including the subjective dimension of our thoughts and emotions, as well as the objective world of matter and energy. Everything is accelerating, and thus we are also beginning to experience the direct consequences of our thoughts and actions more quickly than before. When we lie, cheat, steal, or hurt others, a corresponding misfortune soon happens to us. What used to take months or years to manifest, now takes only weeks or days. Within this new environment, there is no escaping from our personal karma.

The movement of every object is merely the result or reflection of the prior movement of its spiritual equivalent. The delay between the original spiritual movement and its eventual physical movement is decided by the size of the object in question. At the shortest, the delay is a matter of days; at the longest, the time can extend to several years. As the Age of Day approaches, however, this time-lag is steadily decreasing, and recently it has become remarkably short. The spiritual world is now in an unprecedented turmoil which tells its own story of the change to come, the change that will be the end of the world. – *The Nature and Behavior of Evil Spirits. HT*

During this period of transformation, there may be cataclysmic earth changes and extreme weather conditions. The earth may generate earthquakes, hurricanes, tidal waves, fires, droughts, tornados, and blizzards. Human civilization will likely suffer political turmoil, economic chaos, famine, and social dislocation. All nations and every region of the world will be affected. Nothing will be exempt from radical change, as all of the negativity in the world is dredged up and cleansed. The corruption and lies that society is based upon will be exposed to public scrutiny. All of the suffering that this causes will be part of the birth pangs of a new world coming into being. Throughout this turbulent time, large numbers of people will undergo personal transformation and spiritual awakening. The amplified level of Light will shine on everyone and everything.

If one's spirit is pure, one can pass through this critical time with relative ease, no matter what form it takes. – Last Judgment. MK

The extent of suffering that will occur during this transition will depend upon the collective level of humanity's consciousness. Only those who have already been purified, both spiritually and physically, will be able to adjust to the higher frequencies now beginning to enter into our world. Many others may become ill, go insane, or perish. This is why Meishusama was given Jyorei to share with the world at this point in history: to help as many people as possible to successfully make this transition. People who hold peace and love in their hearts, and are genuinely concerned about the welfare of others, will help to usher in this great transformation from Night into Day. They will remain relatively untouched by much of the suffering that occurs around them.

The great changes that result will be completely unprecedented in the history of the universe. There will be destruction and creation on a scale that has never been experienced before. As the corruption of the spiritual world is swept away and all is made clean, this change will inevitably be manifested faithfully and completely in this world of ours, and the transformation that it will cause is beyond imagination. – *Repent for the End of Night Is at Hand.* HT

Meishusama was not alone in predicting this coming change. Ancient myths, scriptures, and oral teachings from throughout the world have prophesized about this approaching time. The Bible warns about the apocalyptic end times, followed by the Second Coming of Christ and the establishment of God's kingdom on earth. Hindu scriptures predict the ending of this current dark age, called the Kali Yuga, to be followed by the great golden age of the Satya Yuga. The elders of the Hopi tribe of northern Arizona warn us that we are now in the midst of the "Great Purification" long predicted in their oral tradition. The calculations from the Mayan calendar indicate that the world will soon enter into a higher dimension of reality, called "The World of the Fifth Sun." Details differ from one source to another, but what is significant is their unanimous agreement concerning an approaching great purification followed by a golden age.

According to Professor Bannerjee of the University of New Mexico, earth's magnetic field has lost up to half its intensity in the last 4000 years due to a slowing of the planet's rotation[1]. Paralleling this, the earth's background base frequency, known as the Schuman Resonance Frequency, is rapidly rising from its traditional level of 7.83 hertz to much higher levels. Geologist and computer scientist Greg Braden, in his book "Awakening to Zero Point," suspects that this increase of frequency might be responsible for the feeling many of us have that time is speeding up. He also claims that we are experiencing an intensification of our emotions and increased difficulty remembering things because our emotional body and memory are closely connected with the Earth's magnetic field. Braden predicts that when the lessening magnetic field strength reaches zero, and the earth's base frequency reaches 13 hertz, there will be a magnetic pole shift and a reversal of the planet's rotation, which will cause extreme weather conditions, earthquakes, and social unrest.

Meishusama was a modern prophet whose urgent goal was to help all of humanity. He was not just promoting inner growth and healing, but also

---

[1] National Geophysical Data Center (NGDC): http://www.ngdc.noaa.gov/seg/geomag/faqgeom. shtml#q8a

perfection in the objective world. In his mind, the inner and the outer are inseparable. For that reason, he dedicated himself to healing and transforming not only individuals, but also society and the physical environment. People's hearts must be purified of greed, selfishness and malice. Society must learn to take care of everyone, even those who are disliked or unpopular. Government, business, culture, medicine, education, religion, and ethics—all must align themselves with higher values and principles. The earth, water and air must be purified of all pollution. The fulfillment of this ideal vision will coincide with a dramatic rise in the collective spiritual level of humanity.

According to Meishusama, God works out the divine plan through people. The prophesied changes are going to happen, but our attitudes and actions will determine how mild or harsh they will be. Therefore, each of us has an important part to play in helping to usher in this new world. Each of us can look for ways in which we can promote peace in our environment and harmony with our neighbors. Together, we can help usher in this Age of Light through our combined efforts to serve God and humanity.

The world of man will end as the first buds of God's world shoot forth.
– Last Judgment. MK

The arrival of the Age of Day will accompany the emergence of a new, enlightened condition within humanities' collective consciousness. Those who survive will have been purified and transformed in body and soul. Meishusama prophesied that even the material substance of the world would be transmuted into something resembling translucent crystal, rather than the dense, opaque matter we see today. The world that survives these changes will be permeated with Divine Light—and will literally be a "World of Light." This will be an age when people learn to honor and appreciate their individual differences, rather than feel threatened by them. Individual actions will be motivated more by generosity and kindness rather than greed and spite. Mankind literally stands on the threshold of a profound awakening in consciousness and the corresponding birth of a new civilization. This will be the dawning of a Paradise on Earth, and the fulfillment of humanity's long-held dream of universal brotherhood and peace on earth.

After tens of thousands of years of waiting, the process nears completion.
— God's Plan. MK

Truth, Virtue, and Beauty

The ultimate aim of God is the creation of an ideal world of truth, virtue and beauty, as all those with true faith know quite well. The aim of the devil is the complete opposite, and this is starkly obvious; it is to incite falseness, vice and ugliness. I scarcely need to explain the nature of falseness and vice for these two foul things are well enough known to everybody. — Heaven Is a World of Beauty. HT

The goal of Meishusama's life, for which he worked tirelessly, was the creation of a world embodying the universal values of truth, virtue, and beauty. The ancient Greek philosopher, Plato, championed these same three ideals over two thousand years ago. These values characterize branches of Western Philosophy concerned with reality, ethics, and aesthetics.

As an inner experience, truth is attained through self-investigation; virtue is an expression of purity of intent; and beauty is a subjective experience resulting from the perception of balance, harmony, and proportion. Truth engages the mind; virtue, the will; and beauty, feeling. Commenting on beauty, anthropologist Margaret Mead wrote, "Art is the language of the heart; that is, the language of the emotional structures."

A person's character is made up of three critical components: their thoughts, words, and deeds. A person's thoughts are subjective because only the thinker can perceive them. Actions are objective because others can observe them. Words, however, translate the subjective into the objective because our inner thoughts are outwardly communicated to others. When purified and developed to the highest level, our thoughts, words, and deeds can become significant vehicles for helping to transform the world into an ideal place embodying truth, virtue, and beauty.

Truth

The fact that people become ill indicates that they have strayed from the Truth in some way, and the same is true for the fact that [their] illness cannot be cured. The corruption of politics, the decadence of ideas, the increase in crime, the distress caused by tight money, inflation and deflation—all are caused by our straying from the Truth. If we do not stray from the Truth, then honesty will be as successful as we hope, for society was made by God to be like that. A society of Virtue and Beauty will be born, and man will be able to live a joyful and fortunate life. In other words, the paradise on earth of which I speak will become reality. – The Embodiment of Truth. HT

Truth has many levels. At the highest level, truth is the spiritual dimension that is experienced by mystics, saints, and seers. It is the primary concern of theology and metaphysics. Truth, on a more worldly level, relates to the mental disciplines of logic and mathematics, and to the physical world of the material sciences. Although the highest spiritual truth is eternal and unchangeable, its verbal expression in the world of form is subject to change in accordance with current cultural values, religious ideas, and philosophical theories.

The opposite of truth, which is falsity, is the cause of much suffering in the world. On a personal level, self-deception (which is basically lying to oneself) contributes to most of the psychological problems we see today. It is the lies that we tell ourselves that torture our minds and lead to errors in our actions. Similarly, relationships based on deceit are doomed to fail. About this, Meishusama said, "To make other people honest, first discard your own lies and deceptions." *(Honesty. MK)* Not surprisingly, most psychotherapy is concerned with helping people to become more honest with themselves and with others. Honesty and sincerity are crucial for the development of individual maturity and for maintaining healthy relationships.

In a time of universal deceit, telling the truth becomes a revolutionary act.
                                                                      – George Orwell

Meishusama says that the world is currently suffering from "a culture of external forms," a world enamored by false glamour and obsessed with personal status. Recognizing what is truly important amidst this confusing swarm of stimuli is the basis for wisdom and inner peace.

Ultimate truth is direct knowledge of God. The more we perceive the spiritual reality within ourselves, the more we perceive it everywhere else: in people's hearts, in nature, in beauty, and in lives lived consistent with spiritual principles and values. This is both seeing and living truth at the deepest level, beyond the scope of the mind, with its endless internal chatter. This spiritual reality is the most profound meaning of Meishusama's expression, "the point within the circle." In a human being, this point is the indwelling spirit, the individual spark of God located within each of us.

Relative truth, however, is more concrete and obvious than ultimate truth because it refers to facts that can be verified in the objective world. For instance, one can easily look outside to see if it is raining, taste soup to see if it is hot, or listen to hear if people are talking in another room. Relative truth lies within the jurisdiction of common sense and can be accurately measured by science. When a statement correlates with the facts, we say that the statement is true.

How nice it is to hear a person say, white is white. – Honesty. MK

According to Meishusama, nature itself is truth—not an abstract truth, but a truth that is both felt and visible to those who are observant. He says, "To understand the world, to find the answer to the deepest problems, you usually need to do no more than look closely at the world of nature." *(Impasse. HT)*

The natural world is capable of managing itself without the need for outside intervention. Nature rejuvenates itself from within. All of creation is spontaneously evolving towards greater complexity and intelligence. The wisdom of nature is vast and impersonal, yet nurtures the growth of countless life forms, each with their own uniqueness and individuality. Nature reveals a higher truth not based on rationality or logic. When one seeks inner peace, one can benefit greatly from visiting nature, where there is silence, tranquility, and profound beauty. In nature, it is much easier for us to find these same qualities within ourselves.

If the pure truth had been expounded, human society would not have the appearance of deep suffering which it has at the present day."
– The Embodiment of Truth. HT

Virtue

To become a person with a purer spirit, you must do good deeds and increase your store of virtue. It takes a fair amount of time and self-sacrifice, but it provides a way of rising rapidly up in the spiritual world by tens of strata.
– The Strata in the Spiritual World. HT

Virtue refers to an inner quality that is revealed by our actions. It relates to morals, ethics, justice, and the general sphere of social interaction as judged by common standards of right and wrong. Although morality and social standards may vary significantly from one society to another, some universal agreement in these areas is necessary in order for there to be cooperation and harmony among the peoples of the world. We can find this consensus in such universally valued qualities as kindness, generosity, courage, modesty, honesty, and loyalty, to name a few. The golden rule, "treat others as you would have them treat you," is a useful general guideline for ethical behavior. To do this effectively requires us to place ourselves in the shoes of other people and try to see the world through their eyes.

Virtue is also action that does no harm, and that benefits others as well as our own self. It is selfless action that contributes to the larger common good. Concerning virtue, Meishusama says: "Anyone, even if he is a prominent figure in society, can and should find pleasure in avoiding the snares of dubious entertainment and vice, while spending any spare money he has towards the welfare of society, performing virtuous acts, helping those in need, turning to God, and sometimes taking his family out to the cinema, theater, or on a holiday." (*Virtue Is Pleasure. HT*) One can imagine Meishusama adding that last phrase as a humorous twist to the more lofty sentiments expressed in the earlier part of the sentence. Always advising moderation and pragmatic values, he was therefore quite sincere about suggesting recreational family pastimes.

Meishusama describes acts of vice as "lying, making others suffer, and creating problems and troubles in society. The fact is, however, that far too many people care only about themselves and act without giving a thought to the problems and interests of others. This is the worst possible kind of behavior and will never find favor with God. *(To Be Loved by God. HT)*

Greed and selfishness originate from feelings of lack: lack of love, lack of security, or lack of self-worth. A person emotionally wounded by others often internalizes this pain and then wants to hurt others in retaliation. As the wounds build up, this person may become inwardly driven by anger to take revenge against all of society. Many of the criminals that we see today who prey on others through robbery, assault, or murder, were themselves once victims of emotional or physical violence. Thus, anger breeds more anger, and violence breeds more violence.

As the Buddha says, "He who causes suffering shall suffer. There is no escape." Therefore, the only way out of this vicious cycle of pain and more pain is to make a radical break from the past and to begin acting in ways that alleviate suffering and promote happiness in others. The intention to help others is the essential foundation for virtuous action, and it also results in greater personal happiness for both the giver and receiver. Unfortunately, this profoundly simple formula is all too often ignored in our obsessive pursuit of what is often meaningless and superficial.

Each time we extend ourselves for the sake of others, we accumulate virtue and our level of happiness rises. As Thomas Jefferson, one of the founding fathers of the United States of America said, "Happiness is the aim of life but virtue is the foundation of happiness." There is no need for us to wait for some distant future to obtain our reward, because with each act of charity our character instantly improves. The truest virtue occurs when we do a good deed without any concern for self-gain, and when we also surrender the outcome of that deed to God or to the highest good. Our intentions are as important as the deed itself. Furthermore, doing things with a gentle and loving heart tends to produce the best of outcomes and is also the most rewarding to both the giver and the receiver. All acts of genuine kindness and goodwill move us up a step in the spiritual world.

Although virtuous actions may bring us closer to God, there is always the possibility of acquiring salvation through grace, which does not depend upon our actions, and is unearned. God is full of mercy and love. The joy resulting from spiritual emancipation can be said to be the product of both good works and of grace, each contributing to the beneficial effect of the other. Virtuous

behavior makes us more receptive to grace, which uplifts our spirit and consequently promotes further virtuous behavior.

*As to salvation, I would like to make it clear that true salvation of spirit cannot
be brought about by humans. It is God who acts on this, and humans are mere
instruments to assist Him. However, being allowed to work as one of God's
instruments is truly a blessed thing.*[2] *– KW*

Beauty

The purpose of art is the elevation of the human spirit. – Meishusama

Beauty occurs when the balance and perfection existing at the highest levels of the spiritual world (sometimes referred to as God's Realm) are expressed
in the physical world through art or nature. The spiritual world, in all its varied
dimensions, permeates our ordinary world, both transcending and including
it. A great artist often obtains a heightened experience of reality, in which the
ordinary world is perceived in an extraordinary way, with greater sensitivity,
depth, and appreciation. Depending on their knowledge, skill, and experience,
they are then able to communicate this glimpse by way of music, painting,
writing, or other artistic forms.

If the artist is sufficiently receptive, he or she may receive inspiration
from the loftier heights of the spiritual world. Sometimes higher beings, such
as a person's guardian spirit, may provide assistance. However, Spirit is the
true source of all great art and intellectual discovery. It falls upon the artist
to capture this inspiration and then translate it into works of art. About this,
Meishusama writes, "When an artist is working creatively or when an inventor
is trying to solve a problem, they often get ideas in what we call 'a flash of
inspiration.' This is, of course, guidance provided by their primary guardian
spirits." *(Guardian Spirits. HT)*

While viewing or hearing great art, if the viewer or listener is sufficiently
sensitive, he or she can also receive a glimpse of the spiritual world, a world

---

[2] Meishusama, "Judge Not," *Shumei Magazine*, vol. 262 (March/April 2006).

of timeless beauty and radiant Light, which produces feelings of peace, harmony, and joy. Art, like love, accepts all things. It reveals the Light shining beneath the surface of things. But it is not just the world of the spirit that art finds engaging, for it also delights in the textures, shapes and sounds of the world around us. Art embraces the senses as well as the imagination. It is both rational and irrational. More than anything else, art demonstrates the essential unity of matter and Spirit, of passion and purpose, and of form and formlessness. By reconciling these and other dualities, art heals. It makes whole that which is fractured.

All forms of beauty, like all possible phenomena, contain an element of the eternal and an element of the transitory—of the absolute and of the particular.
– Charles Baudelaire

Nature is Spirit made manifest. It is a perfect synthesis of Spirit and matter, without ego or artificial contrivance. The world is God's artwork expressed through such things as mountains, rivers, flowers, trees, oceans, and sky. Seeing the Himalayas, a Pacific Ocean sunset, or the Aurora Borealis, can be a life changing experience. Nature's beauty incorporates both individuality and universality, as each and every thing, although part of larger groups of things, has a unique color, shape, movement, or sound. Nature, although inwardly still, is wild and exuberant in its diverse expression. About this Meishusama comments, "Again, a flower, a leaf, the beauties of natural scenery, and every living thing from beasts, birds and fish to the last tiny insect - all of them show the wonders of God's works, and who can fail to marvel at them?" (*The Truth about Health, God's Way to Health. HT*)

Beauty is certainly a soft, smooth, slippery thing, and therefore of a nature which easily slips in and permeates our souls. – Plato

Interrelated Values

Truth, virtue, and beauty are mutually interrelated. To choose truth over falseness and to prefer beauty to ugliness is, at the same time, a moral attitude. Hence, philosophical values and aesthetic values cannot be divorced from moral values. The revelation of truth, to see things as they are, is good, because as the saying goes, "To know all is to forgive all." Such insight leads to compassion, which is both virtuous and beautiful. Similarly, to selflessly do that which serves the greater whole is also beautiful and in alignment with the highest truth. And when one's every action is graceful and beautiful, then it is also virtuous and honest. Such behavior is never false, never causes harm, and eventually leads one to truth. It is deeply sincere and has great integrity. Meishusama described truth as the way, virtue as the deed, and beauty as the heart. As personal traits, truth, virtue, and beauty each reflect an aspect of makoto, and as outer values, they each lead to the establishment of a "World of Light."

8 LIVING A SPIRITUAL LIFE

God is both immanent and transcendent. God exists within everything, and everything exists within God. The whole is within the part, and the part is within the whole. This paradoxical and seemingly dualistic nature of God is called Miroku Omikami. Miroku Omikami is that which encompasses everything. The apparent presence of opposites in the nature of God is due only to the limitations of imagination and logic, both of which cannot grasp undivided Oneness. In the spiritual life, this Oneness has the attributes of harmony and balance.

The Purpose of Life

Meishusama always cared for balance, which could be seen in both his lifestyle and in his published teachings. His great effort to elevate human souls was balanced by his natural gift for enjoying the simple pleasures in life. Rather than separating these two activities, he cultivated both simultaneously. Each supported the other, because by helping others to grow spiritually, he became happier, and by radiating happiness, he was able to draw more people to himself and thereby influence them in a positive way.

The ultimate and the immediate are not separate, but are actually one undivided whole. A flower growing beside a road, a raindrop splashing on a pond, a ray of sunlight shining through clouds—all of these can reveal God's presence if a person's mind is absolutely quiet and his or her heart is sufficiently open. God, when viewed as the transcendental reality beyond this world of ignorance and suffering, can best be approached through gradual purification and elevation of the soul; whereas God, when viewed as the immanent reality existing within this world of time and space, can best be approached by living fully in the here and now, with love and gratitude.

Consequently, from Meishusama's perspective, life has not one, but actually two overriding purposes: the spiritual development of the soul, and the simple enjoyment of the present moment. One may appear distant and the other close, yet happiness and enjoyment depend, to varying degrees, upon both the sacred and the secular. Two things contribute to our sense of happiness: the soul's spiritual purity, and also the amount of peace and harmony in one's outer environment. In the joy that comes from experiencing beauty, both the inner and the outer come together, because outer beauty can only be appreciated to the extent that one is inwardly capable of perceiving it. Thus, the higher our spiritual level, the more we live in a world of beauty.

Each of us also has two primary tasks in life: to learn to love self and others completely and unconditionally, and to help create Heaven on Earth. The first is inner directed, and the second is outer directed. These two soul tasks support the attainment of our two life purposes because each of them helps us to grow spiritually and each contributes to our overall enjoyment and happiness in our day-to-day lives.

Spiritual Growth

The spiritual clouds that cover our soul are the chief cause of suffering. These clouds not only darken and distort our experience, but also strongly influence the conditions and circumstances of our daily life. The more we eliminate spiritual clouds and elevate our soul, the more capable we will be of enjoying the simple, ordinary things in life. "Therefore to become happy and fortunate you must make all possible efforts to purify your soul and make it light so that it reaches the highest level possible. There is absolutely no other way. And this is the great significance of Jyorei," writes Meishusama. *(Jyorei and Happiness. HT)*

Through the experiences of many lifetimes, each individual soul goes through various stages of purification, accumulates wisdom, and gradually progresses toward final union with God—that loving Presence which is our ultimate source and fulfillment. Activities that create spiritual clouds, that create impurities in the body or soul, contribute to both current and future suffering. Because happiness is dependent on our spiritual level, our leisure activities should also support spiritual growth, or at least not detract from it.

Put simply, the purpose of life is happiness, and this happiness is synonymous with the inner peace and radiance that comes from a life attuned to Spirit. Despite popular opinion, happiness does not come from the pursuit of selfish preoccupations. Rather, happiness results from making a meaningful contribution to others. This is why, in the Bible, Jesus Christ says, "It is better to give than to receive." A friendly concern for others that translates into concrete action helps the soul progress upwards in the spiritual world. Through service to others we receive Toku Energy (spiritual merit), which fosters refinement of character.

Each soul evolves in its own unique way during its journey through life. The further the soul proceeds on the journey, the more pure it becomes. By purifying oneself, one also contributes to the purification of the world by radiating more Light to others.

God gives everyone a mission in this world. He gives them special characteristics and special talents. He gives them physical existence and takes it away again, and He makes us all move ever forward towards the ideal object of Eternity. Good and evil, war and peace, destruction and creation are all not more than processes that are necessary to this evolution. – The Strata in the Spiritual World. HT

Enjoyment

The saints of ancient days wrapped themselves in sackcloth, but I do not.
– Art. MK

Although spiritual growth determines our capacity for true happiness, by itself it is incomplete. If spiritual realization was the only purpose of life, we would then be encouraged to devalue pleasure as no more than a meaningless distraction from that pursuit. This point of view promotes an ascetic lifestyle that rejects the pleasures of the world, including people, art, food, and nature. This ascetic attitude differs from Meishusama's way because it lacks love, and beauty.

Meishusama was a gregarious man who experienced life to the fullest. He did not view life as a problem to be solved, but rather as a gift from nature to be enjoyed and appreciated. Meishusama was well-known for his infectious sense of humor. He had a gift for sharing delight in the comic absurdity often found within ordinary circumstances and events. Meishusama loved going to the movies, dining out with friends, gardening, visiting art museums, and attending concerts. Rather than overly dwelling on the rampant sin and corruption of the world, he preferred to enjoy the good things in it. Meishusama wanted to transform and redeem the world. *More than anything else, he wanted people to be happy.*

The beauties of the birds, flowers and trees, bird-song and distant hills, the pale graceful moon and the gentle breeze—all are made by God to please and comfort mankind. – The Glory of Faith. HT

Desire and Oneness

To be human is to be driven by desire. Some desires are primal, such as the need for food and shelter, some are instinctual, such as the urge for sex or physical pleasure, and some are ambitious, such as goals for fame and fortune. But what all desires have in common is that they constantly compel us to seek fulfillment in the future, while ignoring the here and now. Because of this, the present moment always feels incomplete and unsatisfying. Big houses, new cars, good jobs, soul mates, long vacations, and stylish clothes—these things may bring a degree of happiness, but such happiness is usually only short-lived. We may become temporarily happy after acquiring these things, but soon enough, new desires will emerge, and we will then return to seeking new things. This is why worldly things, although enjoyable, are not sufficient for creating happiness that endures.

When we obtain the things we want, our desires tend to subside, and we become contented and peaceful for a while. But it was really the lack of desire that made us happy, not the outer thing that we obtained. Unfortunately, though, when new desires emerge, we go back to being dissatisfied again.

Deep down, what all of us really seek is to become free of division, because all divisions (both inner and outer forms of it) cause alienation, fear, and conflict. These feelings are the underlying cause of desire. They cause us to desire positive feelings, which at their deepest source, originate from unity—not division. This is why worldly objects do not bring lasting happiness. They do not satisfy our deepest need, which is to experience a state of inner Oneness with all that is; a state in which there is no underlying division—only unqualified unity. Most of us are not conscious that this is what we are really seeking, but if we investigate deeply, it will become self-evident to many of us. Only when this most fundamental desire is fulfilled—the desire for unity and love—will we be truly happy.

The first peace, which is the most important, is that which comes within the souls of people when they realize their relationship, their oneness with the universe and all its powers, and when they realize that at the center of the universe dwells the Great Spirit, and that this center is really everywhere, it is within each of us.
– Black Elk (Sioux Medicine Man)

The Present Moment

By staying focused on the present, we move closer to this state of unqualified happiness. The pleasant company of family and friends, a meal of delicious food, an arrangement of beautiful flowers, and the rich sound of a live concert: these are not experiences to be dutifully endured as a means toward an end. Rather, we experience these things joyfully for their own sake, for it is the nature of joy to be fully satisfied with the present moment.

Everything has beauty, but not everyone sees it. – Confucius

Although we encourage everyone to help create a perfect world, when this perfect world finally arrives, then what will we all do? Should we continue to search and strive for perfection? But when the world is finally perfect, there will not be anyone left in need of saving, or anything left to improve. The only thing left to do will be to relax and enjoy life. It will finally be time to celebrate!

But we do not need to wait until then to celebrate. Maybe we should start celebrating here and now instead of postponing it until later, because how can we promote joy and happiness in the future if we do not feel it in this very moment? It is hard to make others happy if we ourselves are miserable. Only joy creates more joy, just as only love creates more love.

Although purification and self-cultivation are essential for our spiritual growth, we can also grow spiritually from living joyfully in the present moment in playful activity—activity done without ulterior motives or future objectives. To be fully present, the mind must become very quiet and alert, rather than obsessed with thoughts about the past and future. Meishusama called this the "instantaneous self," Henry Bergson's term for a state of mind that reacts immediately and intelligently to whatever arises in the moment.

Need there be a purpose to love, kindness, joy, or beauty? Is there a reason or objective to the innocent delight of a child's play? Where is the enjoyment in dancing if a goal is attached? The simple pleasure of immediate experience is often its own reward.

Using activities or people merely to fulfill an objective—even a spiritual objective—is unwise. Nobody likes being treated as an object, because when we objectify people, we deny them their humanity. Similarly, to objectify our own life, or to regard our experiences as mere stepping-stones to a distant, abstract goal, is to not live fully in the here and now. Instead, it is a life lived in perpetual anticipation of the future, rather than in relaxed enjoyment of the present moment. Obsession with the future distracts us from the eternal silence that exists, unnoticed, within the present moment. This present moment is the window through which God's Grace enters our life.

A Balanced Life

On the other hand, if mere enjoyment were the only purpose for living, then there would be no meaning or justification for higher principles. All values would have secondary importance in comparison to momentary pleasure. Kindness, loyalty, honesty, generosity, altruism, fairness, and many other human virtues would have value only because they are pleasant, not because they reflect something higher. For most people, the pursuit of pleasure would become their overriding concern.

But eventually hedonism can become empty and meaningless, not to mention exhausting. Plus, our attraction to pleasure always coincides with an aversion to pain. They go hand in hand. And since no one can control everything, then none of us can avoid experiences that cause pain. Each of us will inevitably experience suffering in one form or another during our lifetime.

However much we enjoy life, the fact remains that everything decays and falls apart eventually, including the things that give us pleasure. We all get sick and die, as well. This means that our pleasure and enjoyment will also end at some time or other, and we will then be left with nothing, not even a life purpose. This leads to inevitable frustration, rather than enjoyment.

Based on the above analysis, it should be clear that the simple pursuit of pleasure will not lead to lasting happiness. Spiritual growth needs to be added to the pursuit of pleasure in order to give it greater depth and lasting fulfillment.

These complementary life purposes, of spiritual growth and simple enjoyment in the present moment, are mutually supportive. The greater the purity of our spirit, the more capable we are of being present in the here and now, and of appreciating all the beauty that is around us. Equally true is that the more capable we are of enjoying the present moment, the more we can learn and grow, and thus progress further in our spiritual development.

Only a balanced pursuit of both spiritual growth and enjoyment of the present moment can create true happiness. This balanced and moderate way of life is referred to as "Kannon's Way."

Attachment and Faith

Suffering is subdued and dispelled by putting everything in the hands of God.
– Signs of Divine Mercy. MK

We tend to grasp at the things that give us pleasure, while simultaneously running away from the things that cause us pain. This leaves us at the mercy of changing conditions. There is no security in this way of living because everything is unpredictable. That which brings us joy today may be gone tomorrow, including our family, our friends, and even our own physical body. Everyone dies eventually. So, to depend solely on the transitory things of this life for happiness only guarantees eventual suffering when they disappear.

Most of the suffering we experience is not caused by the actual conditions and circumstances we encounter, but rather by our attachment to these things. By insisting that life conform to our personal desires—and this is what is meant by attachment—we set ourselves up for frustration, anger, or depression. In reality, life does not usually turn out exactly the way we hope it will. Sometimes it ends up better and sometimes worse. The more we cling to our personal desires, the more we also suffer from a combination of anxiety about the future and regret over the past.

Attachment is the underlying cause of much suffering visited on other people and on themselves, and of much bitter strife. – Egotism and Worldly Attachment. HT

Usually our desires are driven by blind momentum, not wisdom. Sometimes our desires seek to fulfill authentic needs, whereas at other times they chase after mere whim or fancy. Most of us have probably experienced times when following our desires has led to disappointment or disaster. Because of this, it is sometimes better not to get what we want, especially if we cannot act wisely.

Part of the problem is the common assumption that the world we live in is a dangerous place, full of random chaos and uncontrollable accidents, as well as devoid of either meaning or purpose. In such a bleak world, it seems we have no choice but to struggle desperately for mere survival.

Meishusama counters this materialistic interpretation of life by teaching that the physical dimension is only a field of effects, not causes, and that the true cause, or source, of everything is in the spiritual world. If we look inside our minds, we will discover that everything we experience originates in our own consciousness. As far as we are concerned, nothing exists until it first registers in our consciousness as a perception, thought, feeling, sensation, or intention. Our inner experience can be interpreted as the subjective aspect of the spiritual world, and our outer experience, the objective aspect, just as our skin that has both an inside and an outside. If we do not experience something, or at least hear or read about it, then how do we know that it exists? This question is mirrored in a traditional Zen Buddhist 'koan' or riddle: "If a tree falls in a forest and nobody is there to hear it, does it make a sound?" Everything starts with our experience. To a large extent, we create our own reality by what we experience and by how we interpret our experiences. We then draw those things to us that energetically resonate with what we hold within our consciousness. Thus, the nonphysical dimension is the cause, and the physical is the effect.

The universe is not composed of blind forces acting upon inert matter. In reality, these forces and substances are but gross expressions of subtler realities that are not easily perceived by our ordinary consciousness. Quantum physics reveals that the universe is an endless ocean of particles invisible to our senses; that each particle is comprised of still-tinier particles; and that, at deeper levels, these particles are made up of pure energy. Similarly, Meishusama saw Spirit in all things. To him, the world was conscious and intelligent. The further we expand our own consciousness, the more we can perceive this conscious intelligence operating through all things.

All the experiences and events in our lives have meaning, whether we recognize this or not. The world is fundamentally spiritual, not material, although it may seem solid and stable when touched, tasted, or seen. Everything is permeated by invisible Light. Truly grasping this fact can transform our inner clouds of doubt and fear into clear skies of faith and trust. Then, instead of struggling with life, we begin to cooperate with it. We begin to trust that life will do what is best for us, and that it will give us those experiences that are most appropriate for our spiritual growth and long-term happiness.

Faith is different from belief, which is based on preconceived ideas. Many of us cling to various preconceived ideas, concepts, and opinions for the security they offer. But hidden within these beliefs are the seeds of doubt, whereas faith is free of doubt because it is based on trust in the unknown. To have faith is to let go and allow the universe to unfold in its own natural way. As Meishusama states, "The primary aim of faith must be to remove self-will and worldly attachment from the hearts and minds of people." *(Egotism and Worldly Attachment. HT)* Not being attached to outcomes promotes a sense of inner peace, which gradually spreads outward to the world around us. Faith does not need to control life, but instead flows gracefully with the natural unfolding of events. "Thus, as the feelings of attachment are swept away, the spirit ascends higher and higher in the spiritual world." *(Egotism and Worldly Attachment. HT)*

Of course, this does not imply that we should be careless and not plan for emergencies. Life is always full of challenges, so it is wise to be cautious. By preparing for the worst, we give ourselves the luxury of expecting the best.

It is always good to save money, buckle our seatbelts, and to lock our doors at night. This frees us from worry, allowing us to welcome whatever arises. Instead of blind faith, we should adopt a pragmatic faith, in which we also include taking responsibility for the details in our lives. Humans were given the faculty of intelligence in order to use it, not to ignore it.

To have faith is not unusual. To trust that we will continue to breathe throughout the night while we are sleeping is an act of faith. To trust the bank with our money, to trust our car to run safely, and to trust that water will pour out from our faucets, are all acts of faith. Even trusting that the sun will come up each morning demonstrates faith. We could not function well without trusting the various things in our lives to operate correctly.

True faith promotes detachment from results, allowing us to live a more peaceful and harmonious life. Faith, then, is the trusting but detached relationship between desires and outcomes. When we are inwardly detached, our behavior becomes free and easy rather than compulsive and stressful. This detachment should not be confused with apathy, which is motivated by resignation, fear, or laziness. Authentic detachment can express itself in either action or inaction, depending on circumstances. And, it is deep inner faith that supports this detachment.

I think that faith is the only possible way to help the world, which has lost and abandoned all its moral values. – Good and Evil. HT

There are times when circumstances may require decisive action. However, if done with faith, this action will not come from closed-minded willfulness, but from open-minded awareness. We each need to do our part while trusting God to do the rest. Instead of doubt, we need faith. True faith puts us in alignment with the higher power that directs all things, which is divine love and intelligence. Only when our hearts are pure, and when we are motivated by love, can we truly serve the greater good. In these cases, we become mere agents of a higher will. Even when we act with faith, there is no guarantee that the outcome will turn out well. Regardless of the immediate outcome, we need faith that eventually all will be well. In other words, we turn the final results over to God.

This perspective is not the same as simple "positive thinking," which artificially superimposes a positive interpretation over negative experiences.

Although it is good to have a positive attitude, positive thinking, when taken to extremes, can lead to mental blindness and the unwillingness to deal with negativity in oneself and in others. With faith, however, we do not need to have an answer for everything, nor do we need for life to always go our way. We no longer demand that life conform to our personal agendas. Faith trusts that all is the way it should be, and that all is well.

We must reach the mental and spiritual condition in which we do what we can as mortals and leave the rest in the hands of the Almighty, having perfect trust in God. – The Glory of Faith. HT

Hoshi (Selfless Service)

True happiness is found in helping others to be happy. – Common Sense. HT

Outwardly, at the level of physical form, we are each separate from one another, but inwardly, at the level of Spirit, we are all interconnected and part of a greater whole. The quality of our relationship to this greater whole is crucial to our sense of peace and well-being. In particular, when our relationship to this larger totality is based on service, we align ourselves more closely with that totality. Each time we help someone to feel happier, all of us benefit.

Being of service to others is one of the most effective ways for us to discover genuine happiness within ourselves. In Shumei, this service is called hoshi. Volunteering to help our family, friends, coworkers, or neighbors with simple tasks is a good way to begin doing hoshi.

Hoshi is a selfless form of service in which we dedicate our efforts to a purpose larger than ourselves. Within Shumei, people perform hoshi in order to support the organization in its greater mission of serving humanity. Usually, hoshi consists of such ordinary tasks as sweeping, mopping, wiping, or scrubbing. It is kept simple, basic, and physical, and therefore vital. When, as a form of hoshi, we physically clean something, we are simultaneously cleaning the interior of our soul, following the principle that the inner reflects the outer and the outer reflects the inner. This is why hoshi emphasizes physical labor—often the simpler the better—because such action helps to purify those ingrained impulses and tendencies within us that lean towards selfish behavior. Hoshi, when done with sincerity, promotes a heart of giving.

Put the benefit of others before your own profit. – Faith Means to be Trusted. HT

When we give freely of our time and energy, we generate Toku Energy, which is the spiritual Light we receive from helping others. Toku Energy is the spiritual merit we earn from performing good deeds with an open heart. Such action brightens the aura, elevates the soul, and generates inner happiness. Our selfless intentions create an inner glow that attracts others and exerts a positive influence upon them. Toku Energy is also the basis for good luck (some would say good karma) because it acts like a magnet to draw positive things to us. Thus, the more Toku Energy we accumulate, the better will be our future success and good fortune. However, the best rewards come when we do not seek personal gain, but instead concern ourselves with how we can be of service to others.

It is also possible to serve others in nonphysical ways. We can begin by treating people with simple courtesy and kindness. Cultivating a light and friendly attitude that brings comfort and joy to others is an outward expression of this kindness. By this simple practice, our heart begins to open, we rise to a higher spiritual level, and our capacity for kindness increases. As Mother Teresa once said, "We never know how much good a simple smile can do." *(The Joy in Loving)*

Eventually, as our desire to help others increases, our sensitivity to their inner needs increases as well. We begin to notice suffering that is not visible to the outer eye. And because of this, we become increasingly interested in helping those around us to feel better physically, mentally, and emotionally. We learn to answer rudeness with friendliness, selfishness with generosity, and hostility with kindness. We begin to radiate sympathetic warmth to those in need of love, especially those who are the least lovable or who seem the least deserving.

People often help humanitarian organizations because collective efforts can assist humanity in ways that we, as solitary individuals, cannot. There is power in groups, and this power can be used for many good purposes. Spiritual organizations often engage in humanitarian work, and by dedicating their work to God, they elevate it to a higher level. They usually view their missions as ways of serving God. Of course, God does not need anything because there is nothing outside of God. But the Creator does have an objective: the evolution of the world into divine Light. So, the best way to serve God is by serving others, especially by doing whatever we can to help them grow spiritually. Each of us can become a humble servant of God by dedicating our lives to fulfilling the divine plan for the transformation and spiritual awakening of all creation.

Based on this understanding, hoshi can also be viewed as a way of helping a spiritual organization in its mission of spreading Light. Hoshi is a spiritual discipline, and is not to be engaged in casually, since it provides a practical path to become closer to God. It does this by helping us to transcend selfishness. We can practice hoshi by doing physical or mental labor or by donating money. Any form of voluntary service that is practical and helpful, no matter how prestigious or menial, can be considered hoshi when performed with the right attitude.

Hoshi should not be done for the sake of recognition or reward. That would make it self-serving rather than selfless. Usually it is more appropriate to give anonymously, without seeking credit for it. As Meishusama writes, "Displayed virtue is false virtue. Concealed virtue communicates with God." *(Faith. MK)* However, this does not require us to be secretive, because oftentimes in order to be effective, others need to know of what we're doing.

My advice is that you do good without craving recognition. Perform good deeds even when people are not paying attention. God will return blessings to you many times greater than the value of your deeds.[1] – *KW*

Hoshi serves both God and humanity. This natural balance between idealism and practicality brings both inspiration and effectiveness to the act of hoshi. No one knows what the final results will be, and there is no need to know. What is important is that we do our best, while trusting in God

---

[1] Meishusama, "On Being Humble and Flexible," *Shumei Magazine*, vol. 263 (May/June 2006).

to handle the outcome. As stated by Krishna in the Hindu scripture, the Bhagavad-Gita, "Do your duty, always; but without attachment. That is how a man reaches ultimate Truth; by working without anxiety about results."

Surprisingly, when we reach out to assist others with sincere intent, we become happier ourselves. If we perform hoshi with gratitude for the opportunity and privilege of serving God, then our souls will shine with joy and our work will shine with excellence. Just be happy to serve. All hoshi, whether big or small, has value because it contributes to the greater good. It often comes as a surprise to people when they discover how much joy and camaraderie exists within volunteer groups. The volunteers are paid in self-satisfaction and happiness, not money. Selfless action purifies our spirit and opens us to the beneficial influences exerted by our guardian spirit. It also tends to liberate us from self-absorbed moods and preoccupations because the self is forgotten in the act of giving. Generosity reinforces a sense of abundance, whereas selfishness, by its very nature, is a miserable condition, whether we get what we want or not, because it arises from a belief in lack.

I slept and dreamt that life was joy. I awoke and saw that life was service. I acted, and behold, service was joy.
              – Rabindranath Tagore, Indian poet, playwright and essayist

We are naturally motivated to serve others when we see ourselves in them. As our consciousness expands to include others, we begin to find that their sorrow becomes our sorrow, and their happiness, our happiness. An unexpected benefit of this expansion of consciousness is that we now have more reasons and opportunities to be happy than we did previously when we were only looking out for ourselves. More and more, we find that when we help someone feel happier, we also feel a corresponding increase in happiness ourselves. As a result of this, we feel less isolated and cut off from others, and instead, feel more connected to them. This is why it is better to give than to receive—because giving is receiving. By acting generously, we find happiness, which is what each of us is fundamentally seeking. Therefore, pray to God to use you, body and soul, in service to the greater good. Holding this intention in your heart will re-orchestrate your priorities accordingly, and will gradually purify your being and lead to a state of undisturbed joy. Through selfless giving, we discover that, as the philosopher William James stated, "We are like islands in the sea, separate on the surface but connected in the deep."

In the conventional way of thinking, there is the role of the giver and the role of the receiver. But from a higher perspective, this and all other dualities fall away and there is only the transcendental Oneness of God, which includes all beings and all things in its all-encompassing totality. Thus, to serve others is to serve God, and to serve God is to serve one's very own self. From a higher perspective, there is no separation, but only unity. Everything partakes of God's love, which is the same love that can be found deep within one's own heart.

Living a life of selfless giving is the highest expression of hoshi. When this becomes constant, then all of our actions are forms of hoshi, because giving is now an established way of life. Like Kannon Bodhisattva herself, we have become a pure instrument through which God's wisdom and compassion can effectively manifest in the objective world.

Since receiving a new life, his eyes have become gentle, his face radiant and bright. – Faith, MK

The Instantaneous Self

A direct, undistorted perception is the only true perception, and this is a function of the instantaneous self. – Henri Bergson. HT

The natural world has a pattern, an order that varies constantly according to the seasons, the weather, and the time of day. The nature of this pattern is similar to the movement of water in a stream or the wind currents in the sky. Although the natural world cannot be defined in words, it is, however, possible to attune oneself to its nonverbal rhythms of ebb and flow by living fully in the moment.

Unlike man, nature is unselfconscious. Nature is devoid of anxiety and stress. Hawks, bears, and rabbits do not worry about tomorrow's meal or the following day's shelter. For them, each day takes care of itself. They also do not concern themselves about what others think about them, and thus remain free of shame, guilt, and embarrassment.

Letting go of our preoccupations with the past or future gives us the clarity to respond appropriately to whatever challenges come our way. What works well one moment may not work well the next, because each situation is different. Consequently, to apply an old solution to a new problem is usually ineffective. Each response to each problem needs to be fresh and new if it is to be appropriate to the situation. Living in this way brings us into harmony with each moment. Writes Meishusama, "The 'instantaneous self' is a state of consciousness that reacts exactly at that instant when a person sees or hears something. It is not hampered or distorted by preconditions, prejudices, received ideas or other obstructions; it is just like the spontaneous reaction of a child." *(Henri Bergson. HT)*

Infants live in a state of pure experience, unmodified by recurrent thoughts or accumulated memory. There is a profound wisdom in their innocence and vulnerability. As Jesus Christ said, "Unless you change and become like little children, you will never enter the Kingdom of Heaven."

As adults, we too often regret the past and worry about the future, and as a result tend to miss the essence of life, which only occurs in the here and now. Nothing we do can change something that has already happened in the past. Guilt, remorse, and grudges over past events only poison the present. These feelings are unproductive and futile. Similarly, fretting about what might happen in the future is also unproductive and futile because, no matter how much we worry, we cannot control the movement of the stars. Anxiety is caused by the obsessive desire to avoid pain, but ironically, this anxiety is itself a form of pain. Instead of protecting us from harm, chronic worrying actually harms us in the present.

The extent of our bondage to both the past and the future is determined by the amount of spiritual clouding that dulls our perception. But the Light of awareness has its own innate power to dispel the darkness. Each time we choose open-eyed alertness over blind reaction, we move closer to the Light and closer to our own inner freedom.

Only when we let go of our personal concerns and agendas can we fully live in the present moment. The "instantaneous self" is capable of responding uniquely to each situation because it does not operate based on old preconditioning and prejudices. When living in a state of openness and alertness, we are able to immediately grasp vast complex details in the surrounding environment, and then coordinate and prioritize them into meaningful patterns. The appropriate response then emerges from within us naturally, before the mind has a chance to interfere and disrupt things. This natural unconditioned response reflects a deeper intelligence than does the conditioned self.

When practicing any form of martial arts, it is vital for practitioners to quiet their minds and to allow their bodies to act spontaneously, without any mental interference. Trying to plan and calculate the next move only slows down the body. This is because the body is much faster than the mind. It can respond almost instantly to a person or situation if the mind does not get in the way. Thinking about the future only distracts the martial arts practitioner from the immediate situation. In addition, as soon as he begins to visualize his next move, he immediately telegraphs his plans to his opponent, thereby allowing his opponent to outmaneuver him. Only when he is spontaneous can he surprise his opponent. So, to be truly effective in martial arts, he must not focus on any particular thought, situation, or person. His attention should not be preoccupied with anything in particular. It must be silent and alert, and keenly aware of all things simultaneously. He needs to move without trying, see without looking, and feel without touching. The instantaneous self always acts in this way, smoothly and effortlessly.

Similarly, the body can operate more effectively when playing a piano, typing, or driving a car if the mind does not try to control or interfere with the process. Our hands, fingers, and feet are capable of rapidly performing numerous movements simultaneously without the need for any mental oversight. In such activities, we need to let go and trust our bodies. Then our consciousness can guide our physical movements perfectly.

From the perspective of a spiritual vantage point, the whole or true nature of things is always apparent.[2] – KW

Each moment and each situation is different from that which occurred previously. Everything is constantly changing—nothing stays the same. None of us are immune to this constant change, because we, too, are always chang-

---

[2] Meishusama, "Seeing from a God-Centered Viewpoint," *Shumei Magazine*, vol. 165 (May, 1994).

ing. Old thoughts and opinions are based on the past, and therefore can only offer us old solutions to new problems. Only by living fully in the present can we clearly perceive what is needed in each situation, and then respond quickly and appropriately. Spirituality is not about having mystical visions; it is about effectively and harmoniously taking care of everyday affairs.

If the mind is made blank and receptive, however, the new ideas can be absorbed with little trouble. – Henri Bergson. HT

A quiet mind allows us to easily recognize "the point within the circle," the most significant aspect of a situation, event, or problem. With this knowledge, we can then adjust our behavior and make the most appropriate response. By relinquishing our conditioned mind, we allow Spirit to act through us, unimpeded. This requires the discipline of surrendering our thoughts to God and maintaining an alert consciousness. In our awareness of the present, the physical and the spiritual come together as one. The Sufi poet, Rumi, declares: "Past and future veil God from our sight; burn up both of them with fire."

Cultivating the "instantaneous self" strengthens our higher nature, freeing us from the excessive influence of our animal spirit, which is always consumed with chasing pleasure and avoiding pain. The animal spirit has no real freedom because it is dominated and controlled by desire, whereas our divine spirit is fundamentally free because it remains untouched by events and circumstances.

Waiting for future fulfillment is self-defeating because it conditions us into the habit of perpetual postponement. And when the anticipated future finally does arrive, we cannot really enjoy it because the mind is already one step ahead of itself, always chasing the next thing. Living obsessed with the future is inherently frustrating because life can only be enjoyed in the here and now, not later. As the Buddha said, "Life can only take place in the present moment. If we lose the present moment, we lose life."

Both past and future are merely imaginary thoughts in the mind. When the mind's endless chatter subsides, we find ourselves grounded in the present moment, and a deeper spiritual awareness is then revealed within this inner silence. To discover this awareness, we need to let go of thought and pay attention to what is currently happening around us. The more successful we are in this practice, the more this silent awareness is revealed to be our pre-existing condition. The only reason we did not notice it before is because it was too obvious, similarly to how fish are unaware of the water in which they constantly live and breathe. When we rest in silence, the mind is unable to superimpose rigid boundaries between self and other, good and bad, or Spirit and matter. Mental distinctions and judgments fall away, and what remains is undivided presence. Our awareness then expands to embrace everything, and in this openhearted expansion we find true inner peace.

Only a silent mind is capable of finding deep inner guidance from the real source of inspiration and creativity. Eckhart Tolle, in his book, *The Power of Now*, describes this source as that which is "none other than the power of your presence, your consciousness liberated from thought forms."

The Point in the Circle

As people tend to see things from the perspective of outward appearances, they usually don't grasp the true essence of things. People usually judge by the outer shell. This is very dangerous.[3] *– KW*

We currently live in a time of superficial fascination with outer appearances and external forms. This way of seeing things is shallow. By focusing only on outer appearances, we fail to see the deeper significance of things. Such blindness therefore prevents us from acting wisely. Meishusama compared this spiritually impoverished condition to an empty circle—a circle without a central point. People who walk through life in such a superficial manner lack a sense of inner direction or meaning. They lack inner depth.

The world we live in is of course spherical, but a sphere by itself is empty, nothing more than a lifeless ball. To put this in human terms, a person who is empty is not alive, but if a soul enters into the emptiness at the center of his being, he becomes alive and is capable of action. The soul is

---

[3] Ibid.

like the point in the circle. – *The Point in the Circle. HT*

Much of the art that is produced today is devoid of soul. This art has no depth of feeling or experience. Rather, what we see is cleverly constructed forms, which, although initially pleasing to the eye, soon become boring. Such art lacks the ability to touch people deeply, or to inwardly transform them, because it has no spiritual center. In other words, it has no point within its circle.

Similarly, the purpose of food is to nourish us and to give us pleasure. But unfortunately, much of the food that we buy at restaurants and supermarkets, although superficially pleasing to the taste buds and the eyes, weakens and poisons us through lack of nutrition and the presence of toxic chemicals.

Modern medicine typically treats only the outer symptoms of a disease or illness, not the cause. Usually it prescribes painkillers and other medications that do not address the underlying problems, but only cover them up. The symptoms may temporarily disappear, but eventually they almost always return, even worse than before. This approach to medicine offers no real cure, but at best, only short-term relief. A more intelligent approach to health would be to investigate the root cause of the illness and treat it appropriately. How else can a real cure be found? That root cause is the point within the circle.

This is a clear sign of the nature of the society that we are living in—a society that only looks at the surface of the material world and does not perceive the vital underlying reality of the spiritual world. – *A Sense of Justice. HT*

To find the point in the circle requires the ability to perceive the true purpose or intention of a thing. It is a matter of recognizing what is essential, and not being distracted by what is unessential. Armed with this knowledge, one can then take action that is both intelligent and practical.

The question is not what you look at, but what you see. – *Henry David Thoreau*

When listening to people, it can be useful to ask, "What are they trying to say? What is the point they are trying to make? What is their real motive? And how can I help them?" These questions prompt us to see beyond people's external appearances or behavior, and to see how they truly think and feel. Through this inquiry, we gain a glimpse of their very soul—the point within their human circle.

When working or playing, it is best to put your heart fully into the activity. Otherwise, not only will the quality of your work or activity suffer, but also the experience itself will become boring and meaningless. It will have no life in it —no point within its circle.

Spirit is invisible to the outer senses because it lies deep within all things. It is the central point within the circle, the secret power that animates all things. Spirit is also that which drives the evolution of all of creation. As Meishusama phrased it, "The basis of this movement, the still point at the ultimate center, is the Divine Will." *(The Nature and Behavior of Evil Spirits. HT)* A life without awareness of Spirit lacks depth and is devoid of real happiness. Visionary scientist and futurist, Willis Harman, wrote, "Most of us are living at the periphery of consciousness while intuition invites us into the center."

As your intelligence and spiritual perception deepens, you gain the capacity to discern the essence of things without having to rely solely on sensory observation or logical analysis. And with increased awareness, irrelevant details become less distracting or important. You become capable of instantaneously understanding the entire pattern of a problem, and of going straight to the heart of the matter. Additionally, your ability to perceive beauty increases, as does your sensitivity to the feelings of others. About people who have reached this level, Meishusama writes: "Their intelligence and spiritual perception deepen tremendously, and they have become able to grasp the reality of things and situations." *(The Strata in the Spiritual World. HT)*

All of Meishusama's teachings and efforts were directed towards the spiritual upliftment and redemption of the world. This redemption will be accomplished by ridding humanity of its spiritual clouds, and by revealing the vital truth hidden within human beings, as well as within art, medicine, politics, science, and the natural world. This truth is the central point within the circle of existence, and is what humanity was put here to discover.

As I have often said, the world is only ninety-nine percent complete. It is waiting for one final touch to bring it alive. If we put the point in the circle, this will be the final touch that transforms the whole world. To put it another way, the power of one small touch of good will destroy all the evil in the world. To bring truth into this world of vanity and emptiness will be like adding one point to a circle smeared and obscured with blackness, and through the power of this one small point, dispelling the blackness and revealing pure white. In other words, we will give the world its soul back. We will revive this civilization that has been like a corpse for so long, and bring to birth the New World. – *The Point in the Circle. HT*

9 KANNON'S WAY (Dynamic Balance)

I advocate a faith in Kannon that is not only different from popular beliefs about Kannon, but has many significant principles completely opposite to theirs. This faith requires no excessive dedication, and places the highest importance on gratitude as a way of responding to the daily blessings we receive. This type of Kannon faith never encourages extreme asceticism. It understands that self-imposed, severe practices often lead to great personal suffering. Because of its heavenly character, Kannon's Way is not related to practices that invite suffering. In this regard, Kannon's Way is a moderate form of spiritual practice.[1] – KW

Life exists because of balance. Living cells require a balanced ratio of sodium and potassium to function correctly. Every living organism depends upon a proper balance between anabolism and catabolism—creative and destructive metabolic forces—to maintain their health and vitality. Plants and animals require a moderate range of weather conditions—neither too hot nor too cold—to survive. Ecosystems, both large and small, depend on numerous mutual co-dependencies to sustain themselves. Introducing just one new species into it can disrupt or destroy the delicate balance of the entire system.

The universe is in constant motion and change. To survive and prosper, we need to constantly move and change as well. Similarly, water that sits still for too long becomes stagnant, while water that moves and flows stays fresh. The water in a river, by constantly bending and turning, eventually reaches the ocean. We also need to bend and turn like a river if we wish to achieve our goals and objectives.

Kannon's Way is a way of living that embodies flexibility, balance, and

---

[1] Meishusama, "Avoid Asceticism," *Shumei Magazine*, vol. 269 (May /June 2007).

moderation. People with such characteristics are patient, tolerant, and easygoing. They value peace and harmony, and also enjoy laughter and excitement. They are like a fresh spring breeze, both soothing and invigorating. They tend to go unnoticed by others because they do not push and pull at the world. They seek the path of least resistance. In many ways, they are the true peacemakers of the world.

The essence of Kannon's Way lies in maintaining order and propriety.

– Propriety. MK

Key Principles

Daijo and Shojo

As is commonly known, in Buddhism a distinction is made between daijo and shojo. These concepts, however, still leave room for an expansion of their meaning.[2] – KW

Meishusama borrowed two words from traditional Buddhist terminology, shojo[3] and daijo, and redefined them to encompass two fundamental principles that apply to all things. Shojo is the principle of inwardness and daijo the principle of outwardness. Shojo is fire, which burns upwards; daijo is water, which flows laterally. Shojo is the inclination towards spiritual growth; daijo is the inclination towards service to others. Shojo unites individuals with God; daijo unites people with people. The former is driven by the desire for truth and freedom; the latter is motivated by generosity and love. Freedom without love is joyless and uncaring; love without freedom is deluded and emotionally binding.

---

[2] Meishusama, "The Daijo Way," *Shumei Magazine*, vol. 267 (January /February 2007).

[3] The term 'shojo' traditionally refers to Hinayana Buddhism, the original form of this religion. Hinayana means 'small raft.' Daijo, on the other hand, refers to Mahayana Buddhism, which is the large raft. The implication is that Mahayana is the greater vehicle, one that can carry more people to salvation, while Hinayana is considered elitist and severe.

On a mundane level, shojo represents conservatism, and daijo represents liberalism. Shojo is analytical and detail oriented, whereas daijo is holistic and focuses on pattern recognition. Shojo looks at the trees, whereas daijo sees the forest.

A shifting balance always exists between shojo and daijo. It can be a stable balance, an uneven balance, or a destructive balance. Living things require a harmonious balance that supports their overall safety and comfort. In Taoism, this changing interplay between polar opposites is explained by the principles of *yin* and *yang*.

Kannon's Way is a manner of thinking and behaving that promotes peace and harmony in one's environment. The shojo way leads to wisdom and the daijo way leads to compassion. When we incorporate both of them in our lives, they lead to spiritual growth and personal happiness. The inner spirit of Kannon is often referred to as Izunome, which is the point at which the spirit of water intersects with the spirit of fire.

Two great civilizations had emerged, the vertically inclined Eastern, and the horizontal Western. To express it in different terms, Eastern civilization is characterized as shojo, and Western is daijo by nature. In contrast, Eastern thought is complacent and insular. And that of the West is observed by how it has spread laterally.[4] – *KW*

There are many aspects to shojo and daijo and they are not always reducible to clear cut definitions. Shojo and daijo can be understood as personal attributes or even forces of energy. To better understand this, here is a list of some shojo and daijo traits:

---

[4] Meishusama, "Creating the World of Light," *Shumei Magazine*, vol. 251 (May/June 2004).

Shojo	Daijo
Strict	Lenient
Vertical	Horizontal
Fire	Water
Sun	Moon
Masculine	Feminine
Principled	Tolerant
Yang	Yin
Inward	Outward
Salvation through effort	Salvation through grace
Exclusive	Inclusive
Analysis	Synthesis
Conservative	Liberal
Distinctions	Similarities
Elitist	Egalitarian
Individual	Universal
Narrow	Wide

Meishusama feels it is important to have a healthy balance between these two polar opposites. He writes, "Shojo draws distinctions between good and evil, and tends towards commandments and precepts; its virtues are easily understood by people. Daijo, on the other hand, draws no distinction between good and evil, and tends towards liberalism. Its virtues are correspondingly difficult to perceive." *(Daijo and Shojo. HT)* These two principles are not in opposition to each other but instead are complementary.

Conflict of Opposites

All strife is the result of the illusion of separateness caused by the mistaken perception that life is composed of fundamental dichotomies. This perception divides people into "us" and "them." The more separate we feel from something, the greater its potential threat to us. We are conditioned to view conflict as a struggle between two opposing sides where one must win and one must lose. We make distinctions between good and evil, and then project these judgments onto others. Our side is usually seen as morally superior, while the other side is judged as immoral and corrupt. We feel that we are right and they are wrong. Choosing sides only increases the distance between people, increasing conflict rather than lessening it. Emotionally-based judgments that generate anger and resentment are the true source of most conflicts. Then logic and facts come later, usually twisted to justify one's position at the expense of the other.

These conflicts are all based on the logic of conflicting opposites, an emotionally polarized position that does not recognize any middle ground. Such dichotomies leave little room for compromise or reconciliation and can actually reinforce the very thing we wish to defeat. This principle is summarized in the popular adage, "What you resist persists."

Co-Dependency of Opposites

The shojo faiths, which emphasize only the benefit of the individual, and the daijo faiths which sacrifice the individual, are both mistaken and not complete. In order to achieve complete relief, both the world and the individual must be equally helped.[5] *– KW*

Opposites are mutually dependent. A valley cannot exist without the mountains that surround it. A tree cannot grow its branches upwards without its roots growing downwards. A conversation cannot happen without talking

---

[5] ibid.

and listening. The bottom of a wheel cannot move upwards without the top of the wheel moving downwards. In order to walk, the right leg must cooperate with the left. Buyers need sellers and sellers need buyers. Harmony supports melody and melody supports harmony.

The principles of shojo and daijo are complementary, not mutually exclusive. Neither one is right or wrong, nor better or worse. Together, they create a natural balance and an integrated whole. Understanding this principle of the co-dependency of opposites helps to reduce feelings of hostility towards our opponents because we begin to recognize their necessity within the larger scheme of things.

The co-dependency of apparent opposites can also be illustrated by the following example: according to quantum physics, subatomic matter is composed of either particles or waves, depending on how we choose to observe it. To see an electron, one of the smallest elements of matter, we must shine light on it. The more light we shine on the electron, the faster it moves, until it becomes a wave, not a particle. Conversely, the less light we shine on the electron, the slower it goes, until it becomes a particle, not a wave. Yet, how can we see a particle without light? And how can we locate a wave if it is moving too fast? What, therefore, is the true nature of an electron? Are we altering its original condition by shining light on it? If so, then its true nature is that of a particle. But if we cannot see it, then how can we be sure? The ambiguous and interdependent nature of these two aspects of the electron is sometimes referred to as a "wavicle," a term that stresses their mutual identity. Neither can be separated from the other, yet neither is alike.

Outer space is only recognizable by the planets, stars, and galaxies that inhabit it and, through contrast, define it. And without empty space, we could not see these celestial bodies because everything would be too crowded. Furthermore, without the space in between these objects, they would all fuse together into one indistinguishable clump. Thus space defines form, and form defines space.

From the infinitely small to the infinitely large, everything depends on everything else, and we are all part of this vast interdependency. We support the universe and the universe supports us.

Dynamic Change

All of life is constantly changing, and this dynamic mutability sustains the overall existence of everything. There is a time to sow and time to reap. Winter flows into spring, which goes into summer, and then fall. These cycles of change can be seen in our personal lives, which begin at birth and progress through the phases of growth, maturity, decline, and death. After a period of time spent in the spiritual world, the soul returns to a new body and begins the process again.

Life is not opposed to death and winter is not opposed to summer. They evolve into each other through perpetually recurring cycles. Life works best when we accept and harmonize with these cycles of change and equilibrium, rather than resist them.

Change is often threatening to us. Quitting one's job, moving to a new city, ending an old relationship or starting a new one—any of these can turn out badly. So, rather than take risks, we often seek the security of predictable situations.

Nothing stays the same. When we look inside our minds, we discover that our thoughts are constantly changing from one moment to the next. Similarly, the breath within our lungs constantly changes with every inhalation and exhalation. Even our most dependable relationships change and evolve over time, whether we want them to or not.

Living things are always moving and evolving, whereas only dead things stay the same. Life differs from rocks, which sit quietly and immobile. Instead, life resembles a rushing stream, twisting and turning, splashing and swirling, always changing from one moment to the next.

To embrace change is to embrace life. The more we can approach life with wide-eyed wonder, the more every second becomes new and exciting. This is how we find inner peace and fulfillment.

Holism

The whole is greater than the sum of its parts. A car is more than just the engine, wheels, transmission, brakes, and seats. Only when all of these components are built and assembled correctly will it run properly. A person is more than just a collection of skin, bones, nerves, and internal organs. It is the harmonious synergy of all of these various elements that guarantees a healthy, functional body. An orange is more than just skin, rind, pulp, juice, and seeds; it is a unified pattern that integrates all of these individual parts.

From a vertical perspective, a person has many levels to his or her being, such as physical, emotional, mental, and spiritual. Together, these make up the totality of that person. From a horizontal perspective, a living thing cannot be separated from its environment. If we pull a plant out of the ground and leave it on the kitchen floor, it will probably die. Or if we deprive a person of oxygen or water, that person will not survive for long.

The totality of a creature includes not only its many levels of experience and behavior, but also its horizontal extension into its natural environment. Everything belongs within a larger context, both vertically and horizontally. The more clearly we can see the total picture, without leaving anything of significance out, the more effectively we can promote balance and harmony both within ourselves and throughout the world around us.

Attitudes and Behavior

Non-Dual Awareness

Pairs of opposites arise from the perspective of the perceiver. Hot and cold are judgments based on comfort level. Gain for one person is often a loss for another. Near and far are relative to one's location. Pain and pleasure go hand in hand. As soon as we take a stance or position, the pairs of opposites come into place.

Non-dualism is the recognition that pairs of opposites are co-dependent and inseparable from each other. Consider the following pairs: can "up" exist without "down" or "big" without "small?" What is "dark" without "light" or "inside" without "outside?" Could we recognize "good" without comparing it with "evil?" Does beauty have meaning without ugliness for contrast? Each half of these pairs is only recognizable through contrast with the other, and therefore depends on the other for its very existence. This is the logic of "both" rather than "either / or."

According to Meishusama, God transcends the dualities of good and evil. He writes: "There is no good or evil in God Himself. In God's eyes, good is indistinguishable from evil. This idea is also expressed in the familiar saying, 'Good and evil are as one.' From this perspective, we humans cannot grasp the true nature of good or of evil."[6] *(KW)*

Opposites are often rather arbitrary and, therefore, difficult to determine. An ant travels fast in comparison to a snail but slow in comparison to a grasshopper. At what point is fast considered slow, or slow considered fast? We may think we are standing still, yet the earth is traveling at enormous speeds through space in relation to the sun and the other stars. So, how can we determine motion or stasis? A yacht is huge in comparison to a speedboat, but is tiny in comparison to a luxury liner. So, how can we define big or small? What one person considers hot weather another considers cool. At what point does cold become hot or hot become cold? So much of our judgments are relative to one's position, preconceptions, and subjective values.

Do individuals make choices and are they personally responsible for their actions? Or do genetics and social conditioning determine their behavior? Is there fate or free will? Based on the principle of non-dualism, these can be two sides of the same coin. Neither fate nor freewill is the complete truth, but is only a one-sided point of view. Meishusama teaches that everything is determined by the conditions in the spiritual world, where there is no sharp distinction between fate and free will or between thought and action.

To cultivate Kannon's Way, it is important to look at the other side of any polarity or conflict that comes our way. This requires inner stillness and active listening. There are always two sides to everything; both are present in any given situation. When faced with an interpersonal conflict, take a moment and imagine how it must feel to be the other person or group. Temporarily suspend identification with one's own position to understand the other's point of view. Only after understanding and sympathizing with both sides of a conflict is it possible to act intelligently and promote the greatest harmony for all concerned. With practice, one begins to see the whole picture, undivided and complete, and eventually attains the union of shojo and daijo within one's own character.

---

[6] Meishusama, "Judge Not," *Shumei Magazine*, vol. 262 (March/April) 2006.

Open-Heartedness

It is vital that the big powers of the world of the future avoid trying to spread their colors to other countries, and instead try to make those other countries' colors brighter and more beautiful. This kind of policy will follow the will of God and bring about the New World. – God the Artist. HT

Conflict can easily arise when people are confronted with the extreme variety of opinions, values, and objectives that others may hold. How can we accommodate everyone if there are conflicts of interest? Whose needs are the most justified? Whose views are correct? People with closed hearts and closed minds see only differences everywhere and frequently find themselves struggling with others because of their limited perception. To create peace and harmony with others, we must look for what we have in common with them. As the Taoist sage, Lao Tzu, wrote, "People rivet their eyes and ears upon differences amongst them. The sage, with childlike innocence, sees one humanity in all."

We can make better, more informed decisions when we listen to all points of view. By doing this, a consensus can be reached which does not foster hostility or opposition from anyone. Each point of view is regarded as one of a variety of colors in a large palette of paints. A great painting can only be created if all the colors of the rainbow are available to the painter. Although the colors may vary, the actual substance of paint does not, and the primary purpose of this substance is to express beauty. The more colors we value, the greater the possibility of creating art that has richness and depth. Peace is created in the world when everybody feels acknowledged and appreciated. It is important to respect differences, while striving for unity.

Take the case of a thief. If you take the shojo approach to reforming him, you will attempt to persuade him by taking him to task. The daijo approach is first to get close to him, and then, when the opportunity arises, to point out that what he is doing is not really profitable and is causing him more anxiety than it is worth, and in this way, guide him from evil to the path of righteousness. – *Daijo and Shojo. HT*

When we open our hearts to others, we begin to see everyone as part of our extended family. We start to see the good in them despite their outward behavior. With this feeling in our hearts, we are less likely to fight with people because to do so would be like fighting with our own self. It would be like our right arm struggling with our left arm or our mouth yelling at our ears. Once we truly perceive the common humanity we share with others, we can no longer dismiss their needs or desires any more than we can dismiss our own. Instead, people are embraced as extensions of ourselves.

If someone behaves badly, pause for a moment before passing judgment. Be big hearted enough to give them the benefit of the doubt. First assume that they meant well, rather than intended to hurt or offend. By generously assuming this possibility, most conflicts will be prevented. Remember, each person feels that their behavior is justified, no matter how harmful it may appear to others. If someone throws a valuable possession of yours away, do not immediately get upset. Find out if maybe they were trying to be helpful, rather than inconsiderate or mean. What looks valuable to one person may appear like trash to another. And even when people do intend to hurt others, often this is because they too were hurt earlier, and so they want others to also know what that feels like. This knowledge does not excuse their behavior, but it can remind us of times when we may have also felt that way. An open heart begins with an open mind. By listening and communicating with kindness instead of reacting and accusing with anger, most conflicts can be avoided, and peace and harmony can be promoted. This is the heart of compassion.

Kindness is a language which the deaf can hear and the blind can see.
– Mark Twain

Not only is compassion for others essential, but so too is compassion towards oneself. Only then can it be considered to be universal compassion. The quest for spiritual growth can become a burdensome source of unhappiness if we hold extremely high ideals and then judge ourselves harshly for not attaining them. This self-judgment saps us of our inspiration and lifeforce and tends to hinder our progress. Therefore, it is important to be gentle with ourselves and to remember that no one is perfect. A balanced perspective concerning our imperfections and our better qualities is the best way to support our spiritual growth. Our lives become happier when we balance intense dedication to personal growth with easygoing humor and self-acceptance.

Although there is great benefit to be gained from self-improvement, it is equally important to accept ourselves just as we are. This is the basis of self-love. Only when we accept ourselves—both the good and the bad parts—can we accept others as they are. Unconditional love accepts people just as they are now, rather than holding idealized expectations about how they should be. This type of love inspires us to treat everyone with tolerance and kindness.

Expanded Perspective

One of the largest problems we humans face is that of people judging each other. It is completely wrong to be judgmental of others. When people judge others as either good or evil, God simultaneously judges them. Before passing judgment upon others, judge yourself and deeply reflect upon yourself. When the urge to judge others arises, stop and deeply reflect upon yourself. It is completely wrong to call others either good or evil.[7] – KW

The tendency to ignore the big picture contributes to short-sighted judgments and foolish decisions. Actions that appear evil may actually end up doing good and actions that appear good may end up doing evil. According to Sigmund Freud, "Neurosis is the inability to tolerate ambiguity." Healthy, mature people realize that life is made up of shades of gray, rather than only black and white. In truth, there is always a degree of uncertainty in most everything.

We may generously give money to a homeless man, only to later discover that he used the money to get drunk and beat his wife. Or we may chop down a forest to build homes for our community and then watch in horror when a rainstorm causes a mudslide on the now barren land that washes everything out to sea. What we thought were good actions may prove otherwise if they end up hurting others. From the victim's standpoint, our "good actions" would be considered bad rather than good. How we interpret things depends on our

---

[7] ibid.

perspective.

From the ashes of a forest fire comes fertile soil, followed by new growth. To the burnt trees, the fire was bad, but to the regenerated forest, it was good. Similarly, one person's gain is often another person's loss. From loss comes gain, and from gain comes loss.

With the approach of winter, plants and trees begin to die. Yet, without the harsh snowfalls of winter, the rivers would dry up in summer, causing agriculture to fail and people to starve. Everything goes in cycles: sometimes creating abundance, and sometimes creating scarcity.

Oftentimes, good people are driven to do bad things out of desperation. They may steal to eat, or lie and cheat to survive. And sometimes people feel compelled to hurt others because they themselves have been hurt in the past. There is an old French proverb, "To know all is to forgive all." By suspending judgment, we give ourselves enough time to collect all the facts. It should be no surprise to discover that there are at least two opposing points of view in any conflict. Instead of choosing sides, we need to gain insight into the feelings and motives of others. The best way to do this is by putting ourselves in their shoes and trying to see things from their perspective rather than expecting them to behave according to our own values and standards. By doing this we can become true peacemakers rather than promoters of conflict.

Helping others without distinguishing between good and evil is the true meaning of Kannon's unending compassion. – Infinite Compassion. MK

Detachment

It is obvious that the characters of most people on this earth contain both a sense of egotism and a feeling of attachment to the world. These two are very closely related. When people examine problems which appear very complicated and fail to find easy solutions to them, almost always it is because of this combination of egotism and worldly attachment. – Egotism and Worldly Attachment. HT

Everything is transitory, including our family, friends, homes, cars, money, and careers. Each of us will eventually grow old and die, and all of our hopes and dreams will be left behind. Nothing stays the same, and even long-term relationships change over time. Our possessions wear out, our bodies decline in health, and our memories fade. To cling to these things causes needless suffering because no amount of clinging will slow down the passage of time.

To find happiness, we need to cultivate a certain measure of detachment. Detachment is an acceptance of all that arises in life, both pleasant and unpleasant. The more we cultivate detachment the less our happiness is held hostage to the outcomes of life's events. Detachment is different than suppression, which blocks sensitivity and awareness. When we suppress, we become dead. For instance, some people take psychiatric drugs to manage painful feelings such as guilt, anxiety, and depression. These drugs suppress symptoms but do not eliminate the problem. People who are medicated by psychiatric drugs tend to be cut off from their feelings. Their emotional responses are stifled and their sensitivity is reduced. Not only do they feel less pain, but they also feel less joy.

Detachment is not the inability to feel. Detachment actually increases one's sensitivity to the richness of life. It makes one more sensitive to the feelings of others, to art, beauty, and the broader scope of life's enjoyments. Detachment frees one from compulsively dwelling on the future or the past. It is not that those who are detached do not experience life's unpleasant realities or enjoy its pleasures, but they do so without avoiding the one, or grasping at the other.

People who are detached still care about peace, harmony, and beauty, and want everyone to be happy, but when trouble inevitably does arise, they have a more balanced reaction. They are able to do this because attachment has been replaced by a peaceful trust in the Higher Power to orchestrate everything perfectly.

This trust allows us to maintain an inner distance from both our own problems as well as the problems of others. The more we cultivate detachment from the dualities of pleasure and pain, gain and loss, and praise and blame, the more we will be able to see life's laughter, joys, sorrows, and tears through the eyes of God. We become free from egoic involvement with the experience of our lives. We will find that the world does not revolve around us any more than the universe revolves around the sun.

The whole world now becomes our concern, beyond the narrow boundaries of our personal lives. In a sense, the world becomes our extended body, with each part essential to the proper functioning of the whole. From this larger perspective, the ups and downs of our individual lives take on less importance. Our minds become clear and our hearts peaceful. The happiness of others becomes the source of our own happiness. The smile of another becomes our own.

Since I realized this, I have made the utmost efforts to rid myself of self-will and attachment, and as a result have found ease for the sufferings of heart and mind, and have enjoyed constant success in the affairs of the world.

– Egotism and Worldly Attachment. HT

Flexibility

The true religion is at times vertical, at times lateral; it adapts itself to the time, place and situation, diversifying through myriad forms and metamorphoses to accomplish its work in the world. – Daijo and Shojo. HT

Adapting to changing circumstances requires flexibility of character. Sometimes we need to change not only what we do, but also what we think, as new information reveals itself to us. This requires openness and humility on our part. If we become attached to our previous position because of pride or stubbornness, we cannot continue to learn and grow. Inevitably, we will begin to make mistakes because of our ignorance. In the *Tao Te Ching*, Lao Tzu says, "A blade of grass bends in the wind and survives, but an oak tree resists and breaks." Different people may require different treatment, and our response to each person must be unique. Sometimes we must be lenient and sometimes strict, sometimes we should speak and sometimes remain silent. In his dealings with people, Meishusama would vary his teaching depending on the person or the situation. This allowed him to be effective wherever he went.

Sometimes, when raising children, we need to be strict, and at other times lenient. If people are being selfish and unkind towards others, we may need to confront them, while at other times it may be better to respond with love and understanding. There are times when we need to hold people accountable for their actions and other times when it is important to investigate the circumstances and conditions influencing them. Sometimes, we can walk forcefully with a strong purpose and at other times we can relax and enjoy the scenery. Sometimes we act shojo and at other times daijo. Each moment and circumstance is different and requires a unique response. This dynamic range of possible responses is one of the features of Kannon's Way. It is the practical principle of adaptability and moderation.

We also need to learn to be flexible in our timing. Not pushing headlong into things before circumstances are favorable, nor hesitating for so long that we are too late, is the key to success. We need to wait for the right moment. Meishusama writes, "When I plan to do something new, I never rush to make a final decision. Instead, I take enough time to see the thing objectively and from various angles, and repeatedly deliberate upon it to ensure that it is not only right, but also beneficial in the long run for the well-being of society. Having completed these mental processes, I then wait for the right opportunity. However, most people do not have the patience to wait for the best time. They start a project before it is obviously feasible. So they get stuck in the gap between their blueprint and their miscalculations, then hurry to recover, only to make the situation worse. Finally, they end in failure. To repeat, what is essential here is to be patient until the right time comes." [8] *(KW)*

Meishusama illustrates this flexible approach to life with the analogy of steering a car while driving on a curved road. To manage the turns, we need to constantly adjust the steering wheel from left to right and right to left, always moving forward. Meishusama writes, "First, you should adjust your way of speaking to your listener. Speak suitably to an old man, speak gently to a lady, speak philosophically to an intellectual, and talk common sense to an ordinary man. If you do so, your listener will become interested and listen with pleasure and appreciation." *(Henri Bergson. HT)*

Persons embodying a true balance of shojo and daijo will be fluid in their behavior, sometimes demonstrating masculine qualities and at other times more feminine qualities. Spirit is beyond gender and is quite capable of acting in whatever manner is appropriate at the time.

Moderation

In this world, everything is easy if one observes moderation.

– Spiritual Cultivation. MK

---

[8] Meishusama, "Wait for the Right Moment," *Shumei Magazine*, vol. 268 (March / April 2007).

People who are unbalanced often swing from one extreme to the other, reacting with panic, rage, or despair at the drop of a hat. Or, they may become overly elated, throwing caution to the wind and acting with reckless abandon. Many bounce back and forth from elation to depression, from starvation diets to gluttony, or from overblown idealism to deflated cynicism. The middle ground seems to always elude them. Although intensity can add richness and depth to our experiences, when taken to extremes, it causes discomfort or pain and can even be destructive.

It is best to find a middle path. Be neither too generous nor too cheap, neither too open-minded nor too opinionated, neither too aggressive nor too passive, and neither too strict nor too permissive. When cooking a delicious meal, the taste should be neither too sweet nor too bitter. When driving, the speed should be neither too fast nor too slow. It is best to wear lightweight clothing during hot weather and heavy clothing during cold weather. And during conversations with others, it is best to balance one's talking with one's listening in a natural flow of give and take.

A person practicing Kannon's Way seeks balance and moderation at all times and will not overreact with too much emotion and excitement; nor will they suppress emotion or excitement. Just as the ability to walk down the street depends on the balance and rhythm between the right and left legs, so too does this person seek balance between action and inaction, depending on circumstances. They do not become proud with success or shamed by failure. When complimented, they remember their faults and, when criticized, remember their virtues. This inner practice of remembering the opposite side of things keeps them balanced and undisturbed despite the ups and downs of life.

Although we may find ourselves in the midst of conflict, it is not always necessary for us to choose sides. If we always cling to our shojo principles, we may become intolerant and aggressive. If we indiscriminately adopt too much daijo, we can become overly permissive and passive. Recognizing that most things come in pairs, and are mutually dependent on each other, provides us with the wisdom needed to resolve most conflicts.

The person who is not biased towards either side of a conflict listens to both sides with sympathy and objectivity. These people win the trust and confidence of all concerned and are truly the peacemakers in the world.

Being able to see all points of view allows us to compromise and to find the most effective solution. This is another sign of moderation. An intelligent person will take into account all the various factors in a situation before taking action. When we go to extremes we usually ignore some important facts or concerns. We risk being thrown off balance by our blindness, making it difficult to respond effectively to new developments. This tendency to ignore the obvious is caused by attachment to personal preferences. If we find ourselves acting in extremes, we should ask ourselves, "What am I missing that is important?"

To practice Kannon's Way, one never does things partially, nor does one go to extremes of action.[9]– KW

Common Sense

The first thing we must deal with as regards this problem is to ensure that faith and the expression of faith do not become separated from the dictates of common sense. – Common Sense. HT

Common sense depends on the ability to honestly look at things just as they are without the blinders of personal biases or preconceptions, which usually lead to poor decisions because they block one's ability to be well informed. Just as a car driver needs a windshield free of dirt and grime to see the road clearly, so too does one need an open mind and an untroubled heart to see reality clearly. Only then can one make sound judgments and then act intelligently.

Never be swayed by fixed ideas or preconceptions. – True Faith. HT

Common sense is a very practical attitude that values simplicity and useful results. It is the ability to recognize obvious solutions even when others fail to notice them. A person with common sense distrusts dogmatism and fanaticism because these narrow mindsets indicate an attachment to

---

[9] Meishusama, "Kannon's Way," *Shumei Magazine*, vol.264 (July/August 2006).

abstractions rather than to concrete evidence. Instead, this person trusts his or her senses and prefers simple, down-to-earth solutions to most problems.

There is a popular story that is not factually true, but nonetheless still serves to illustrate the use of common sense. Back in the early days of space exploration, neither the Russian nor the American astronauts were able to record scientific data on paper because their ball point pens failed to operate in zero gravity. The American solution was to spend millions of dollars to invent a special pen that could function in weightless space. The Russians, however, simply switched to using a wooden pencil. The American's made use of science and technology. Their solution was brilliant, but wasteful. The Russians, however, made use of common sense. Their solution was simple, easy, and inexpensive.

Common sense can be summarized as the ability to notice the obvious rather than be distracted by what's irrelevant or inconsequential. This is then followed by practical action.

Our conduct also needs to be consistent with Kannon's Way. When we act, it is very important to locate our heart within the binding knot that connects vertical with horizontal. In a way, this connecting point is common sense, and this is the underlying reason that we set a high value on common sense.

However, in our society, people who abide by common sense are seen as mediocre, and those who deviate from it tend to be seen as special. We should keep this in mind. For it is a fact that the reputations of those who are monomaniacal are ephemeral, and those people never accomplish anything truly great. As history clearly shows, eventually, by their very nature they invite their own failure.[10] – KW

Humor

An environment where you can enjoy things with cheerful laughter, and where you can make others laugh in the same way, will naturally lead to a heavenly

---

[10] Meishusama, "Vertical and Horizontal," *Shumei Magazine*, vol. 269 (May/June).

state. In this way, laughter contributes to the resolution of disputes and to the creation of a peace-loving atmosphere. And to establish peace on earth, it is necessary to eradicate conflicts[11]. – KW

Understanding that life is often ironic and full of unexpected contradictions can encourage a humorous attitude towards our experiences and bring joy to our hearts. Humor is based on incongruity and surprise. It arises from the sudden perception of two things that do not really belong together, such as a team of military generals caught wearing a ballerina dresses, or flames coming out of a shower head instead of water. Oftentimes there is a dark or negative component to humor, such as when a dignified person slips on a banana peel and falls on the floor, or when someone's pants fall down while giving a speech. The greater the discrepancy between what is expected and what actually happens, the funnier the result. A sense of humor depends upon one's ability to stand back and experience circumstances from an impersonal perspective, as if watching a bad movie in which everyone is acting out of character. Laughter arises spontaneously when we look at things from this perspective.

Man plans and God laughs. – Hebrew Proverb

Life is ironic. Despite our best efforts, things rarely turn out the way we expect. Life is too full of surprises for that to happen. One may sometimes wonder if there is some evil tormenter hiding somewhere up in the sky who actually enjoys giving us garlic flavored ice cream, mismatched pairs of socks, and leaky umbrellas. Yet, one must ask why it is that we get so angry when annoying things like this happen to us, but find it so funny when similar things happen to others? Maybe it is because we do not take other people's misfortunes personally, as we do our own problems. In other words, as American social and political humorist, Will Rogers, said, "Everything is funny as long as it is happening to somebody else."

If we could give up our incessant demands for life to turn out the way we want, then maybe we could find a bit of humor in all the imperfection that

---

[11]Meishusama, "Roundness," *Shumei Magazine*, vol. 270 (July/August).

exists around us. The difference between drama and comedy is in the level of personal involvement in the story. The less involvement, the lighter the story tends to be. Often, with the distance of time, we are able to laugh at a painful incident that earlier we took very seriously. Jokes directed towards one's self as the object of humor are usually enjoyed by others. Jokes directed towards specific events or situations are only sometimes appreciated. Jokes directed at another person are usually viewed as an insult by that person.

We can use laughter to neutralize the frustration and hurt that life sometimes brings us. It can be beneficial to take a moment and imagine that your life is a comedy and that you're eating popcorn while watching it. See how silly you look with that frown on your face and your fists pounding angrily on the table. Then ask yourself, "What's so terrible about a flat tire, a burnt pot of rice, or bad haircut?"

A sense of humor is the reward we receive for relinquishing our heavy chains of expectation and attachment. Humor can bring pleasure and enjoyment to the most trivial of things and, most importantly, frees us from morbid self-preoccupation.

Meishusama himself was renowned for his wild sense of humor. A friend who came to visit him one evening ended up leaving with a stomachache because of all the non-stop laughter he experienced there. Meishusama's jokes ranged from the ironic to the absurd and from satire to slapstick. He commented that most religions were sadly lacking a sense of humor, but that, in his opinion, heaven was full of laughter. Even during the depths of war and government oppression he was still able to find things to laugh about.

Laughing at ourselves when things go wrong may not change the circumstances much, but at least we will not suffer internally anymore. That's one of the most significant factors about humor. Humor actually transforms darkness into light. Humor does this by acknowledging darkness rather than by ignoring, denying or repressing it. Some of the best jokes come from fear, pain, or anger. Bad circumstances offer some of the best opportunities for making good jokes because humor thrives on darkness. Humor accepts negativity while simultaneously liberating us from the suffering that usually accompanies it. Humor shows us that we can be happy whether it rains or shines, whether we are rich or poor, or whether we are healthy or sick.

Malicious humor, on the other hand, derives from narrow-mindedness and a closed heart. People use sarcastic humor to ridicule and condemn others while failing to recognize their own personal shortcomings. If these malicious people were to sufficiently expand their consciousness they would begin to see themselves in others rather than judge them. Then their laughter would be a sign of friendship, not animosity. It would express sympathy for others. This type of humor has a healing effect on everyone.

Humor delights in the incongruities of daily life. A funny joke has the miraculous power to transform a potential catastrophe into a liberating experience. Humor widens our perspective so that we see things in a larger context. It helps us accept our day-to-day existence with a light heart and an even mind and promotes an easygoing tolerance of other people, helping us bridge our mutual differences. Laughter pulls us out of our head and into our body. It leaves our opinions, judgments, and hidden agendas behind and returns us to our senses, allowing us to simply enjoy the here and now. When we laugh from the bottom of our hearts, we become like little children, full of innocence, wonder, and delight.

Laughter is flowers in heaven. – KW

A Life Filled with Joy

The more liberated from spiritual clouds a soul becomes, the more it is capable of dancing to its own internal rhythms rather than blindly conforming to the outer dictates of society. Such souls trust their own internal wisdom rather than the beliefs and opinions handed down to them by society. They are free of self-conscious doubt and thus behave in an easy and natural way. They intelligently adapt to circumstances rather than unconsciously react to them. There is often a lighthearted playfulness in their behavior. Such souls are able to express the freedom and joy of Spirit itself while simultaneously maintaining an inner balance and harmony with all people and all things.

I tend to work playfully. So, engaged in a task, there is never any struggle. For me, my work is like a luxurious hobby. Among the many images of Kannon is the *Yugyo*[12] Kannon, and the spirit of this Kannon suits me best. When I carry out tasks in this spirit, I can do a much better job. On the other hand, when I feel I am struggling with a heavy burden, and am all tired out doing things I am reluctant to do, then things do not go as I wish.

This light-hearted approach is the opposite of what people used to believe was best, and I see that most of my students also share this outdated view. When they work too passively or too strenuously, their efforts inevitably turn out badly. For example, when you are asked to visit someone who is sick to give them Jyorei, if you go with the spirit of joy, the person will begin to recover, and that good result will encourage you to continue helping him or her. In this way, both you and the person will enjoy the results. So, the more joy you find in what you do, the better the result will be.[13]– KW

With each new step along the path of spiritual growth, our awareness expands and we gain new knowledge and insight about ourselves and others. At each step, it is important to accept and embrace this new knowledge and insight, as this will help us to integrate it. Then, we are ready to proceed to the next level of spiritual development. In this way, we build our own spiritual ladder, step-by-step, towards the final destination of eternal salvation and Oneness with God. The end of the journey is not a final step on the ladder, but an embracing of the entire ladder itself. And it is not we, as individuals, who embrace the ladder, but the universe itself that embraces the ladder through us. This is an example of Kannon's unconditional love for all things.

If we truly understand the principles of Kannon's Way and learn how to live according to them, spiritual clouds will not accumulate at all. At the same time, one will become a person who constantly gains toku energy. Not only will one be free from sickness and misfortune, but also be blessed with health, longevity, and prosperity, not only for oneself but also for one's family and friends. Finally, one will be able to live a life filled with joy.[14] – KW

---

[12] Yugyo means to act or behave with a light heart and enjoyment, free from attachments to results and suffering.

[13] Meishusama, "Work with Joy, Not Pain," *Shumei Magazine*, vol. 268 (March /April 2007).

[14] Meishusama, "The true cause of sickness is found in the soul," *Shumei Magazine*, vol. 264 (July /August 2006).

10 JYOREI

If we can only find a way of curing sickness then it is inevitable that cures for poverty and strife will follow. And if these are achieved, then humanity will have found the basic conditions for happiness. – Jyorei and Happiness. HT

Divine Light

The ultimate source of all peace, joy, and inner fulfillment is God, the absolute highest reality. In its purest expression, God's blessings manifest as divine Light, which emerges out of the world of the ultimate mystery. Although this ultimate mystery cannot be known objectively, it can be known subjectively, in the center of our being, as our own divine spirit. At the level of pure Spirit we all share in the Supreme Being's unbounded love and serenity.

God's Light (Miroku Omikami) extends throughout the cosmos, infusing all things with its sublime radiance. Without this Light, nothing could exist. The Light is what gives expression to the clouds in the sky, the fish in the sea, and the thoughts within our minds. This Light is the mysterious energy that animates our heart, our lungs, and our breath. Through the healing practice of Jyorei, this mysterious energy is concentrated, focused, and directed toward others for the purposes of individual health, happiness, and spiritual transformation.

Most of us, because of the numerous impurities that have accumulated in our souls over the course of many lifetimes, are unaware of our inner relationship with God. To find true inner peace, it is important to realize that

God's presence is not located far away, but actually resides deep within our own hearts. We each have a spiritual cord that directly connects us to the Creator and allows us to constantly receive His divine grace, whether we feel it or not.

Another expression of God's grace is Jyorei, which is the Light of Spirit made tangible. This Light is an expression of God's unconditional love. Through receiving the blessings of Jyorei, our spiritual clouds—the root cause of all suffering—are dispelled. Jyorei purifies our body, mind, and spirit, thereby assisting our soul in its long journey toward subjective Oneness with Eternity.

The Creator gave this divine power to Meishusama to heal and awaken as many people as possible. They, in turn, were often encouraged to share it with other people so that the blessings could spread still further. Jyorei is now being shared with people in many countries around the world, including the six continents of Asia, Africa, North and South America, Australia, and Europe. Thus, as one candle lights another, the world grows increasingly brighter, until every corner is set ablaze in radiant Light.

The appearance of Jyorei in the world today coincides with the emergence of a greater intensity of spiritual energy entering our dimension and our planet at this time. We are approaching a new age in which the element Meishusama calls the spirit of fire is growing stronger, promoting increased miracles of healing and spiritual awakening. "The advent of Jyorei in the material world is, of course, a harbinger of the ideal world to come, for Jyorei is at the very heart of the Age of Day," writes Meishusama. (*The Strata in the Spiritual World. HT*)

Jyorei and Happiness

The fundamental cause of unhappiness is spiritual clouding. And there is a sure means of clearing this clouding of the spirit; there is Jyorei.

– Jyorei and Happiness. HT

In ancient times, before the creation of books and organized belief systems, people did not need to be convinced of the existence of a higher power that exerted a profound influence in their lives. They intuitively knew this. For many, life revolved around Spirit, and the deeper their connection with it, the greater was their inner peace and harmony. But in our modern world of cell phones, fast cars, cable television, iPods, and the internet, this connection with the sacred dimension seems to have become lost. Thus, it is no wonder that so many people nowadays find their lives rather empty and meaningless. They suffer from a poverty of the soul that cannot be healed by endless entertainment or by the compulsive accumulation of more and more things.

Increasingly, people are coming to realize that the answer to their deepest problems comes not from large bank accounts, long vacations, or small bottles of pills. Many are now turning to various forms of spiritual healing, meditation, or prayer for help with their physical and emotional problems. Not only do these practices offer relief, but they also provide them with direct experiences of something beyond the ordinary, mundane world. Amongst these various practices, Jyorei is drawing special attention from people because it incorporates healing, mediation, and prayer combined into one simple, but powerful process.

Jyorei is a simple, yet profound healing technique in which spiritual Light is directed toward people for their overall health and happiness. Through the experience of Jyorei, we enter into communion with the silent presence of God, and then allow this silent presence to move through us. *Jyorei, in Japanese, means "purification of the spirit."* The energy of Jyorei dispels the spiritual impurities within people's souls and also eliminates the physical toxins that have accumulated in their physical bodies. This does not imply that people's souls or spirits are polluted, but only that they are covered up, just as the sun gets covered by clouds in the sky. These spiritual clouds are the true cause of human suffering. Removing these clouds does not cause the sun to shine brighter; it merely reveals that which was hidden. What then begins to emerge from behind the clouds is our divine spirit, which is innately peaceful and happy, just as the sun is innately warm and bright.

Methods that need to use the functions of the five senses to reach and purify the soul can never produce very profound effects, for they use the corporeal flesh in order to touch the incorporeal and invisible spirit. Jyorei, as practiced by us, works directly on the spirit, purifying it and filling it with Holy Light. The results are incomparably superior to those of any physical methods. To think of it in terms of conventional medical treatment, Jyorei can heal diseases that have previously been considered as incurable. – *Sermons and Precepts. HT*

There is more to healing than repairing broken bones. Healing is about mending broken hearts and calming agitated minds. Most importantly, it is about renewing the spirit. Although Jyorei is most often introduced to people as a form of physical or emotional healing, *its primary purpose is for spiritual growth. Through spiritual growth*, we eventually arrive at a heart full of love, joy, and serenity.

Strife, poverty, disease, and other forms of suffering arise from excessive clouding within the spiritual world. Each of us creates spiritual clouds by our incorrect attitudes, beliefs, and actions. These clouds are the true cause of our current problems.

All suffering originates from either reactionary purification or proactive purification. Both can be unpleasant, but each has different causes and results. Reactionary purification is caused by life-denying experiences, such as exposure to environmental toxins or our own negative thoughts, emotions, and behavior, whereas proactive purification is caused by life-affirming experiences such as Jyorei, appreciating beauty, eating healthy food, or performing good deeds. These life-affirming experiences, in themselves, are usually quite enjoyable, and usually result in pleasant feelings afterwards, although occasionally an unpleasant effect may occur if something toxic suddenly gets released from within a person's physical or spiritual body. Although both forms of purification discharge accumulated toxins and negativity, proactive purification is more positive because it prevents the generation of new spiritual clouds. Both eliminate the bad, but the proactive purification also promotes the good.

Reactionary purification does not tend to improve things long-term because it only discharges surface-level toxins, not deep-seated ones. It also does not prevent new toxicity from occurring. Reactionary purification can sometimes be quite unpleasant. For instance, a flu infection will often discharge some toxins from the body through phlegm, runny nose, diarrhea, sweating, or vomiting, but it does not usually produce significant improvement to one's overall health. At best, reactionary purification will release just enough toxins from the body so that one does not become overwhelmed by them, but not much more.

On the other hand, proactive purification, such as that caused by Jyorei, is usually mild. It tends to discharge greater amounts of toxins from the body than does reactionary purification, and also lessens the tendency to generate future toxicity. Oftentimes proactive purification is either unnoticed or can actually be quite pleasant, producing feelings of comfort, serenity, and well-being. Over time, not only does proactive purification improve physical and emotional health, but it also fosters spiritual growth.

In this modern world it is almost impossible for us to avoid all forms of toxins and to avoid generating new spiritual clouds. Therefore, it is advisable to receive Jyorei on a daily basis. The proactive purification caused by Jyorei is similar to taking a daily shower to wash away sweat and grime or to washing one's clothes frequently. Both Jyorei and showering make one look and feel better. If one neglects to do one's laundry regularly, one's shirts and pants may become so dirty that some of the stains will not come out no matter how hard one scrubs. Similarly, if one neglects to generate proactive purification regularly, one may accumulate so much mental and physical toxicity that they become embedded in one's mind and body. The more one experiences proactive purification, the freer of toxicity one becomes, and therefore the less suffering one is likely to experience in the future.

One does not need to endure the suffering of reactionary purification if one simply avoids exposure to physical and mental toxins and refrains from engaging in negative actions. The suffering occasionally caused by proactive purification, on the other hand, is but a minor discomfort when compared with the increased health and happiness it can produce in the long run. Therefore, a wise person will always choose proactive purification over reactive purification.

The key to understanding Meishusama's teachings is the distinction between these two types of purification. *It is better to purify ourselves of spiritual clouds in a painless or pleasant way rather than through unnecessary suffering.* The best way to promote proactive purification is through trying to help as many people as possible, and the practice of Jyorei is especially well suited for this purpose. Making others happy can also be a great source of personal satisfaction and fulfillment.

Often, healing people's physical illness is the first step towards promoting happiness in them. The next step is the healing of their mental and emotional problems. At other times the reverse is true, and the person's inner nature will be the first to show signs of healing. The body and mind are interconnected, and each affects the other. Oftentimes, problems originating in the mind or from past lives must be healed before conditions in the physical body can be addressed. Although the true source of these problems lies in the spiritual world, most people are looking for immediate, tangible relief from their pain rather than abstract explanations. Nevertheless, it is important to understand that the real healing is actually occurring on a spiritual level.

Jyorei strengthens the divine spirit's influence over us while simultaneously purifying the corrupting influences of the animal spirit, thereby lessening the latter's excessive control over us. The animal spirit is basically narcissistic and selfish by nature, subject to greed, lust, and aggressiveness. As the spiritual body becomes cleansed, the animal spirit resumes its rightful place as the servant of the physical body, not its master.

Spiritual purification opens us up to the beneficial guidance of the guardian spirit, bringing us increased inspiration and good fortune. It promotes inner harmony between the divine spirit and the animal spirit, and supports the soul's progress in its journey towards greater spiritual awareness and happiness.

Not to commit evils, but to do all that is good, and to purify one's heart—this is the teaching of all the Buddhas. – Gautama Buddha, The Dhammapada

Spiritual growth occurs through the purification of thought, feeling, and intention. Through the power of Jyorei, the desires that we hold within us become less negative and compulsive. As selfishness and immaturity are transformed into greater concern for the welfare of others, we begin to relate to others in a more positive manner and begin to see the world as a friendlier place. This attitude is the opposite of alienation and separation, which causes anguish to the soul. Spiritual growth expands our awareness into greater and greater levels of perceived unity. We begin to feel a kinship with everyone and everything, including the natural world around us. We see that there is no need to exclude others from this kinship because of personal judgments or animosity.

Meishusama says, "If you do not make others happy, you can never be happy yourself." (*About Myself. HT*) This simple motto does not advocate trying to subserviently please other people all the time, but rather to open our hearts to others, and to feel their pain as our pain, and to feel their happiness as our happiness. If we have an open heart, then how can we be happy when those around us are miserable? This sensitivity generates spontaneous feelings of empathy for others as well as the altruistic motivation to help them.

As the Light within us increases, we also begin to recognize its presence in others. This perception is the basis of love. Love helps us see beyond our various outer differences by revealing to us our common humanity. Love unites us inwardly. It makes us care about each other.

Love is the true motivation for practicing Jyorei. There is never a charge for Jyorei other than donations based on gratitude. These donations, if given, go to support Shumei's altruistic activities, not the Jyorei giver, who offers it freely. The only personal gain the giver of Jyorei receives is the satisfaction derived from helping others.

The act of helping others purifies our soul and raises our spiritual condition to a higher level. When we serve the greater good, we receive Toku Energy, which benefits us in the spiritual world. Toku Energy is the Light that comes back to us because of our good deeds. Of all the possible ways we can help others, to help them spiritually is the best because its effects are the most enduring. Everything else, such as houses, cars, and people, comes and goes. When we die, only our spiritual wealth can be taken with us. Jyorei is one of the simplest, yet most profound, ways to help people spiritually, as well as to generate spiritual wealth.

> I have not only succeeded in focusing these radiations on to one part of the body and dispelling the clouds of the spiritual body, but I have also perfected a technique to increase the power of everybody's radiations.
>
> – *Natural Power. HT*

Jyorei is a unique healing method in that it is very easy to learn and practice. The primary requirement for practicing Jyorei is an altruistic concern for helping others. It does not require any special breathing techniques, concentration, visualization, mantras, or difficult bodily movements. Jyorei also does not require faith, nor does it depend on the innate power of the person giving Jyorei. Its blessings are not earned; they are given. It could be said that Jyorei is a gift from God and Meishusama to humanity.

The Practice of Jyorei

The method of Jyorei given by our organization bathes the inner spirit in divine Light instantaneously and awakens the spirit to True Life at a stroke. As this transforms people in a way that we can describe as 'effortless,' it obviously relegates sermons and precepts to a position of secondary importance.

– The End of Suffering. HT

A Jyorei session is usually conducted with two people: one giving, and the other receiving. If both are qualified to give Jyorei, then afterwards they can trade places so that the former giver can then be the receiver and vice versa. When transmitting this energy, we simply raise our arm to project healing Light out of our hand. When our arm gets a little tired, it is time to switch hands. The arm and hand should not feel stiff or strained, but rather, relaxed and loose. No effort is required. Healing is about allowing the energy to move through us, rather than feeling that we are doing something special to make this happen. The Light of Jyorei is not our personal possession; we are merely voluntary conduits for its expression. This energy comes from God (or Spirit), with assistance from Meishusama, and it is our privilege to be allowed to share it with others and to work for the betterment of humanity.

As human beings, there are generally two ways that we can give to others: either through kind words expressed by our mouths or through generous actions performed by our bodies. Jyorei, however, comes from neither of these two sources, but originates from a third source: the eternal Spirit that transcends all things. Jyorei is one of the very few ways that the average person can give to someone on a spiritual level without relying on words or physical actions to do so.

As mentioned earlier, Jyorei is given using the arms and hands only. Neither talking nor verbal prayer are needed to give Jyorei, as that would only distract from the session. Some people can feel the energy traveling down their arms and out their hands as it radiates to the person in front of them. But even if the givers feel nothing, they know in their hearts that the transmission is occurring.

The best way to give Jyorei to others is with a quiet mind and an open heart. Let go of your various worldly concerns, and focus on love or gratitude. If distracting thoughts come up, just surrender them to God. Stay focused on the act of giving Jyorei, without effort or strain. Especially, let go of the need for particular results. Remember, the main point is to relax and allow.

If the success of our efforts depended on us, we might fall short. But this action is divinely inspired and is much greater than any one of us. Therefore, we need to put our egos aside while giving Jyorei. Successfully doing so is much like blowing away the clouds in the sky, revealing the bright sunshine of Spirit that was formerly hidden. The sunshine of Jyorei is waiting for the chance to break through the cloud cover so that it can light up the world around us.

Some of us may feel that Meishusama is guiding and assisting us in the transmission of Jyorei. This feeling can help us to relinquish personal credit for the effects of Jyorei by acknowledging either Meishusama or God as the true giver of Jyorei, rather than us. We are merely the physical instruments being used by them for the healing.

People can give Jyorei even when they are sick, depressed, or angry, but it is best to bring as much purity as possible to the Jyorei session. Sick people, however, find that by sharing Jyorei with others, they themselves become healthier. Those with emotional problems also find more inner peace and happiness from sharing Jyorei. Some people feel that the act of giving Jyorei benefits the giver more than the receiver. This adds a new perspective to the words of Jesus Christ, who said that, "It is better to give than receive."

When we hope for something, we often find that it is impossible to bring it about, but once we have almost forgotten about it, things suddenly go as we want them to. Even the giving of Jyorei follows the same pattern. The more eager one is to heal the patient, the less effective the cure is. When, however, one does not let such thoughts enter one's mind, but simply gives Jyorei as a matter of course, or when one does not know whether the patient is curable or not, but gives Jyorei anyway, the cure is unusually easy and effective. – *Trust in God. HT*

Attachments block the Light. Even attachments to the results of Jyorei, although altruistic, can reduce the flow of energy. To thoroughly align ourselves with divine power requires detachment, which comes from faith and trust in a higher power. Although good intentions are valuable, the attachment to a desired outcome is not. Trust and allow divine intelligence to work through you.

When receiving Jyorei, it is best to have an attitude of openness and gratitude. Simply quiet the mind and open the heart. This does not add to the Jyorei energy, but rather puts one in a more receptive state. Although a spiritual orientation may be helpful, the results are not dependent upon it. Even people who fall asleep while receiving Jyorei, benefit from it. This is also true for those who might be unconscious or in a coma. Neither the giver nor the receiver needs to believe in the power of Jyorei for it to work. This healing through divine Light can even be effective with people who are skeptical or disbelieving, and can also benefit animals and plants. Each individual has different personal beliefs, attitudes, and needs, and our intention is to always respect those differences.

The recipient normally sits from two to four feet from the person giving Jyorei. First, Jyorei is directed to the forehead. Next, the recipient is asked to lower his or her head, and then Jyorei is directed to the top of the head. These areas of the body are especially sensitive to spiritual influences, and from there the energy will travel down to whichever part of the body needs healing.

Some may wonder why we do not direct energy to other parts of the body, especially to those areas where there is pain or dysfunction. Although it does not hurt to do so, usually this will merely treat the symptoms of a problem, not the cause, thereby resulting in only short-term benefits. For example, a stomachache might be caused by food poisoning, an ulcer, emotional stress, a pinched nerve, parasites, a spiritual disturbance, or even a physical injury. These problems, in turn, may have still deeper causes on a physical, emotional, or spiritual level. In other words, diagnosis can be complicated and difficult. Although it is important to know the cause of a problem so that we can deal with it on a practical level, this knowledge does not usually affect how we give Jyorei. We do not usually send energy to the stomach when someone has a stomachache because that would only be dealing with the secondary effects, not the root cause. Instead, we usually direct energy to the forehead and the top of the head. Just as the nutrition in food (if we swallow it through our mouth) will go to wherever in the body it is needed, so too, Jyorei (if we direct it to these two vital spots) will go to wherever it is most needed within a person.

It is important to remember that Jyorei is divine energy, and that it works on many levels, not just the physical. Jyorei intelligently interacts with our whole being to guarantee the best outcome. Most importantly, Jyorei clears up the spiritual clouds that underlie all problems. And as these clouds dissipate, our awareness expands, allowing us to discover what is contributing to our problems and what to do about it. For example, sometimes we need to improve our diet, eliminate toxins from our homes, get more exercise, become more considerate of others, change jobs, or get more sleep at night. There are also times when Jyorei produces seemingly miraculous healings, without the need for any change on our part. Jyorei both weakens the bad and strengthens the good. It works in more ways than we can imagine. Therefore, our job is not to diagnose an illness or problem, but only to share Light with compassion and trust.

The forehead area (some people refer to this as the Third Eye Chakra) gives us access to the frontal part of the brain, including the pituitary and the hypothalamus glands, which are located deep inside the brain, directly behind the bridge of the nose. The hypothalamus is a cluster of brain cells that sort out messages to and from the rest of the body, and responds accordingly through the pituitary gland, which in turn produces the specific hormones that the body needs. These hormones are then circulated in the blood to the body's organs and tissues, including other endocrine glands. The hypothalamus is currently considered by many to be the master gland of the entire endocrine gland system, which is responsible for regulating many of the essential biological processes in the body. Thus, when we direct Jyorei to the forehead and the area behind it, the rest of the body is affected. Most significantly, directing Jyorei to this location also awakens inner spiritual perception and mystical consciousness.

The top of the head (some people refer to this as the Crown Chakra) gives us access to the pineal gland, which is located in the central part of the brain, just behind and above the pituitary and hypothalamus glands. The pineal gland produces and controls various hormones and neurotransmitters, such as melatonin and serotonin, which influence many important physiological activities, including our moods and energy levels. Thus, when we direct Jyorei to the top of the head, we are affecting another area vital to our general health and well-being. Transmitting Jyorei to the top of the head causes the energy to flow downward, thereby purifying and healing the entire body in the process.

Together, these two points promote homeostasis and balance within the body. Receiving Jyorei on the forehead emphasizes purification of the spiritual body, whereas receiving Jyorei at the top of the head has a greater healing effect on the physical body. Of course, spirit and body are interrelated, so each affects the other to a large extent.

The usual amount of time spent during a Jyorei session is just five minutes, although longer sessions are also beneficial. However long the session, we cannot judge or quantify Jyorei based on duration because Jyorei is spiritual in nature, and Spirit transcends time.

When you give Jyorei to someone, always keep your heart aligned with God's love. If you do so, good results will surely follow.[1] *– KW*

The Experience of Jyorei

What joy I feel at my life's renewal and even more so for the opportunity to give Jyorei. – Affiliation Ceremony. MK

---

[1] Meishusama, "Being Daijo," *Shumei Magazine*, vol. 267 (January /February 2007).

The power of Jyorei can often be experienced through one or more of our five senses. In recalling a healing session, recipients often report feeling heat in various parts of the body or all around it. Other common experiences include: tingly sensations on the skin, feelings of gratitude or joy, subtle pressure in the head, calming of the breath, weightlessness of the body, subtle lights of various colors, faint inner sounds, the smell of flowers or incense, or deep inner peace. Some people even report spiritual visions of Meishusama or Kannon Bodhisattva.

If a person feels a bit sleepy or tired after receiving Jyorei, it may be because their body is redirecting its own internal energy to assist in the healing process. This may be similar to the tiredness one feels after eating a big meal; it is temporary, and will soon pass after the digestive process is complete. Such tiredness, after Jyorei, is a good sign because it indicates that a deep cleansing and healing is occurring within the body. Therefore, during these times, it might be helpful to lie down and rest for a while.

When people start receiving or giving Jyorei they often notice dramatic changes in their lives. The more often they engage in Jyorei, the more dramatic the results can be. Jyorei frees us from future suffering by purifying us of internal toxicity. Meishusama views all purification as an opportunity to learn and grow. It provides us with the opportunity to re-evaluate our lives and to seek inner guidance. Rather than resisting or complaining about our various hardships or pain, it is better to keep in mind that this discomfort is only temporary, and inevitably leads to greater health and happiness. Knowing this, it is better to feel grateful for the purification. Gratitude has a way of transforming even the most difficult of situations into something of inexplicable beauty.

Our blood can be viewed as a physical manifestation of the soul. Because of this direct link, when Jyorei is used to purify the soul, it also purifies the blood. On the physical level, as the body becomes free of toxins, the immune system gets stronger, and other biological processes move to a deeper state of balance, harmony, and vitality. Meishusama writes, "The spiritual clouding we are talking about also has a physical equivalent or expression, and this is poisoning of the blood and the accumulation of purulent matter in the body." (Sin and Sickness. HT)

Meishusama often refers to Jyorei as purification by the spirit of fire, and when people are receiving it they feel heat. This heat can be a sign of physical healing, as the body will often raise its internal temperature in order to subdue harmful viruses or bacteria, such as when we have a fever, or to flush internal toxins from the system, such as what happens in a sauna. Jyorei also appears to activate the lymphatic system to further facilitate detoxification. Sometimes people who have received numerous Jyorei sessions will experience powerful elimination symptoms such as runny noses with dark, thick discharges, skin rashes, tremendous sweating, boils, diarrhea, and even pus oozing out of their skin. These symptoms are usually the result of medicines, environmental pollutants, and other poisons that the person has ingested or been exposed to in the past. Sometimes physical toxins can also be inherited from a person's ancestors. Meishusama explains that symptoms such as these are the outer effects of inner lumps of accumulated toxins melting and discharging from the body.

A useful distinction can be made between the symptoms of sickness caused by purification (proactive purification) and sickness caused by environmental pollutants such as contaminated food, bacteria, parasites, venom, pollen, smog, radiation, chemicals, or polluted water (reactionary purification). Although both types of sickness can be considered forms of purification, one is favorable, and the other is not. Purification caused by Light leads to greater health and happiness, whereas purification caused by toxins only slows down the gradual descent into ill health. With the former, it is good to appreciate the healing we are receiving, whereas with the latter, it is good to isolate and identify the cause of the discomfort, and to avoid further exposure to these substances whenever possible. This is a common sense and practical approach to dealing with sickness.

Sometimes one can help reduce the discomfort of purification by drinking plenty of water, which helps to flush toxins out of the internal organs and the lymphatic system. Additionally, as common sense tells us, eating foods with lots of fiber can assist in pushing sluggish toxins out of the digestive tract.

The lymphatic system is one of the body's most important means for eliminating toxins and metabolic waste products. But unlike the bloodstream, which is constantly circulating throughout the body because of the pumping action of the heart muscle, the lymphatic system depends on physical movement (including breathing) to carry these toxins out of the body. Therefore, some light physical exercise, such as walking, can be helpful. An added benefit of exercise is that it stimulates the bloodstream to carry active components of the immune system to where they can attack and eliminate viruses, bacteria, and other pathogens. In general, it's important to pay attention to the current needs of one's body, and care for it wisely in order to go through one's physical purification smoothly and effectively.

Although many people feel or perceive such sensations as heat, pressure, vibration, or light when receiving Jyorei, it is not necessary to feel anything to benefit from the healing sessions. Some people never feel any immediate sensations from Jyorei, but nonetheless still benefit from the increased health and spiritual growth that it promotes. The important thing to look for when evaluating Jyorei is its practical effects in one's life.

Experiencing the various miracles produced by Jyorei gives people the opportunity to re-evaluate their beliefs about life. Is there a higher power or intelligence somewhere that has the ability to dramatically affect their lives? This is the beginning of faith, which can inspire one to transcend one's limited conditioning and to step into a larger life, a life dedicated to spiritual values and to serving the greater good.

Testing out new things before coming to conclusions about them is often wise. Therefore, a little skepticism is welcomed. Cynicism, on the other hand, may not be so helpful. Cynicism not only closes the door to new experiences, but also drains the joy out of our lives. During the healing session, if we can keep our hearts open, then the full benefits of Jyorei will enter our being unobstructed. Jyorei is a form of non-verbal prayer in which peace, love, and joy are the means of prayer as well as the end result. To feel grateful for the Light is to fully participate in this prayer. This prayer is not one of ritualized words, but of silent communion with the sacred.

Sickness that purifies body and soul is a gift from God. – Sickness. MK

Although Jyorei can be given anywhere, and is not entirely dependent on the surroundings or a person's personal beliefs or attitudes, nonetheless, Jyorei is influenced to varying degrees by the following factors: the spiritual level of the giver, the physical health of the recipient, the spiritual vibration of the physical environment, the strength of the spiritual connection or cords between the people exchanging Jyorei, the number of people exchanging Jyorei at the time, the mood or attitudes of both the giver and receiver, the intention of the giver and, finally, God's Will, which cannot be measured. It's good to consider these factors, but not obsess or worry about them. What is most important is to be grateful for the divine blessings that Jyorei offers.

Although the Light of Jyorei is always the same at its source, our attitudes and receptivity greatly affect the power of its transmission. Because we are the physical transmitters of this energy, we have a sacred obligation to be as clear a conduit as possible. Letting go of self-preoccupation, distracting thoughts, and attachment to results allows the Light to move through us unimpeded. The more humility, purity, and love we bring to the session, the more both the recipient and we ourselves will benefit. Jyorei will be stronger and more effective when one embraces these positive attitudes.

It is important to realize that the higher the spiritual level of the source, the finer and subtler the radiations will be. This is a basic principle. And although radiations from the human body are all extremely powerful, it can be imagined that the power of these varies according to the individual, and that the power to transmit Jyorei to others varies with the power of the radiations. – *Natural Power. HT*

Furthermore, the thicker the aura of a person who gives Jyorei, the better will be the healing results of his cures. And, as he saves more and more people through Jyorei, he will receive more and more gratitude and appreciation, his aura will become even thicker, and the results of his healing will climb to new heights of splendor. – *Spiritual Radiation and the Aura. HT*

People are attracted to Jyorei for a variety of reasons. Some are looking for relief from their suffering, whereas others are more concerned with helping people. The latter view is a wonderful way for a person to be of service to their family, friends, and associates. Both, however, receive internal purification, spiritual growth, and greater personal happiness from sharing Jyorei.

Jyorei is the Light that will unify the peoples of our world and heal their aching hearts and troubled minds. It dispels spiritual clouds, which are the invisible influences that cause our suffering. As the clouds obscuring the soul are dispelled, the radiations of the spiritual body begin to increase in strength and power. Meishusama states, "The true object of our attention should be the soul, not the body." (*Natural Power. HT*)

At the deepest level, sharing Jyorei strengthens our inner spirit. The stronger and more radiant our spirit, the happier and more positive we become, and the more capable we are of helping others. With progress, we become increasingly motivated to create love and harmony in our environment. Our aesthetic sense becomes more developed and we become more sensitive to the conditions of the world around us.

It is important to remember that God is using us as an instrument to heal and transform the world spiritually. As Meishusama says, "Human beings do not have the power to perform miracles; only God can perform them." *(Religion is a Thing of Miracles. HT)* The quickest way to realize a perfect society is to purify the spiritual bodies of as many people as possible. The more people actively share Jyorei, the sooner will our world transform itself for the better. Each of us can make a difference in the lives of those around us. Anthropologist Margaret Mead said, "Never doubt that a small group of thoughtful, committed citizens can change the world; indeed, that is the only thing that ever has."

The Ohikari

When I take a brush and write, the writing on the paper is vibrant with life. If this paper is folded and put around someone's neck as an Ohikari, their feelings become radiant, and miracles start to happen. – The Savior of the World. HT

For an individual to give Jyorei, it is first necessary to attend a series of formal introductions, followed by an initiation into divine energy. At this time, there is a brief ceremonial reception of an Ohikari, which is a sacred silk amulet that is worn around the neck. Inside the Ohikari is a reproduction of one of Meishusama's hand-painted symbols for Light, written in Chinese calligraphy. Each Ohikari carries Meishusama's blessings and healing power within it.

Something is considered sacred when it carries a high spiritual vibration, communicates spiritual wisdom, or symbolizes a spiritual quality. Each of us has a spiritual dimension deep within our being, and wearing the Ohikari helps remind us of this dimension.

Wearing an Ohikari reinforces the connection we have, through powerful spiritual cords, with Meishusama and God. Through these cords we receive the power of Jyorei as a gift from God and Meishusama. The Ohikari is symbolic of the Light that each of us carries within the center of our being. Meishusama writes, "The Light given out by myself is carried instantaneously to the inscription of each and every Ohikari by spiritual cords. This process very closely resembles that by which a central broadcasting station sends out radio signals to any number of receivers. My spiritual body radiates light waves through the spiritual cords." (*The Principles of Jyorei. HT*)

Many have reported a sense of spiritual protection while wearing the Ohikari. The powerful vibrations emanating from it can help to raise our level of awareness, strengthen our intuition, lift our mood, and draw good fortune to us. To wear an Ohikari is a great privilege.

We need to take special care of the Ohikari. How we treat it is an outer reflection of the care and respect we give to our soul. In our busy lives, it can be easy to ignore and neglect our spiritual life. Taking thought to be careful with our Ohikari reminds us of our connection to the spiritual world and of the need to think and behave in ways that enhance our spiritual condition.

Life is not a chain of haphazard events, but is actually an intelligent reflection of the conditions in the spiritual world. Our relationship to the Ohikari is more profound than our relationships with ordinary objects. What happens to the Ohikari is a reflection of our life at this time, and by association, our current inner condition. There are no accidents. For instance, if we discover a foreign element, such as a strand of hair, inside of the outer pouch of the Ohikari, it may reflect a spiritual impurity within us that requires our attention. Similarly, if we were to accidentally drop the Ohikari, it may reflect a certain carelessness about our spiritual life. In these cases, it acts as an outward reflection of an inner condition that needs to be examined. It can also point to problems we have with our personal relations or with our finances. Or, we may be carrying an emotional burden within our hearts that needs to be addressed.

If something unfortunate happens to the Ohikari, the owner of the Ohikari is advised to consult with the person designated to support his or her spiritual growth. Through dialogue with this person, the Ohikari owner can receive help in unraveling the hidden meaning of this incident, and also in discovering ways to improve the current situation.

The conditions and circumstances surrounding our Ohikari often have great meaning and significance. What initially can appear as a problem may actually be an important message from the spiritual world offering us spiritual guidance (if we can interpret it accurately). If ever there is a need to purify our Ohikari, it may signify that our soul also needs extra purification. It can also be an encouragement to discover God's Will or to resolve to do better in some area of our lives. Incidents of purification are gifts from the spiritual world for which we can be grateful. They are opportunities to change our destiny for the better, and often these incidents can lead us in the direction of greater peace and harmony.

A special donation is requested to provide for the initiation into Jyorei and to thereby receive an Ohikari. The choice to begin sharing Jyorei is a momentous decision to live a life of generosity and service to others. It is a choice to look beyond one's own personal needs by focusing on the needs of others. Many have discovered that genuine happiness does not come from the selfish pursuit of personal desires but actually comes from the act of giving. They begin to experience a joy and fulfillment that is untouched by the daily circumstances in their lives. The initiation donation is a concrete expression of this commitment to giving.

The Nature and Source of Jyorei

There are several organizations other than Shumei who also study the works of Meishusama and who also practice Jyorei, each with different approaches or different techniques for directing energy. In this book, we are expounding on Jyorei as practiced by Shumei, which puts greater emphasis on a person's attitude and state of mind rather than on learning elaborate techniques and procedures.

Although there may be positive benefits from using the more elaborate Jyorei procedures, there are also advantages to the simpler approach which humbly relies on the highest power in the universe to effect change. Our human intelligence is quite limited in comparison with that of our Creator, and therefore, by putting our trust in this Being, we do not need to concern ourselves with having to diagnose people or give special treatments to them. By surrendering our personal will to Divine Will, we become aligned with the ultimate source of Jyorei, which is also the ultimate source of life itself.

Interest in spiritual matters is becoming increasingly popular in modern society. Among these various fields of interest, the subject of spiritual healing is drawing special attention, perhaps because it is experiential as well as practical. Some of the more popular forms of spiritual healing are Reiki, Chi Kung, Mahikari, faith healing, acupuncture, and laying on of hands. Although these techniques all deal with transmitting energy, there are also some fundamental differences between each of them.

Within the electromagnetic frequency spectrum there are many different types of energy, such as microwaves, X-rays, gamma rays, radio waves, ultraviolet rays, infrared rays, and cosmic rays. What they have in common is all are forms is of pulsating energy. Yet scientific instruments can detect significant variations in the wavelengths and power of each of these types of energy, which thereby produce significant differences in their quality and functionality.

Light is something invisible that, through vibration, makes all things visible. To see something, we must shine light on it. But the light itself remains invisible, no matter how bright it is. We can only know light by what it does, not by what it is. Despite all the scientific explanations, light's fundamental nature is still a mystery cloaked in brightness.

Most of us can only see light indirectly by its reflection off of physical objects. Along with the familiar spectrum of colors that most of us can see, there are also other colors that we cannot see, such as infrared and ultraviolet. These latter two color spectrums differ from the colors of the visible spectrum because they vibrate at different rates of speed. A similar distinction can be made between radio and television broadcasting signals as compared to X-rays or gamma rays. It would be impossible to transmit the former via the latter. Again, these examples merely stress the actual differences between various types of energy, regardless of whether they are physical or spiritual in nature.

From the highest perspective, we can say that everything originates from Spirit, including the energies of the electromagnetic frequency spectrum. Meishusama writes, "The true nature of the Spirit is this: it is the fundamental source of all energy and it is the directing power behind the creation, movements, activities, and changes of every single thing in this vast and infinite universe." (Natural Power. HT) Spiritual energy emerges directly from Spirit, whereas physical phenomena emerge indirectly from Spirit, with many intermediary causes or sources in between. In other words, the things of this world have many levels of origination, depending on how dense, complex, or artificial they are. For example, although sunlight, like all things, ultimately comes from Spirit, its more immediate source is the sun. The sun is the material source of sunlight, and Spirit is the immaterial source of them both. In the case of water from a faucet, the local river is the intermediary, or material source, whereas Spirit is the primary, or immaterial, source. The purer the spiritual energy, the closer it is to Source, and therefore, the more it mirrors the qualities of Spirit.

Some people have asked whether Jyorei and Reiki are similar or possibly even the same energy. Both are described as originating directly from Spirit, without any significant, intermediate sources in between (such as the sun, which is the intermediate source of sunlight, or a kitchen faucet, which is the intermediate source of tap water). In truth, everything originates from Spirit, but this does not make Reiki and Jyorei identical, just as it does not make apples and oranges the same, either. As a glass prism refracts light into a spectrum of diverse colors, so too, does Spirit manifest in a variety of energies and forms. Before hitting the prism, the light is pure and undifferentiated, whereas afterwards it takes on various qualities of this world, such as color and shape. At the level of appearances, there is always diversity. Also, many people who have experienced both forms of healing report that the energies feel different from each other.

Not only does the type or quality of energy used by Jyorei and Reiki differ, but so, too, do their techniques. According to our understanding, Reiki practitioners visualize various symbols while transmitting energy, plus they are allowed to touch the recipient. Jyorei does neither. The set of points on the body that Reiki directs energy to differ from those that Jyorei focuses on.

The ideal motive for sharing Jyorei is the pure desire to alleviate suffering and to help make the world a better place. Jyorei practitioners are altruistic, with the strong desire to help humanity. They never charge money for their services, unlike many other healers. Jyorei is always given freely and unconditionally.

Despite the various differences, many Reiki practitioners and other types of healers are also dedicated to serving humanity, and therefore we support them in their mission.

Although Jyorei is universally beneficial, it does not empower harmful microorganisms within the body, such as parasites, yeast, bacteria, or viruses. Jyorei might possibly strengthen these organisms if they were to be isolated on a Petri Dish in a laboratory, but Jyorei will not do so when they inhabit the interior of someone's body. This is because life is a hierarchy composed of increasingly complex biological structures: cells are composed of colonies of molecules, internal organs are composed of collections of cells, and bodies are composed of groups of internal organs. The larger and more complex generally takes precedence over the smaller and simpler. Thus, the body makes use of Jyorei to strengthen itself and to inhibit harmful microorganisms while simultaneously promoting the growth of friendly microorganisms. In all cases, the smaller become subservient to the larger, not the other way around. Similarly, the interior organs also become strengthened and begin to work in harmony with each other for the sake of the greater overall functioning of the body.

Meishusama claimed that he received the power of Jyorei from Kannon, the Japanese name for the popular Buddhist deity of compassion, who instilled a mysterious orb of golden Light within his abdomen. (Some refer to this deity by the Chinese name of Kwan Yin.) This was the immediate source of power for Meishusama and his disciples. Jyorei is a gift from Kannon to Meishusama and to humanity.

I have in my body a Ball of Light about two inches in diameter. This has been witnessed by more than one person. Infinitely powerful Light waves are given out by this Ball. The fundamental source of the Light energy of the Ball is to be found in the spiritual world. The Orb of Kannon constantly and infinitely replenishes this Ball's Power with Divine Light rays that are directed at me. This is the power of Kannon, the mysterious Power, the *Myochiriki,* as it is often called. This Ball is the same as that borne by Nyoirin Kannon. – *The Principles of Jyorei. HT*

Kannon can be viewed as an outward expression of God: His power of compassion. An analogy would be the flames at the perimeter of the sun that are distinct from the sun itself while simultaneously remaining an integral part of its overall body. The flames are a part of the sun but not the sun itself—the same but different. Understood in this way, Jyorei can be described as originating from both God and Kannon, who are inwardly the same although outwardly different. Although there are numerous images of God, the reality behind them is identical. The mind's identification with various names and forms is what creates the illusion of multiplicity.

Although the source of Jyorei is a divine mystery beyond human under-standing, the way it functions can be partially explained in terms of the three symbolic elements: fire, the power of heat and expansion; water, the power of fluidity and movement; and earth, the power of coldness and contraction. The energy of Jyorei is primarily composed of fire, which melts and dissolves toxins, and secondarily of water, which flushes the liquefied toxins out of the body. When one gives Jyorei to another, its power first passes through the physical body of the giver and then penetrates the physical body of the recipi-ent. Through this process, the element of earth, which is inherent in the hu-man body, is integrated with the energy of Jyorei, resulting in the combination of the three elements of fire, water, and earth operating in dynamic unison. The earth also symbolizes the solid, tangible results that can be felt in the mind, in the body, and in one's interpersonal relationships.

When these three elements are mixed together, power or energy is created.
– The Spirit of Fire, The Spirit of Water, and The Spirit of Earth. HT

For most of us, these various subtle distinctions are not so important. What is significant is the spiritual source of Jyorei—the boundless wellspring that is beyond our limited world of observable phenomena. Jyorei comes from the infinite vibration that is Spirit itself.

The Effect on Humanity

This world can be liberated by performing genuine works of healing.
– Meishusama IV, MK

According to Meishusama, our minds are interconnected with others through numerous spiritual cords. Taken together, this results in one huge interwoven field of consciousness—the collective consciousness of all of humanity. Biologist Rupert Sheldrake, author of *A New Science of Life: The Hypothesis of Formative Causation*, refers to these fields as 'morphogenetic fields,' or 'form-generating fields.' They are the collective memory and intelligence of the species. According to Dr. Sheldrake, each species of plant or animal has a unique, nonphysical memory bank that feeds them the information necessary to survive and reproduce, and which is the real source of their instinctual knowledge. This morphogenetic field can be viewed as the biological equivalent of an electromagnetic field, one that determines the form and inherited behavior of various species.

Dr. Sheldrake postulates that when a large enough percentage of a particular species learns a new skill or acquires new knowledge, it then automatically (through morphic resonance) becomes available to the entire species. Through this psychic networking, individual races and species are able to learn, grow, and adapt to changing circumstances. This principle has been referred to as "The Hundredth Monkey Effect." Following this logic a step further, if enough people, beyond a certain threshold, evolve to a higher spiritual level, then possibly the entire human race may rise up to that new level as well.

> In the entire process of cosmic evolution you see a spiritual process as well as a material process. You can't separate the two. – *Rupert Sheldrake, Ph.D., evolutionary biologist*

Every time a person is healed of negativity or is raised to a higher level of consciousness, that person exerts a positive effect on the mental and behavioral aspects of this morphogenetic field. Thus, as each individual progresses, so too does everyone else. The Light from Jyorei, through its beneficial influence on millions of people, and therefore on this field, may be helping to purify and uplift all of humanity. In Meishusama's terminology, we could say that everyone benefits from Jyorei, either directly or indirectly, through the spiritual cords that link us all together in an invisible web of relationships. Therefore, Jyorei is not just a gift to individuals, but also to humanity as a whole.

At its highest level, Jyorei is an experience of Oneness. When we give with love and receive with gratitude, we touch everyone through our shared collective awareness. Love and gratitude, empowered by divine Light, are capable of dissolving the inner barriers of alienation and separation that have troubled humanity for countless millennia. Through Jyorei, we can each help in the transmutation of this world into a realm of radiant beauty and Light.

11. NATURAL AGRICULTURE

The foremost principle of Natural Agriculture is, as Nature itself clearly teaches us, an overriding respect for nature. – A Great Agricultural Revolution. HT

Fundamental Principles

Meishusama developed the principles of Natural Agriculture through his own personal experience in farming in the late 1930's. The reason that he started farming was originally to help farmers who at that time were experiencing dire hardship and poverty because of poor harvests. Many had to abandon their farms and move to the cities. The condition of the farmers was so devastating that Meishusama could not overlook it. He felt compassion for their suffering, and wanted to find a practical solution. How could farmers increase their crop yields and reduce the general food shortage? How could they avoid the toxic chemical residues in food left over from pesticides, as well as improve the food's overall nutritional quality?

Natural Agriculture is a spiritually based form of farming that does not use chemicals, fertilizers, or manure, and pays special attention to the farmer's spiritual relationship to the environment. As such, it is both a spiritual discipline and a practical vocation. The expression that "some gardeners have a green thumb," because of what appears to be their natural talent for growing things, could also apply to practitioners of Natural Agriculture. The attitude of the farmer plays an essential role in the quality of his or her crops. Especially important is the emphasis on love, respect for nature, and gratitude.

From his early stages of farming, Meishusama maintained a firm belief in the power of nature. A proper relationship between the growers and nature was essential for growing healthy food. This relationship is based on gratitude. Three principles—love, gratitude, and respect for nature—are at the foundation of the Natural Agriculture movement. These principles arise from our realization of our fundamental Oneness with all things, including our unity with all of nature.

Philosophical Overview

Contemporary View of Nature

Based on his experiences with medicine earlier in life, as well as his later experiments with fertilizers, Meishusama came to have serious doubts about the mentality of controlling and suppressing things—whether illness in the human body or insects and disease in plants. He felt that this tendency to control was contrary to the principles of nature because such control caused more harm than good. Humankind had lost its way in its over-reliance on technology to dominate nature. Nature now suffered the consequences of this misdirection.

Meishusama would agree with the popular English philosopher, Alan Watts, who ironically suggested that the bulldozer could be the most appropriate symbol for the modern era. Bulldozers level the mountains and fill in valleys, treating the natural habitat as no more than worthless dirt to be pushed around at our convenience. In our rush for increased consumption, modern civilization has managed, compared to previous centuries, to desecrate the land, air, and water. Our civilization uses technology to dominate nature for the sake of shortsighted goals, while ignoring long-term environmental effects. Our bulldozers shove around massive amounts of earth to create monotonous housing tracts, leaving behind a chopped-up landscape. Natural beauty is sacrificed for the sake of "progress."

Our scientific power has outrun our spiritual power. We have guided missiles and misguided men. – Dr. Martin Luther King Jr.

Our contemporary mentality, influenced by nineteenth century mechanistic scientific models, tends to view the universe as essentially unintelligent. This model conditions us to experience the universe as something dominated by chaotic forces with no concern for life, consciousness, or beauty. According to this model, the universe was created eons ago by a spontaneous explosion known scientifically as the "Big Bang." Much later, life supposedly originated in a freak accident. Intelligence is considered to be the lucky result of "natural selection," or evolutionary adaptation to hostile circumstances. It is no more than a subtle byproduct of physical matter. The psychiatrist Stanislav Grof says this about such theories, "The probability that human consciousness and our infinitely complex universe could have come into existence through the random interactions of inert matter has aptly been compared to that of a tornado blowing through a junkyard and accidentally assembling a 747 jumbo jet." Such a world appears inherently hostile to all life forms, especially to humans with any sensitivity or thoughtfulness. This outlook encourages us to develop an adversarial relationship to the world and to use whatever technological power is at our disposal to dominate nature for our own safety and survival. Humans are thus left feeling anxious about their existence and alienated from nature.

The Intelligence of Ecological Systems

We do not weave the web of life—we are merely a strand of it. Whatever we do to the web, we do to ourselves. – Chief Seattle

An alternate view holds that the universe is inherently conscious and intelligent, with love at the foundation of its existence. We humans are likewise inherently conscious and intelligent, all the way down to the cells in our bodies, with love at the core of our being. Not only humans, but also all the other creatures in our environment contain this innate intelligence and love. Elizabeth Sahtouris, an evolution biologist and futurist, calls this "a living universe." In her book *Biology Revisioned*, she writes: "The dynamic dance of nature is ever conscious at every level, from the tiniest particle to whatever its currently largest configuration, or holon, is."

The earth's ecosystem is composed of chains of smaller, local ecosystems, all interrelated with each other. Each of these local ecosystems is composed of a fantastic variety of life forms, from birds, animals, and insects to trees, grasses, and plants. All are subject to multiple influences, such as sun, rain, wind, soil, and temperature. Nothing exists independent of anything else. A profound intelligence harmoniously orchestrates the diverse elements within each of these ecosystems so that they live in balance. This is not an outside intelligence, but an inner one. It is part of nature itself. This same intelligence regulates the circulation of our blood, and the digestion of our food.

We are not separate from nature, but an expression of it. The natural environment is teeming with life, from the smallest microbes and fungus to giant whales and sequoia trees. We share this world with the animals, birds, and fish; it does not belong to us alone. All of nature is sensitively alive, and responds to kind thoughts and actions.

This interpretation of the natural world is supported by fieldwork on animal behavior conducted by the Russian naturalist and political theorist Peter Kropotkin. Based on six-years of research in Siberia, he concluded that animals in the wilderness bond together in social groups for their mutual survival. In his book he writes, "They [hamadryas baboons] have been observed working together to accomplish shared goals and even risking their lives to save members of their own group. In some species several individuals will combine to overturn a stone in order to search for ants' eggs under it. The hamadryas not only post sentries, but have been seen making a chain for the transmission of the spoil to a safe place; and their courage is well known." Kropotkin's view on nature starkly contrasts with that of Charles Darwin and his theory of evolution, who describes animal behavior as based on ruthless competition for survival. This view is commonly summarized as: "survival of the fittest." Kropotkin, in his writings, gives ample examples of intelligent, altruistic behavior amongst animals. His description of nature is one of harmony and cooperation, where self-sacrifice and sharing form the basis of life in all its diversity.

Nature teaches us a multitude of things in this way. To understand the world, to find the answer to the deepest problems, you usually need to do no more than look closely at the world of nature. – Impasse. HT

Environmental Degradation

In order to understand the larger purpose of Natural Agriculture activity, we need to note the grim state of our world. Our biosphere is sick. The entire planetary ecosystem, handed down to us from generation to generation, is being relentlessly destroyed. There are over one hundred thousand chemicals in the environment today that did not exist a hundred years ago. Well water, streams, and even deep underground aquifers are increasingly polluted from the poisonous runoff of agricultural chemicals such as organophosphates and n-methyl carbamates. Air pollution is everywhere: not only in giant cities such as Los Angeles, Beijing, Cairo, and Mexico City, but also in regions that have burning rainforests and in areas near factories and oil refineries. Massive amounts of topsoil are being lost each year, and it takes hundreds, perhaps thousands of years to recreate just a few centimeters of it. Everyday, approximately 35 to 150 species of life (mostly insects and plants) become extinct. Global warming is melting the icecaps. Rainforests are being destroyed at a furious pace, and the micro-plankton at the bottom of the food chain, deep within the oceans, are dying off. Because forests and micro-plankton create so much of the oxygen on the planet, the future looks grim.

Not only is our surrounding environment deteriorating, but our inner biology also is being traumatized. Hundreds of millions of people are suffering from hunger, mostly because of direct and indirect problems in the existing marketing system. The alarming rate of increase in American degenerative diseases indicates that something is wrong. According to the American Cancer Society, almost one out of four deaths in the United States is due to cancer. (Cancer Facts and Figures 2005. www.cancer.org) Heart disease, diabetes, arthritis, multiple sclerosis, Parkinson's disease, and numerous other chronic illnesses are increasing without any potential cures available. At best, drugs manage these afflictions and lessen suffering on a short term basis. We need to ask the question, "Are the toxins in our environment causing these diseases?"

Only after the last tree has been cut down; Only after the last fish has been caught; Only after the last river has been poisoned; Only then will you realize that money cannot be eaten. – Cree Indian Prophesy

The Impact of Modern Agriculture

Conventional agriculture was designed for mass-produced, single-crop production, heavily dependent on toxic chemicals and the exploitation of cheap labor. Because of its massive use of toxic pesticides, chemical fertilizers, and animal manure, as well as slash and burn practices in forests and jungles, the single crop practice causes environmental degradation. If modern agriculture continues its current practices, in the near future the global environment will become unsuitable for many species, including human beings.

In anticipation of the future crisis resulting from degrading environmental conditions, we need to alter the way we grow most of our food and end the destructive cycle endangering the world's entire eco-system. Beyond agribusiness, the overall global market system perpetuates the existing food production system. This economic system also must change.

We use the most powerful chemical fertilizers, pesticides, and herbicides to force the land to yield large quantities of crops. This process has had the very unfortunate consequences of polluting the land, depleting the topsoil, and producing food that has less and less nutritional value as each year passes. As far back as 1936, an official document by the United States Senate *(Document No. 264)* warned that the soil used to grow fruits and vegetables was seriously deficient in needed minerals. For the last seventy years nothing has reversed this trend, it is frightening to ponder the current level of deterioration.

Another crisis is the alarming loss of honeybees throughout the United States. According to scientists, the domesticated honeybee population has declined by about 50% in the last 50 years. This is dangerous because bee pollination, which most farmers depend on, is responsible for as much as 30% of the U.S. food supply. Similar conditions are occurring in many other countries. The conclusion drawn by most scientists is that pesticide usage, which continues to increase dramatically, is poisoning the bees. Unless something is done soon to protect the honeybee population, many fruits and vegetables may disappear from the food chain. We appear to be approaching an emergency situation in our food supply that will soon affect everyone, both rich and poor alike.

The prevailing trend in our civilization continues to destroy the natural environment and our physical bodies. Advanced technology worsens the situation instead of improving it. People turn their backs, consciously and unconsciously, to the plight of Earth. Most adults do not have a clear picture of the link between the environment and human life. We have come to a point where we must look at modern agriculture in a larger context. With this understanding, we can take immediate and decisive action to reverse this negative trend.

Alternate Approaches

The organic movement and Natural Agriculture originated as a response to our basic right to live healthy lives. Their alternative food production processes are beginning to shift the trend from large, transnational agribusinesses to local-economy oriented businesses. Because of the recent success of the organic movement, critics are appearing who warn us of dire consequences if chemical free farming continues to gain popularity. They label organic farmers as starry-eyed idealists generating mass starvation by replacing conventional farming with "primitive" natural farming, which they claim is inefficient and less productive.

Although modern mechanized farming has been successful in terms of crop yield, its prices do not reflect the hidden expenses from pollution, such as waste management and environmental "clean-up" projects, not to mention health risks to both consumers and farm workers. One way or another, we all pay for these hidden expenses. The cost of dealing with farm pollution is paid for in the form of higher taxes. Because the public indirectly pays, farm pollution is considered a hidden form of subsidization. When we include the increase in medical expenses and lost productivity brought about by farm pollution, the overall cost to society is compounded. If these "external" costs were reflected in the actual prices consumers paid, the financial inefficiency of modern agriculture would be exposed.

David Suzuki, scientist and environmentalist, sums up the viability of organic farming:

> According to a landmark 21-year study recently published in the journal Science, organic farming can produce good yields, save energy, maintain biodiversity and keep soils healthy. The study took place on 1.5 hectares (3.7 acres) of land in Switzerland, using four farming methods and several different crops. Crop yields, on average, were 20 percent lower using organic methods, but they required 56 percent less energy per unit of yield. Organic plots also had 40 percent greater colonization by fungi and microbes that help plants absorb nutrients, three times as many earthworms and twice as many pest-eating spiders.

Guy Dauncey, an environmental activist and author, compares conventional and organic farming productivity:

> In 1998, the Rodale Institute in Kutztown, Pennsylvania, published the results of a 15-year study that compared three ways of growing maize (corn) and soybeans: a conventional chemical rotation method, an organic system involving crop rotation and legume crops, and an organic system using cow manure. The yields were similar for all three systems, debunking the myth that organic methods cannot feed the world.

We commonly think that modern farming methods have been a huge success because, over the past century, they have drastically reduced the percent of the American population directly involved in farming. Large-scale agriculture would supposedly free people to contribute to society in other ways, thereby adding to the overall productivity of the economy. While it is true that the number of small family farms has shrunken enormously during the past 100 years, it has been estimated that the actual percentage of people employed in the total, combined agricultural support industries has remained almost identical. By this measurement, the real increase in productivity has been questionable.

Long ago, farms were more self-contained and provided local regions with most of their food. They did not require the enormous infrastructure of specialized modern agriculture to run their farms efficiently. Now food travels an average of 1,500 miles from farm to table. This requires a massive energy consuming transportation system that delivers food that is neither fresh nor nutritious. When we take into account the millions of people employed in supportive industries, such as farm equipment, agricultural chemicals, specialized production facilities, and distribution, we discover that the independent farmer has been replaced by a gigantic agricultural industry.

Millions of small, independent farmers have been replaced by a handful of giant farming corporations. Instead of being eliminated from the farming industry, however, former independent farmers have found less gainful employment in other agriculture-related industries. Consequently, there has been a migration of population from small farms to mechanized industry, accompanying a massive transfer of wealth from individuals to corporate ownership. In light of these alarming facts, the true value to society of modern farming needs to be reassessed.

If we calculate the devastating cost of pollution, soil depletion, and inferior food quality resulting from modern agriculture, we might ask, "What is the worth of having lost so many of our traditional family farms, the bedrock of our rural society?" In exchange for the supposed efficiency of modern farming industries, great numbers of small towns have shrunken or disappeared because of the transferring of unemployed farm labor from rural areas to large cities.

In stark contrast to modern, mechanized, chemically driven farming practices, the organic movement in agriculture values local production, chemical-free farming, and a healthy environment. The basic tenet of organic farming is that food grown by natural means is safer than chemically grown fruits, vegetables, and grains, as well as more nutritious.

The Practice of Natural Agriculture

Purpose

Natural Agriculture teaches how to achieve sufficient, healthy, and safe food production. In general, the more purified the condition of people, animals, plants, and soil the better will be their overall condition. Eating pure food helps the body release old toxins and gain new strength. And when we spend time either gardening or walking in the woods, we feel purified and rejuvenated by the beauty and sanctity of nature. Nature exists within our own bodies as well as in the surrounding environment, and by learning to trust nature we simultaneously learn to trust ourselves. This overall trust promotes a harmonious relationship between the external world and us, and is one of the keys to inner peace.

One of the higher purposes of the Natural Agriculture movement is to promote a love for humanity and a true respect for nature, both of which are considered to be essential attitudes required for creating an ideal world. Some other purposes of this movement are to foster gratitude in our hearts, to restore a sense of unity between people and nature, and to help people awaken to the sacred dimension in life. Meishusama says that if a non-spiritual person practices Natural Agriculture with diligence, he or she will eventually become spiritual. On a physical level, the movement aims to improve human health by producing harmless, delicious, and highly nutritious foods.

From a spiritual perspective, Natural Agriculture is seeking to produce food that contains a powerful spiritual essence and life force, which can often be tasted as a vital freshness. A healthy condition can be attained from achieving a balance between body, mind, and spirit; and this will be brought about when we have a proper relationship with nature, of which our body is an extension. Natural Agriculture offers a practical opportunity for people to discover their essential relationship with nature and to directly experience a sense of wonder at the miracle of life.

Basic Methodology

As fostered by Meishusama, the Natural Agriculture approach goes beyond most organic farming methods in its fundamental respect for nature. The farmer demonstrates this respect by:

- Not using compost as fertilizer.
- Not using aggressive methods to control pests.
- Viewing plant sickness, wind and rain damage, and insect infestation as necessary forms of purification.
- Growing crops well suited for the local environment.
- Using seeds derived from earlier crops.
- Cultivating a loving relationship to the land, crops, weather, insects, and wildlife.

Therefore, Natural Agriculture does not attempt to suppress pests or counteract environmental damage with either chemicals or natural remedies. This form of farming is very gentle and non-invasive to the land and that which grows in it. Most significantly, it deeply trusts the natural processes of nature. As a result, it does not add nutrients to the soil, which most methods of organic farming do. In addition, Meishusama stresses the fundamental importance of the farmer cultivating a grateful heart along with a deep respect for nature. These feelings are viewed as the spiritual elements that support healthy, abundant crops.

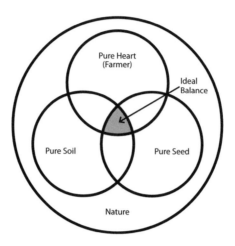

Three Essentials of Natural Agriculture

Principles of Nature

Nature itself embodies truth. For this reason, whatever you plan, it is extremely important to have nature as your guide. Learning from the principles and processes of nature is essential to success. Since the spiritual healing and non-fertilizer growing methods that I advocate, along with other things, have their foundations in this principle, almost no failures occur when using these methods, and the hoped for outcomes always come about.[1] – KW

Natural Agriculture is based on a number of assumptions and principles concerning nature and its relationship to the farmer. These principles offer spiritual guidance to the farmer, as well as a foundation for practical day-to-day work on the farm.

---

[1] Meishusama, "Wait for the Right Moment," *Shumei Magazine*, vol. 268 (March /April 2007).

1. **God created nature and exists within nature**. Humans are not separate from nature or God.

2. **Nature is perfect**. It does not need to be changed or improved upon by us.

3. **Nature is beautiful**. Nature is God's artwork.

4. **Nature is abundant**. It provides us with everything we need for life and enjoyment.

5. **Nature is truth**. This truth is revealed through studying nature and its various processes.

6. **Nature seeks balance**. Sun, rain, wind, trees, grasses and animals—all move toward balance and harmony with each other.

7. **Nature evolves**. All of creation is constantly evolving to higher levels.

8. **Everything has a purpose**. Each and every person, creature, plant, and thing has a mission to help further the realization of Heaven on Earth.

9. **Everything consists of spirit, mind, and body**. Everything has the ability to perceive, feel and react. In this sense, the natural world is conscious and intelligent.

10. **Everything is composed of fire, water and earth**. The invisible force that animates all living things is a product of the intricate mixture of these three spiritual elements.

11. **Nature is holistic**. Everything is connected to everything else. Nothing exists by itself.

12. **Nature is regenerative**. Everything in nature goes through a cycle of creation, sustained existence, and disintegration, after which its various components are recycled back into the larger whole in order to support new creations.

Meishusama did not list these principles as such, although they are clearly implied in his teachings on Natural Agriculture.

The people who practice these truths may not intellectually understand them, but they intuitively comprehend them in their hearts.

The Heart of the Farmer

Plowing in the sunshine, painting when it rains, I happily tend my garden on this late spring day. – Meishusama VI. MK

Natural Agriculture offers an alternative to our destructive lifestyle by advocating the cultivation of humility and reverence towards nature. The Natural Agriculture farmer views nature as his partner, not as his adversary. Rather than dominating the land, he cooperates with it.

Only with profound humility can we learn how to live and work with our natural world. In this regard, we have much to learn from the indigenous traditions living for uncounted millennia in harmony with the environment. "Nature can teach us everything," says Meishusama. *(A Great Agricultural Revolution. HT)* If we observe nature with an open heart, we will begin to discover its innate beauty and divinity. This view of nature as sacred closely echoes that of the Eastern traditions of Taoism and Shinto, as well as that of Native Americans.

By paying close attention to the leaves and soil, the insects and birds, the wind and rain, and the sun and sky, we grasp the interconnection of everything. The growth of a tree affects the sunlight below it, and the movement of the wind determines which crops become pollinated. Observing these phenomena reveals the hidden unity within nature, inspiring awe.

Nature will reveal itself if we will only look. – Thomas Edison

The Natural Agriculture farmer's occupation is more a vocation than an ordinary business. He or she must possess the physical means, diligence, training, and intelligence of conventional farmers, and also a spiritual capacity. Such farmers improve the spiritual well-being of others as well as of themselves. Also, they must love what they do because we are present in the here and now only when we love what we're doing. Along these lines, Nature Farming advocate, Masanobu Fukuoka, states, "Just to live here and now—this is the true basis of human life."

Of course, one should not be mislead into thinking that Natural Agriculture farming is easy. It's hard work. Weeding, plowing, and harvesting can be tedious and exhausting, but so too can many other activities that people voluntarily engage in, such as recreational sports, musical performances, physical exercise, and dancing. On the plus side, though, physical exertion tends to pull us out of our mind, with all its attendant anxieties and preoccupations, and brings us back to our senses so that we can more fully appreciate the natural beauty of the surrounding environment. When we become peaceful and quiet inside, we begin to truly see the beautiful shapes and colors of the plants and trees, smell the subtle but rich aromas of the earth and its diverse vegetation, and hear the sweet songs of birds in the trees, and the gentle rustle of leaves in the wind. The practice of Natural Agriculture is not only practical; it is also a meditation on beauty. And as the effects of this meditation sink deeper into our hearts, we may find that many of our physical discomforts do not bother us so much anymore, and feel more like passing clouds in the sky. We may also find that touching the soil helps to ground us so that the inner tree of our spirituality can take root and grow toward the heavens above.

We must learn to pace ourselves so that, although we work hard, we do not overexert ourselves to the point of pain and exhaustion. It is important to feel happy, not miserable, while gardening because our moods affect the growth of the crops we cultivate. We live in a conscious universe in which everything affects everything else. All of nature, including the soil, the weather, rocks, plants, and insects, respond to our thoughts, intentions, and feelings. What we project outwardly determines what comes back to us. So, if we want a happy world, we need to radiate happiness.

There is another important thing I would like to stress here. Up until now people have believed that conscious reflection of thought and will, which functions as reason and emotion, was limited only to animate beings. To our very surprise, however, even inorganic beings have the same ability; and not to mention soil and plants, which do as well. – *NA*

Plants attached to biofeedback devices in laboratory experiments have demonstrated the ability to respond to a human being's thoughts and feelings. By extension, it is quite probable that the bacteria and microorganisms in the soil will also respond to the farmer's inner state of consciousness. Not only are we all intimately connected, but also from a higher perspective, we are all One.

We are not separate from our environment, for it is what feeds, clothes, and shelters us. When the hills and valleys, forests and meadows, lakes and streams are gone, replaced by endless housing tracks, parking lots, and shopping malls, how will this affect our souls? Do we need the beauty of the natural environment for our basic sanity and happiness? The raw material for creating and maintaining our physical bodies comes from the land. In this regard, we are quite literally not only a product of, but also an expression of, our natural environment. What we do to our environment comes back to us in the food we eat, the water we drink, and the air we breathe. The ecological sciences confirm this basic unity of the organism and the environment, which includes plant, bird, animal, and man. Albert Einstein wrote: "A human being is part of a whole—the universe. Our task is to free ourselves from the delusion of separateness—to embrace all living creatures and the whole of nature."

The Natural Agriculture farmer presumes the existence of an innate intelligence residing within nature, one that is fundamentally benign and life sustaining. The more he studies the natural world, the more wisdom he discovers there. As a result, he is incapable of dominating the environment, but instead, is in conscious relationship with it.

Only when one subject relates to another subject is love possible. This is different from an object-to-object relationship, in which each ignores the inner awareness of the other. When we relate to others as objects, there is no need to be kind or considerate. Objects can be used as a means to an end, whereas subjects are an end in themselves. We can ignore our impact on things but not on conscious beings. Within all things there exists a "point within the circle," an inner awareness. By acknowledging and honoring this awareness within the soil and plants, the farmer activates nature's life force to produce abundant yields. His gratitude towards the life around him for its generous gifts is like the gratitude one feels towards trusted friends.

Therefore, for example, if farmers pray to God—with gratitude—for successful harvests of the rice plants they are growing, their sincere attitude will surely be answered by the plants. Since modern science knows nothing about these invisible things, it tends to avoid dealing with them. This is a seriously problematic tendency that science is still adhering to. – NA

The Natural Agriculture farmer sees his work as an extension of his spiritual life. The hard work is more than made up for by its many benefits—both physical and spiritual. He is not overly focused on future goals because the gentle art of farming is fulfilling in itself.

In stark contrast to this is the one who works at a job only for the sake of a paycheck at the end of the week. Because he does not enjoy this part of his life, he must seek fulfillment elsewhere. Such perpetual seeking fosters misery no matter where one goes because it creates a habit of dissatisfaction. Tending a garden may offer the perfect antidote to these tendencies. Gardening is both therapeutic and life enriching. Many of our inner conflicts miraculously disappear when we touch the soil and nurture new life. Working with nature helps us to slow down and relax. Nature is innately peaceful, and if we remain open, our gardens can communicate this peacefulness to us. Gardening does not have to be full time. Anyone can practice Natural Agriculture farming during his or her spare time.

The Spiritual Basis of Natural Agriculture

Spirituality is at the heart of Natural Agriculture. This spirituality operates on three levels: that of perception, feeling, and action.

1. At the level of perception there is the subtle recognition of an invisible, conscious presence that permeates all things.
2. At the level of feeling there are friendly attitudes towards the natural world.
3. At the level of action there is gentle, cooperative interaction with the soil, the crops, wildlife, and the surrounding environment.

Perception, which is immaterial, corresponds to the spirit of fire. Feelings, which affect and are affected by both the immaterial and the material, correspond to the spirit of water. Actions, which occur in the material world, correspond to the spirit of earth. All three levels of spirituality are essential in order to successfully practice Natural Agriculture.

The consciousness within plants, soil, water and air respond well to positive feelings and gentle behavior. Crops, in particular, thrive when they are acknowledged and appreciated by humans. Therefore, the farmer is encouraged to cultivate such inner qualities as love, gratitude, reverence, joy, kindness, humility, and serenity.

Spirituality is based on attitudes, perceptions, and behavior. Thus, the farmer is encouraged to always:

- Cultivate feelings of love, gratitude, humility, patience, serenity, joy, and wonder.
- Develop sensitivity to the consciousness within all of nature.
- Recognize that everything in nature is interconnected.
- Strive towards balance and harmony.
- Learn from nature and strive to cooperate with it rather than dominate it.
- Value the profound dignity of life.
- Appreciate the sublime beauty of nature.
- Cherish crops as blessed gifts from nature rather than mere merchandise produced for profit.
- Become familiar with each and every plant in the garden or field.
- Mentally communicate with the plants, soil, water, weather, insects, and wildlife in the local area.
- Act with gentleness and kindness.
- Recognize the mutual interdependence of customer and supplier.
- Value customers and co-workers.
- Be grateful for the opportunity to offer healthy produce to customers that can bring them both nourishment and pleasure.

Similarly, customers are encouraged to eat their food with gratitude. Over time, a circle of gratitude forms between the farmer, the crops, and the consumer. Farming in this way fosters a peaceful mind, a joyful heart, and gentle behavior, which can be viewed as elevated expressions of fire, water, and earth, respectively.

Importance of the Soil

The essential activity within Natural Agriculture is the radiating of compassionate love to our most basic resource for living: the crops we raise for food. This love extends to the soil in which the plants grow, as well as to the entire ecosystem that makes up the farm. Honoring and loving the farmland is not simply idealistic, but is also practical because it creates tangible improvements in the quality of the food grown.

Natural Agriculture places the highest importance on the purity and power of the soil, which is the basic substance of our Mother Earth. Topsoil is not simply "dirt;" rather, it is a complex mixture of minerals, organic material and living organisms. This mix of components is crucial for soil to support productive plant growth.

Healthy soil is inherently alive and full of life force. The life force is a mystery that is beyond the grasp of science, with its narrow measurement of objective phenomena. Our connection to the earth is obvious because it is the place where our physical bodies will eventually return after we die. The way to draw the fullest potentiality from the soil is by treating it with kindness. Fertilizers and chemical soil treatments are never used. Only naturally occurring nutrients enrich the soil, but these are not added deliberately. Compost is not used as a nutrient, but only to keep the soil soft, warm, and moist. For this reason, as a general rule, only locally occurring leaves and grass are used for compost, not food scraps or animal manure. In addition, we are strongly encouraged to use seeds produced from Natural Agriculture crops in order to maintain purity.

Consider the differences between the agricultural methods I advocate and current practice. Farmers until today have used fertilizers and human manure, and have achieved some temporarily good results. But these fertilizers kill the soil and make it progressively less fertile. The farmers are blinded by the temporary success of the fertilizers and fail to notice the underlying reality until finally the fertilizers poison both the soil and the people. – Meishusama *(It Is Not True that "Honesty does not pay." HT)*

The soil is the basis of agriculture, and its profound function is too deep for modern materialistic science to fathom. Meishusama writes, "Soil was made by the Creator in order to produce crops to nourish and sustain humans and animals. Therefore, its essential nature is that of a fertilizer; it is, we could say, no less than a great mass of fertilizer. This fact has been unknown before today, and people have mistakenly assumed that fertilizer provided nourishment to crops, and have used all sorts of man-made fertilizers. As a result, the essential nature of the soil has almost been destroyed. People say that Japanese soil is acidic and this is because of the process described above." *(A Great Agricultural Revolution. HT)* Based on Meishusama's insights, soil itself can be considered the primary source of nutrition for life.

Modern commercial farming, with its demand for high crop yields, does not recognize the essential power of the soil. Rather, industrialized methods depend on forms of artificial power such as complex machinery, chemical fertilizers, soil-improvement chemicals, and animal manure. In the long run, as a result of these heavy doses of artificial power, soil can deteriorate enormously, suffering from manure poisoning, over acidity, mineral imbalances, compactedness, and microorganism destruction. This deterioration destroys the soil's innate power to produce truly nutritious crops. In his book, *The Soil and Health*, Sir Albert Howard, a British agrarian, stated, "The using up of fertility is a transfer of past capital and of future possibilities to enrich a dishonest present: it is banditry pure and simple."

In a nutshell, the propagation of our agriculture method can be summarized as a movement to overcome the superstitious belief in fertilizers. – NA

Spiritual Presence in the Soil

Even soil and plants have consciousness. This is an important point that farmers shouldn't neglect. In this sense, it is essential for them to love and respect the soil, and to prevent it from being polluted as much as possible. Since the soil and plants have such nature just as animals do, it is understandable that they would be very upset and resentful if they had human waste or strong poisons poured on the top of their heads. I can imagine that the soil all over Japan is now pretty angry. – NA

Meishusama claims that three universal principles underlie all of physical creation. These are the spirits of fire, water, and earth. The spirit of fire descends from the sun, the spirit of earth rises up from the center of the earth, and the spirit of water, guided by the moon, circulates these two energies. On a chemical level these principles manifest as the elements of oxygen, hydrogen, and nitrogen. Although the spirits themselves are unknown to science, nevertheless, it is the spiritual presence within each of these three elements, and their intermingling within various proportional combinations, that enlivens matter and supports the growth and development of all life forms.

The spirit of fire has the physical attributes of light, heat, and gaseousness; the spirit of water has the physical attributes of fluidity and wetness; and the spirit of earth has the physical attributes of density, coldness, and solidity. When all three principles are present and balanced in the soil, the soil becomes warm, moist, and soft.

The energy X that I mentioned earlier is an undetectable power made by the fusion of the spirits of fire, water, and earth. Although this energy [by its mysterious nature] does not allow me to give it an accurate name, I conceive that it is the source of everything in the universe, and that it is a fertilizing element in itself. Soil is a substance made up of a condensed atmosphere of those spiritual elements existing in a well-balanced three-in-one condition. The density of this spiritual atmosphere is changeable; it increases and decreases according to humans' thoughts. If people love and cherish the soil enough, the spiritual density (liveliness) of the soil will increase. This is the real fertilizer. As you see here, this kind of fertilizer is invisible, and it can hardly be considered as an object of modern science. Actually, I would say that science operates more as an obstacle to discovering the true nature of the soil. – NA

The key to creating healthy soil is a deep inner relationship between the spirit of the farmer and the living spirit within the earth. Because the soil is inherently sensitive and intelligent, it is able to respond to the heart of the farmer. When the soil is kept pure and is touched by a sense of love, its spiritual presence becomes thick and powerful. According to Meishusama, this spiritual presence operates in a manner similar to what is attempted through the use of fertilizer. But unlike some fertilizers, which damage the soil, this presence is the true life force that animates all life. As such, it is essential for growth and health. This spiritual principle is the key to understanding Natural Agriculture. The way to know this subtle force is through our hearts.

Respect and love towards the soil helps fully draw its potential power in yielding crops. The key is to keep the soil free from contamination and to purify it. In response to such attitudes and care, the soil, with a sense of gratitude, will rejuvenate and revitalize itself. – *NA*

Fundamentally, the practice of Natural Agriculture is a spiritual pursuit. When practicing Natural Agriculture, it is important to observe a reverence towards both the soil and its bounty, and to cherish and honor that which gives us nourishment. This requires the spiritual nourishment of the grower, which is the basis of all physical nourishment. Much, therefore, depends on the attitude and commitment of the farmers who choose to pursue Natural Agriculture.

Purification of the Soil

Meishusama has this to say about our attempts to fertilize the soil:

The center of the earth is a huge ball of fire that is constantly radiating heat, that is spirit, to the surface. This takes the form of nitrogen fertilizer given to us by God. It rises up through the surface of the earth and gathers at a certain height in the air, after which it is carried down by rain and soaks into the soil. This natural nitrogen fertilizer falls, as it were, from Heaven, and is of course completely adequate in quantity; it is never too much and never too little.

There is a reason why people started using nitrogen fertilizer instead of this natural type. During the First World War, Germany was faced with bad food shortages and had to increase crop production sharply. . . . The Germans discovered how to extract nitrogen from the air and thereby increased production greatly. Since then this technique has spread all over the world, but the initially good results cannot be carried on for long. Eventually the soil will become over-saturated with nitrogen and weakened, and crop production will consequently fall in quantity. Most people cannot comprehend this basic principle. They stick to their mistaken ideas as a drug addict clings to his drug." *(A Great Agricultural Revolution. HT)*

The huge ball of fire at the center of the earth has both a physical and a spiritual aspect. The spiritual aspect is a powerful energetic presence that sustains the entire planet and all that lives on it. The subtle radiations from this ball of fire rise up through the ground and give vitality to the soil, to plants, and to all living creatures. A sensitive person, when exposed to this force, will feel calmly energized. Unfortunately, when chemicals pollute the soil, a dense layer of toxicity is created that short-circuits the flow of energy to the surface. Urban environments, with their asphalt roads and parking lots, and their pervasive use of chemicals and other synthetic materials, are especially devoid of this vital energy. The loss of this energy in our cities is tragic, for its absence leaves us devitalized and increasingly susceptible to stress and illness.

Crops that have been contaminated by chemical fertilizers and insecticides, although seemingly robust and healthy, are actually weak and sickly inside. And although organic fertilizers and insecticides may seem less harmful, they can also make crops weak and sickly. Like a circle without a point in the center, the plants become hollow shells devoid of life force. Lacking inner strength, they become susceptible to damage by insects, disease and foul weather. Thus the Law of Purification operates to cleanse them of their polluted condition by breaking them down to simpler elements to then be recycled back into nature. Ironically, modern farming's efforts to strengthen crops and eradicate their natural predators actually produce the opposite results over time.

Weeds, on the other hand, do not tend to get disease nor attract so much insect damage. They do not require fertilizers or pesticides to survive in their natural environment, but actually thrive when left alone. Trees in the wild tend to grow large all by themselves, and have been doing so since long before humans arrived on this planet. They also do not require human assistance. How do they do this? The answer can be found in the close study of nature.

Meishusama sees the fundamental cause of human unhappiness as rooted in spiritual clouds. Crops polluted by chemical and natural fertilizers, insecticides, herbicides, fungicides, soil improvement chemicals, and other toxic substances during their production process will promote spiritual clouding in those who consume them, thereby contributing to their unhappiness. Meishusama says that fertilizers invite disease and bugs (who eat the fertilizer), and that parasites feed on organic compost, fertilizer, and manure. These parasites often lay eggs which humans later ingest.

During the first several years after conversion to Natural Agriculture, the soil will continue to be affected by residual chemicals within it, but over time will purify and become rejuvenated. Sometimes, though, when the pollution is excessive, an alternative is to bring in pure soil from another location. Or in more extreme cases, after prolonged use of fertilizer and chemicals, a layer of accumulated toxic residue may be found at a depth of about 30 centimeters beneath the surface of the soil. If a layer of this kind is found, plow the field sufficiently deep in order to completely turn over the soil, allowing it to aerate and break down naturally.

The Mystery within the Seed

Resting within the dark womb of the soil, the humble seed lies dormant, conserving its life energy in anticipation for the arrival of the proper moment for it to awaken. Suddenly, a tiny sprout emerges out of the seed, driven upwards by powerful inner forces. Once again, following a cycle as old as time itself, nature sends a brave adventurer on a journey from hidden darkness to open exposure in the light, reaching up to fulfill its destiny as a fully-grown plant. Soon, if conditions are favorable, it will grow into a tomato plant, a stock of broccoli, a vine of zucchini squash, or a lush head of cabbage.

Although science can analyze and classify the various components of a seed—its chemical makeup, cellular structure, and genetic sequencing—it can never comprehend the awesome mystery of life itself. This invisible life force cannot be viewed in a test tube or studied under a microscope. It can only be known from within, not from without. Life is profound and inscrutable. Without life, our planet would be nothing more than an inanimate heap of lonely rocks and aimless dust, circling endlessly through vast empty space.

According to Meishusama, the only way to understand the mystery of a seed is with the inner sensitivity of one's heart, not with the outer scrutiny of one's head. Love connects us with all things, whereas analysis separates us. Love fosters the growth of life, whereas analytical dissection destroys things by taking them apart. This fact is obvious to any frog trapped in a school science lab.

An incredible intelligence dwells within each seed that is capable of sensing when the optimal conditions are present for the seed to emerge and burst forth as a living sprout. The seed will begin to germinate when the soil reaches the correct approximate temperature range, and there is sufficient water, sunlight, and oxygen available. The seed must also have the inner awareness to sense and interact with the surrounding environment in order for it to respond to these diverse conditions. This inner awareness cannot be measured, but is nonetheless crucial to the successful growth of a plant. Over time, successive generations of seeds grown in the same locality learn how to adapt to their immediate environment, thus becoming increasingly vital and strong in the process. This is why "wildcrafted" herbs and spices are considered by many to be superior to those that are cultivated in even the most optimal of manner. Because of their accumulated wisdom, these native seeds are the most optimal for use when planting new crops.

Within each seed, limited to its particular species, lays the invisible blueprint for a lush cabbage plant, a tall corn stock, or giant sequoia tree. Some sequoias are measured to be over 3000 years old and over 300 feet tall, and yet these trees grew from seeds smaller than a vitamin pill and weighing only 5 milligrams. This fact is amazing to contemplate! The blueprint within a seed is more intricate and complex than the largest manmade building, ship, or airplane. These sophisticated human creations seem trivial in comparison. How these intricate patterns within the seed could be created is a profound mystery sealed within the heart of nature.

Seeds are precious, and it is vital that the seeds used in Natural Agriculture be of the highest purity and vitality because collectively they determine the future of all life on this planet. We can experience a future of health and vitality or one of disease and despair depending on how we nurture the seeds we have been entrusted with. We need only to examine the conditions surrounding the humble seed to discover which destiny we are choosing.

Use of Seeds

Seeds are extremely important. Seeds free from the effects of fertilizer are completely different from those that are artificially fertilized. – NA

A seed is a miniature replica of the entire environment out of which it emerges. The plant that created the seed is a product of the soil, the air, the water, and the sunlight that nurtured and fed it. Thus the seed is a reflection of these conditions. Just as no two locations are identical, no two seeds are identical either. Ask any farmer and he or she will tell you how much the conditions in a garden can differ from one location to the next—even locations that are very close to each other. One location may get too much water, and another may get too much shade. Still another area may have too many rocks, and another may have too much sand. If we look closely at the birds, the insects, and the flowers, we can easily see how unique each one is from the other. Life is indeed an exuberant expression of diversity. Life is also a celebration of individual beauty and intelligence.

Unfortunately, with the continuing expansion and dominance of large, corporate mono-agriculture (one type of crop), the diversity of plants, and especially of seeds, is being dangerously reduced. Variety is nature's way of protecting plant species from being destroyed by disease and unfavorable weather conditions because each variety has unique strengths and weaknesses.

Hybrid plants are increasingly dominating modern agriculture, especially grain crops. According to organic gardener Peter Donelan in his book *Growing To Seed*, "Three crops – wheat, rice, and corn (maize)—account for 50 percent of the calories in the human diet." This makes the quality and reproducibility of grain crops extremely important. He continues, "It is believed by some that hybrids are less nutritious, more demanding of soil resources, and more vulnerable to environmental hazards. Others believe that the additional vigor, uniformity, and increased yields of the modern hybrids are essential for feeding a hungry world and for predictable results in your backyard. The uncontroversial advantage of the standard, non-hybrid varieties is that they breed true [maintain a consistency of quality from generation to generation]."

Genetically modified seeds are those that have had foreign genes implanted into their gene code. Their inner structure is not in harmony with nature, and so should be avoided. Seeds whose genetic makeup is artificially altered do not have the strength and vitality that seeds native to a particular region have. Because of this, use of these seeds threatens the sustainability of agriculture itself. Indeed, some corporations have used genetic modification to create what are called "terminator seeds" because the crops they produce do not create a second generation of living seeds. Farmers who use these seeds are thus totally dependent upon their suppliers each time they plant new crops, and if they fail to get a new supply, they are left with a barren field. Local sustainability is completely lost with such mercenary practices. Commercial seeds also tend to sprout all at once, leaving the entire crop vulnerable to storms, droughts, floods, and other natural forces, whereas Natural Agriculture seeds, with their innate wisdom, tend to sprout at varying times, hence ensuring greater survivability of the crop.

Because of their purity, the most desirable seeds are ones that are obtained from crops grown by the Natural Agriculture method. Seeds from native species and varieties that have been growing in the same area for a long time without human intervention are even better. By developing and adapting to the conditions of a specific locale, they acquire a great strength and vitality. Nature is inherently diverse, with each plant and seed differing from the other. So by using local seeds we help to maintain this plant and seed diversity.

The Natural Agriculture farmer is strongly encouraged to allow a certain percentage of his or her crops to go to seed and to collect them and save them for future use. (They should be saved in a cool, dry place.) These heirloom seeds will continue to adapt to the local conditions of the land, and in the process, become increasingly unique to that farm. Beans, peas, lettuce, tomatoes, or other self-pollinating varieties of plants are the easiest to use as seed crops. Individual plants that demonstrate exceptional qualities are the best ones to choose for this purpose because their seeds will likely produce offspring with those same favorable traits. Heirloom seeds can also be shared with other farmers seeking locally grown, pure seeds, with the hope that they too will begin to save their own seeds from their own gardens and farms.

Seeds are part of the collective heritage of humanity, and are as important to our culture as music, art, and literature. Indeed, it has been said that traditional farming brings culture back into agriculture.

Use of Natural Compost

Look how the soil is covered in a deep rich blanket of withered grasses and dead leaves as autumn deepens into winter every year. This blanket is there to make the soil fertile, and it is this that we should make into fertilizer. You may think that compost supplies nutrition to crops, but this is by no means the case. The essential effect of compost is to keep the soil moist, to warm it and keep it from becoming compacted. Thus the soil absorbs heat and water, and does not become hard. – A Great Agricultural Revolution. HT

One might ask how it is possible to revitalize soil that has lost its mineral content, or has become unbalanced from excessive overuse? To answer this question, consider the fact that trees in the forests and jungles have existed for countless millennium without the need for human intervention to improve the soil. Nature has the ability to rejuvenate herself when left alone or treated with sensitivity and respect.

Evidence has accumulated over the centuries indicating that minerals can transform themselves from one chemical element to another through the agency of living organisms. Professor C. Louis Kervran, of the University of Paris, was nominated for the 1975 Nobel Prize in Physiology for his work on the Biological Transmutation of Minerals in human subjects. Dr. Kervran came to the conclusion that, in humans, these transmutations take place in mitochondrium (cellular components that secrete systemic enzymes). Other researchers have found evidence that microorganisms in the soil might be the agency for similar changes in the land. This transformation appears to occur through the addition or subtraction of protons making up mineral elements. In this way, potassium, with nineteen protons, could be combined with hydrogen, containing one proton, to change into calcium, which has twenty protons. Dr. Kevran postulated the presence of living enzyme activities as the primary catalyst for this transformation in humans.

Earthworms are among the most valuable creatures within the soil. In one of Charles Darwin's last published books, *The Formation of Vegetable Mould through the Action of Worms,* he stated that without worms, vegetation could not survive. Earthworms consume and digest enormous amounts of dry earth throughout their short lives, and in the process transform this earth into rich, vital soil. Darwin estimated that in fields with abundant populations of worms, about one inch of new topsoil could be created every five years.

The point made here is that healthy soil with abundant microorganisms, yeasts, and earthworms has the ability to transform itself and make nutrients available to plants. The correct use of compost to promote soil that is soft, warm, and moist provides the best conditions for these microorganisms to thrive.

Continuous Cultivation

Natural Agriculture recognizes the soil's inherent ability to evolve and adapt to the needs of various kinds of plants growing within it. To maximize this natural adaptive ability, Natural Agriculture farmers are encouraged to practice continuous cropping, the practice of growing the same plants in the same spot year after year. This gives the soil the chance to adapt to the plant and the plant the chance to adapt to the soil. Each exerts a mutually beneficial influence on the other. According to Meishusama, in the long run this method helps increase crop yield.

Advantages

When the original crops absorb chemical fertilizers, they become extremely weak from the poisoning. I have also discovered that this poison provides an attractive diet for insect pests. Furthermore, as I have already mentioned above, these insects can be generated in the first place by fertilizers, and then of course they eat the crops and multiply. – A Great Agricultural Revolution. HT

The Natural Agriculture method, in principle, brings about a drastic decrease in insect damage and helps achieve delicious food as well. When the crops meet with damage by storms or floods, the plants are inherently strong enough to resist being beaten down. Even if they do get harshly beaten, they quickly recover and rejuvenate because of the vitality provided from within. The primary source of this strength is in the roots. "The natural plant has hair roots that are longer and thicker than those of the fertilized plant, and as a consequence is much more firmly rooted," writes Meishusama. *(A Great Agricultural Revolution. HT)*

Conventional farming, by adding fertilizer to the soil, whether chemical or natural, tends to encourage roots to become lazy. The roots are less motivated to reach deep down into the earth for their nutrients. Consequently, they often remain short and shallow, resulting in a weak plant. In contrast, the roots of crops grown by the Natural Agriculture method reach deeper into the ground for their minerals and other nutrients, drawing on the vitality of the earth. These roots are bigger and longer, with a larger spread, providing much greater strength and stamina to the plant. Because of this, the crops are better able to reach their innate potential. The resulting food is safe and rich in nutrition and life force, which greatly contributes to their health-restoring properties.

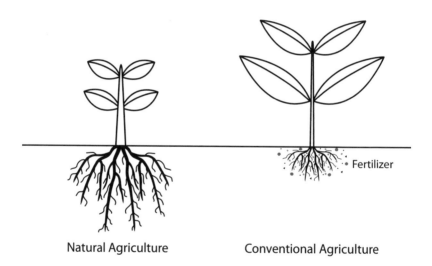

Natural Agriculture   Conventional Agriculture

Comparison between Conventional and Natural Agriculture Methods

Farming as Art

Meishusama calls Natural Agriculture "The Art of Agriculture" because the farmer approaches his work with soil and plants in much the same way as an artist approaches his canvas or stone. Both the artist and the farmer respond from the heart, not the head. Their inspiration is drawn from that which is hidden to the senses but visible to the inner eye of spirit. Natural Agriculture is not merely a scientific method or a collection of techniques applied to farming, but is also an overall spiritual approach to life.

To Meishusama, the world of nature is inherently beautiful in its unself-conscious innocence. Each flower is a gentle song of celebration, and each mountain is a cathedral of towering majesty. Meishusama views nature as the art of God manifesting in earthly reality. In this sense, it is quite suitable to also describe Natural Agriculture as an expression of art and nature as the canvas.

12 ART AND BEAUTY

As our eyes pass over the beauties of nature, an inexpressible joy wells up within us. It would be no exaggeration to call our ideal of heaven on earth "The World of Art," for it is the world of Truth, Virtue, and Beauty, and it is in art that Beauty finds its true expression. – Religion and Art. HT

The Experience of Beauty

The human soul needs actual beauty more than bread. – D. H. Lawrence

In addition to Jyorei and Natural Agriculture, Meishusama puts great value on the appreciation of art and beauty as a way to elevate people's consciousness and to help transform the world. Visiting an art gallery, a concert hall, or going out for a relaxing walk in nature are all wonderful ways to enjoy and benefit from beauty. Beauty lifts us above our personal problems so we can appreciate and enjoy the simple things in life. By contrast, a life devoid of beauty degenerates into a struggle for survival, devoid of meaning, purpose, or value.

Although Spirit itself cannot be made into a direct object of our experience, qualities that emerge out of Spirit can. Love, peace, innocence, charity, gratitude, joy, and beauty are embodied to varying degrees in people, art, and nature. When experiencing great art forms or communing with nature, the spiritual beauty within us touches the inner beauty of the object perceived. This is not an object-to-object relationship, but rather, a subject-to-subject one. In such experiences, objectivity is transcended by something higher and more expansive. Various art forms provide us with an opportunity to be thrown into the moment where we can be more alive and present. At its height, beauty is an experience of the inner unity with all things.

In itself, beauty is transcendent. It transcends all phenomena, including the particular medium, culture, or artist that gives it form. Great works of art are vehicles for the expression of beauty, giving it shape, sound, color, texture, and movement. Neither great art nor great beauty can exist without the other. Art without beauty is devoid of soul, and beauty without art is devoid of substance. Only great art incorporates both in perfect balance.

Art can make us see things we haven't seen before, and inspire us to seek loftier goals. It can change how we feel about the past, present and future and can influence the way we think and act. – Bradlee Sweigart

Meishusama's primary concern is alleviating suffering and promoting universal happiness, and he feels that beauty is central to this. Who cannot feel a serene joy when meandering through a beautiful garden, strolling along the seashore at dusk, or wandering down a pristine mountain path? A simple vase of fresh flowers placed in one's home can bring inspiration and pleasure to one's family and guests, as well as promote domestic harmony. Singing, creative writing, playing a musical instrument, painting, and dancing are also excellent ways to connect with beauty.

A beautiful environment is sure to have the effect of beautifying the hearts of the people who live in it, and crime and evil behavior are sure to decrease. This phenomenon alone will be one of the means of furthering the realization of Paradise on Earth. – Heaven Is a World of Beauty. HT

The Role of the Artist

In the fields of music and art, it is the souls of the artists themselves, as expressed in their various mediums, which most deeply touch the souls of the audience. This is what makes people feel connected through their eyes and ears to works of art. So, if the souls of artists are not spiritually advanced enough, their work will not be truly great. Since artists play an important role by inspiring people through their work, they particularly need to have elevated characters.[1] – KW

Generally speaking, the modern world regards art as a luxury, not a necessity, because people can survive without art, but not without food and shelter. It may be true that cheap trinkets, shallow television series, and crass advertising art have little value, but art that expresses real beauty does have value. According to Meishusama, beautiful art forms are more than mere decoration or entertainment; they are food for the soul. Beauty is necessary because it brings meaning and joy to life. Without it, life becomes impoverished. Although individuals may survive without art, cultures cannot.

Meishusama teaches that life has a greater purpose than that of mere existence. Life is short, but the soul endures. From the vast vantage point of the soul, life's only purpose is spiritual growth. One's spiritual level is what most contributes to happiness because it affects one's general mood and outlook, and also influences the type of people and circumstances that one attracts. People with inner beauty attract other people with inner beauty. In these ways, whatever contributes to one's spiritual growth has enduring value, and beautiful art is one of these contributions.

Meishusama felt that a distinction could be made between art that has spiritual value and art that does not. He felt that much of the contemporary art of his day was ugly, depressing, and vulgar, exhibiting no signs of artistic skill or imagination. It had no higher purpose than to gain recognition or money for the artist. Sometimes the only objective was to shock the public by breaking and defying current social standards and artistic conventions. These criteria, Meishusama felt, were not sufficient.

An artist is only one part of the overall structure of society, and can only produce true art by realizing what his role is and playing it to the fullest. This above all is the duty of an artist.

However, if we think of most of the artists who are active nowadays, we cannot fail to be shocked by their wild and irresponsible behavior. Of course, this is not to deny the existence of a few admirable artists, but for the most part artists seem not so much to have forgotten their duty as

---

[1] Meishusama, "On Being Humble and Flexible," *Shumei Magazine*, vol. 263 (May/June 2006).

to be incapable of understanding it at all. Moreover, they consider that they are "special people," and that egotistical and willful behavior is a demonstration of individuality or a manifestation of genius. Because of this way of thinking, they lead completely selfish lives and are shameless in their behavior. This is indeed a terrible state of affairs. Again, society regards artists as superior in some way and gives them favorable treatment, tolerating most of their excesses. The artists, of course, fall deeper into the illusion of the all-importance of their own egos. To cure this situation, artists must have a character that is far superior to most people's. . . . To put it simply, the mystical power that springs from the artist's soul passes through the written word, through the picture, the musical instrument, the song or dance, and plucks at the strings of the soul of all mankind. This link between the artist's soul and the souls of others is very strong. Because of this, if an artist's character is bad, then all humanity will be debased. And, of course, if an artist's mind is fine and pure, he will elevate the characters of everyone else as well. This is the noblest aspect of art, and the artist must so employ his art as to become a worthy guide for the rest of mankind. – *The Role of Art. HT*

Psychoanalyst Sigmund Freud also held a dim view of many of the artists of his day. In characteristic fashion, he remarked, "The artist is a neurotic...he is doing what he does for honor, power, riches, fame and the love of women."

With this in mind, we may ask, "What is the duty of society to our artists? How can society responsibly support art?" Society has now become so fascinated by the shadow side of people's character that it often fails to appreciate people who are doing good things. We now find it more entertaining to look at people's flaws than at the good things they produce. We have become cynical about human nature, instead of expecting decent behavior from artists and other public figures. Where can we find individuals to respect and admire?

According to Meishusama, two of the most important factors influencing the creation of great art forms are the purity of the artist's soul, and his or her basic intention. If the artist's character is highly refined and is free from excessive selfishness or ego, then he or she will emit a subtle spiritual influence that will be conveyed to the viewer or listener. Some artists of lesser character can also emit such higher influences if their art is created during peak experiences. In both cases, the artist's experience of beauty, along with the great joy and satisfaction they feel while creating their work of art, is communicated to the viewer or listener through the finished sculpture, painting, architecture, music, literature, dance, or play. The outer form of the art—the colors, shapes, textures, sounds, and movements—is not only a vehicle for this inner experience, but also is integral to it. In the best works of art, not a single thing is superfluous or misplaced, and as a whole, there is simplicity of form.

Beauty of style, and harmony and grace and good rhythm, depend on simplicity.
– Plato

The Viewer of Art

Nurture and promote a keen sense of beauty. – Heaven Is a World of Beauty. HT

The world is God's body. It is the outer manifestation of His invisible Spirit. Buildings, cars, trees, and people do not obstruct God, they reveal Him. Those of us who are sufficiently sensitive can experience the divine through an openhearted appreciation of the world around us. This is especially possible in the presence of nature and art because both express beauty. To recognize beauty is to be touched by it, and to be touched by beauty is to be transformed by it. Beauty is a doorway to Eternity.

The arts are not meant to merely entertain, they are primarily meant to express. Something from the artist's inner world of feeling and perception is expressed through his or her art that demands a reciprocal response from the person who encounters it. The arts bring to the surface hidden feelings and values that we do not realize we may have. They call forth something profound from deep within us. Unlike much of the art and music produced by today's entertainment industry, which can be enjoyed in a passive or semi-conscious state, truly expressive art and music require energy and involvement from the viewer or listener for their value to be appreciated.

Viewers of art and listeners of music also have the responsibility to educate themselves about the arts (and society needs to support this education), to cultivate greater sensitivity to beauty, and to refine their own character through spiritual discipline. Otherwise they may fail to appreciate the great beauty that often exists in their ordinary day-to-day lives. Some people can walk through paradise itself but be so consumed by personal suffering that they remain unmoved by the beauty around them. The communication of beauty is a two-way process between the artist or performer and the viewer or listener, depending as much on the openness and sensitivity of the viewer as on the talent and skill of the artist. Objective beauty mirrors the beauty hidden deep within the viewer's soul. During the experience of beauty, this two-way communication dissolves into a unitary communion where there is no separation between the viewer or listener and the artwork or performance.

About the subjective experience of beauty, the Japanese philosopher, Yasuhiko Genku Kimura, writes,

'Beauty is in the eye of the beholder.' This adage is generally understood to mean that beauty is a subjective perception and judgment, different from one person to another, and therefore relative. There is another interpretation: Beauty is precisely in the eye of the beholder because without the [inner] vision that can behold beauty, there can be no experience of beauty. The more we open our [inner] vision for beauty, the more beauty we behold in our eye.

Beauty is a universal quality that is present throughout the universe. Beauty is only subjective in the sense that the kind of beauty that one beholds is determined by the kind of [inner] vision for beauty that one has unfolded. Beauty is only relative in the sense that the degree to which one beholds beauty is proportional to the degree to which one's [inner] vision for beauty is open. (*Beauty as a Path of Peace*)

Therefore, both the artist and the viewer contribute to the experience of beauty—the artist or performer through revealing beauty, and the viewer or listener through his or her sensitivity to and appreciation of that beauty. But this sensitivity and appreciation does not just happen. Beauty, and the recognition of it, must be nurtured. Arts education teaches people how to use their senses. They develop sense-ability. People are better at problem solving and most everything else when they study arts.

Beauty opens our hearts and awakens us to higher values, which then allows us to make better decisions in life. In its highest form beauty produces a sense of wonderment in us, like children gazing wide-eyed at the heavenly stars. Such innocent wonderment is food for our souls.

People with a heart capable of appreciating art are eligible to live in heaven.

– Art. MK

Art Devoid of Spirit

Look about you, look at the literature that plumbs the depths of pornography and cynicism, look at the paintings that go to the extremes of grotesquerie. Amidst the voices of the artists, the clatter of their music, their plays and their films, look deep into your heart and you will know that what I have said is nothing more and nothing less than the truth. – The Role of Art. HT

The essence of art is a mystery. Too specific a definition of art can hamper the creativity that is the essence of art itself. On the other hand, to reject all definitions of art as superfluous concepts, or to dismiss all judgments about art as merely subjective biases, leaves people with no standards to go by. How can people come to a consensus about quality without some form of criteria? Without these, good art cannot be distinguished from bad art, and true talent, when it appears, cannot be recognized or appreciated. This lack of standards is like a ship without a rudder, which is incapable of steering in any particular direction. The end result is an alarming situation in which beauty and refinement are ridiculed, and ugliness and profanity are admired. In our modern era, we need not look far to find numerous examples of this depressing trend.

A belief popular in today's academic world is that all meaning and values are culturally conditioned, and consequently have no objective validity. From this perspective, what one person may judges as good art, another can justifiably condemn as bad art. If everything is subjective—and therefore relative—then who can say which appraisal is most valid? And if we are left with no standards to go by, then how can we reach any social consensus? Some might question the need for social consensus, and instead assert the greater importance of individual freedom. Although individuality is indeed important, we must also remember that we live in societies, and societies make group decisions based on shared values. It's usually groups of people who choose the types of artwork to put in museums, the shapes of buildings to erect, and the ideas and values that are taught in schools; and if they cannot agree on anything, then the person who shouts the loudest will win. If this trend towards cultural relativity continues too far, then soon schools may be teaching that gangster rap music is of equal merit as Beethoven's symphonies or that Shakespeare's plays are no better than urban graffiti. This is not such a wild stretch of the imagination because other forms of rap and hip hop music are already being taught in some of our schools.

In actuality, however, this subjective relativism is not really so unbiased, for this stance often is used to elevate and promote art, architecture, literature, movies, and music that are disturbing, shocking, or merely clever. This may be because sensationalism draws more attention to itself than does subtlety. In such a distorted cultural environment, beautiful works of art are regularly dismissed as shallow, old fashioned, naïve, or merely commercial, and beauty itself is often scorned.

It is sometimes said that everything is art. But if everything is art, then why bother to put anything in a frame or perform anything on a stage? The very fact that we do so indicates that we consider that particular art, music, or play to be uniquely valuable. We are obviously putting it in a special place in order to draw attention to it. On the other hand, if everything is equally valuable as art, then should we put the entire universe inside a special frame or concert hall? And if everything is art, then there is no reason to even use the word art, because a word only has meaning when it can be contrasted with its opposite—non-art. Saying that everything is art is like saying that everything is up, or that everything is big. Up and big have no meaning unless they can be compared with down or small.

The same can be said about the word good. Can all art be good? How can there be good art without the existence of bad art? Value judgments depend on contrast in order to have meaning. And is it really possible to avoid all value judgments?

How often do we see buildings that seem to defy the laws of gravity or some other functional or aesthetic standard that leaves the average person feeling alienated and uncomfortable? Is there any beauty in these structures? When music has so much dissonance, atonality, and disjointed structure that it is impossible for the audience to emotionally relate to it, does this strangeness promote the aesthetic experience or uplift the human spirit? And are works of art that appear ugly to the vast majority of people successes, or failures? Of course aesthetic tastes vary from person to person, but everyone has a threshold as to how much dissonance, atonality, asymmetry or chaos they can appreciate. Beauty is as important to the soul as food is to the body. And where else should people go to experience beauty if not to art?

The role of art is surely to heighten people's emotions, to enrich their lives and to give meaning and enjoyment to their existence. – Religion and Art. HT

Of course, there have been many instances in the past where a piece of music or a work of art was rejected by the public or the critics but which later became highly acclaimed and popular. Examples include Stravinsky's "Rite of Spring" ballet score, which provoked shock and outrage in the concert hall during its debut performance, Richard Strauss' opera "Salome," which caused a riot when it opened, the artist Picasso's painting "The Ladies of Avignon," which was very controversial at the time, and the works of impressionist painter Cezanne, which gained public recognition only after he died. Such instances of rejection usually occur when the piece introduces dramatically original structures, themes, or patterns. The mind is often disoriented, and the emotions disturbed, by that which is new and unusual. People need time to familiarize themselves with the unfamiliar before they can mentally and emotionally connect with it. This type of reaction also occurs in people when confronted by the customs and products of foreign cultures, which they do not understand. On the other hand, most art and music that's popular today will most likely slip into obscurity when current fashions change.

Inaccessibility, in and of itself, is of no inherent value. The difference between noise and music depends on the degree of harmony, structure, and meaning it contains. When there is no pleasure in listening to music or viewing art, can it be said to be beautiful? Of course, music or art that is shallow or merely pretty is often not very pleasurable, and usually lacks genuine beauty as well. One of the challenges for the arts and the artist is to bring out the hidden beauty buried within dark, painful, or disturbing experiences. This is its transformative power. The philosopher George Santayana stated, "The subject matter of art is life, life as it actually is; but the function of art is to make life better."

In modern times, the standards for evaluating art have become so confused that often pornography or clever works of cultural criticism are proudly displayed as examples of leading edge art. These works may touch our senses and our minds, but not our souls, for there is no joy in them. It's the Spirit within art that ennobles it, and when communicated effectively, this Spirit also ennobles the viewer or listener.

Art must be full of laughter and joy, a thing full of interest and excitement.
                                                  – *Religious Pragmatism. HT*

Transformative Art

Beauty is not just for one's own personal satisfaction; it brings pleasure to the eye of the beholder, and in this sense is itself an act of virtue. As the level of civilization becomes higher, so do the things in that society become more beautiful. Think about it. – Heaven is a World of Beauty. HT

When an artist's spiritual awareness is highly developed, combined with a great mastery of the techniques of his art, he or she is then capable of both receiving aesthetic inspiration as well as skillfully communicating it. He or she functions as a suitable vessel for Spirit. The result can be the creation of a work of auditory, visual, tactile, or written art that truly touches a person's soul. Such art appeals to the mind, the senses, and the heart. "Fine art is that in which the hand, the head, and the heart of man go together," wrote John Ruskin, an influential art critic and connoisseur of the Victorian era.

While many artists embody high standards of character that, in turn, are reflected in their work, there are also artists who appear to embody the opposite standards of character, and yet may still produce marvelous works of art. These latter types of artists may suffer from inner torment and depression. Yet during the creative process, while painting, composing, singing, or writing, they get absorbed in higher states of consciousness where everything is experienced as a single flow of ecstatic energy. At this time of pure creativity, the stark division between subject and object is suspended, and they enter into a sublime realm of profound inspiration and inner peace. This is sometimes described as an experience of timeless unity, where everything flows together in wondrous harmony. Unfortunately, this may be the only time when these artists feel free from their tormented lives. This would explain their compulsion to constantly create; it's their desire to be transfixed into a higher dimension. The higher perception that results from this experience is then communicated through the work of art to the viewer or listener. What is communicated is the energy of the artist's vision combined with his or her intention, knowledge, skill, and ecstatic joy.

I dream my painting, and then I paint my dream. - Vincent van Gogh

Viewed objectively, all great or transformative art exhibits qualities of clarity, proportion, integrity, and symmetry—not a rigid symmetry, but one that, like nature, incorporates a degree of asymmetry and spontaneity which gives it life and movement. This is symmetry at a higher, more comprehensive level. It gathers together disparate elements of perception, revealing a greater unifying whole. Great art also has a dynamic energy and passion, either obvious or subtle, which fully engages the viewer or listener. Viewed subjectively, all great or transformative art offers the perceiver a glimpse of reality as seen from a higher perspective—revealing it to be simultaneously extraordinary and ordinary. Through this art, we are given a profound vision of both heaven touching earth, and earth touching heaven. In other words, this art is divinely inspired. It gives us an experience of eternal beauty that transcends our mundane sensory perceptions. In this way, art can be a powerful vehicle for spiritual experience. The novelist and essayist, Albert Camus, expressed this idea well: "Beauty is unbearable, drives us to despair, offering us for a minute the glimpse of an eternity that we should like to stretch out over the whole of time."

Profound beauty has the ability to take our breath away. It awakens our spirit by bringing us a glimpse of the sacred. Through the experience of beauty, our mind stops, and we are transported to a higher realm of radiant splendor. This is one of the most important contributions of art: the ability to bring spiritual perception down into our mundane world while simultaneously lifting our ordinary consciousness up into the divine realm. Unlike more ascetic approaches to spiritual experience, art does not dismiss the world of the senses, but actively embraces it. Art sees Spirit in the world, not above it. Art illuminates the shadowy world of the senses, revealing hidden mysteries within the most ordinary or mundane of objects. This is another example of what Meishusama called 'the point inside the circle.' That point is Spirit itself, which is located in the heart of all things. Through art, we can embrace Spirit as it expresses itself through form.

Nothing is more hallowing than the union of kindred spirits in art. At the moment of meeting, the art lover transcends himself. At once he is and is not. He catches a glimpse of Infinity, but words cannot voice his delight, for the eye has no tongue. Freed from the fetters of matter, his spirit moves in the rhythm of things. It is thus that art becomes akin to religion and ennobles mankind. It is this which makes a masterpiece something sacred.
       – *Hideo Kishmoto, Mahayana Buddhism and Japanese Thought*

This experience of beauty may occur even though the subject matter may be of a most mundane or even disturbing nature. A painting such as Pablo Picasso's Guernica, about the horrors of the Spanish Civil War, or Henryk Gorecki's Symphony of Sorrowful Songs, about the suffering at the Auschwitz Concentration Camp during World War II, can reveal great beauty and spiritual depth, not in spite of, but because of the subject matter. These two pieces radiate a powerful and universal Light from within their outer darkness. Beauty has the ability to transform a negative experience into something sublime and ennobling that nourishes and deepens the soul. This can be done without denying the objective unpleasantness or even tragedy of the subject matter. Just as spiritual love, by its universal embrace, can heal and transform even the most repulsive of things, so, too, does the artist's creative talent reveal the beauty hidden within all things. This inner beauty is the soft breath of God.

Beauty is one of the rare things that does not lead to doubt of God.
                                        – *Jean Anouilh, French playwright*

The Purpose of Beauty in Art

I keenly believe that wonderful artworks should not be secluded, but should instead be shown to as many people as possible, to give them enjoyment and elevate their [character]. In this way, fine arts contribute greatly to the development of culture, and this is the true purpose of art.[2] *– Meishusama*

Art has two primary purposes: to provide pleasure, and to support spiritual growth. Both the individual and society as a whole can benefit from art that elevates the soul, and that promotes heaven on earth. So central is art to civilization that it is not an exaggeration to say that there would be no civilization without it. About the significance of art, Meishusama adds, "The progress of culture is demonstrated most clearly in the appreciation of beauty within that culture." *(Heaven Is a World of Beauty. HT)* A civilization that does not value beauty can hardly be called civilized.

Our highest aspirations are given outer expression in the arts. They ennoble humanity through their gifts of great beauty and sensitivity. The aesthetic experience is an entrance to a transcendental unity wherein all separations fall away. Art explores the heights of the sacred while simultaneously embracing the depths of the profane. From its all-encompassing unitary vision, it cannot reject either heaven or earth because it sees them as one integrated whole. Beauty is a seamless fusion of form and formless, and of spiritual nourishment and sensual pleasure. It also reconciles both the rational and the feeling parts of human nature.

Just as a loving person can inspire us to see the good in others, so too, can great art reveal the hidden beauty that normally escapes our eyes and ears. As the painter Paul Klee stated, "Art does not reproduce the visible; rather, it makes visible." In this way, beauty and love are closely related. Both enrich our lives, and both transform the world around us. As the Christian mystic Evelyn Underhill writes, "All things are perceived in the light of charity, and hence under the aspect of beauty; for beauty is simply reality seen with the eyes of love."

Enjoyment is the other purpose of art. The simple pleasure that art brings is more than enough justification for its existence. This pleasure is a purposeless purpose, because art does not point to a goal outside of itself. Its beauty is its own purpose. Therefore, it is best not to have a purpose in mind when experiencing art, but instead to appreciate art for its own sake, simply

---

[2] Meishusama, "The Origins of the Hakone Museum," *Shumei Magazine*, vol. 195 (November 1996).

because it is beautiful.

The role of art is surely to heighten people's emotions, to enrich their lives and to give meaning and enjoyment to their existence. – Religion and Art. HT

Living a Life of Beauty

Beauty is the purgation of superfluities. – Michelangelo

Beauty celebrates the joy of living. We can easily bring beauty into our daily lives by the way that we speak, behave, and dress, as well as in the appearance and cleanliness of our homes, cars, and workplaces. Simple things like putting flowers in our home or office can significantly raise the atmosphere in these locations. Many people grow flowers in their yards or windowsills for this reason. Making an attractive impression on others by our style of dress is another way to incorporate beauty into our daily lives. Listening to music that brings joy and inspiration, or that deepens our capacity for genuine feeling and appreciation, is both convenient and inexpensive. We can also create artwork ourselves. We do not need great skill or talent to do this, although it can help to take art classes to improve our knowledge and skills. Whatever our personal capacities, it is enriching just to sing, paint, dance, sculpt, write, or play musical instruments because creativity can help expand our appreciation of beauty.

When I decorate my room with a camellia from the garden, I feel the pleasure of the world. – Art. MK

Most important of all is the cultivation of inner beauty, because God lives in a beautiful heart. A warm smile, a cheerful disposition, and actions that are gentle and kind, are all simple ways to express this inner beauty. Such behavior is elegance of the truest kind. Truth tempered by love and elevated by beauty of expression is guaranteed to promote happiness everywhere.

Heaven is a world of beauty, and the hearts of those who live there are beautiful as well. – Art. MK

13 SHINJI SHUMEIKAI

This organization, on the other hand, as my followers know, makes "A world without sickness, poverty, or strife—Paradise on Earth" its central slogan, and works for the benefit of all mankind.

– A Sense of Justice. HT

Organizational Background

General Information

Shinji Shumeikai, also known as Shumei, is an international spiritual organization dedicated to elevating the quality of life for all of humanity. It is committed to creating an ideal state of health, happiness, and harmony by applying the wisdom and spiritual insights of Meishusama to a variety of human activities. Since the founding of the organization, Shumei has been best portrayed as a fellowship that places the highest value on cultivating a grateful heart and praying for the happiness of others. These values are essential to the teachings of Meishusama. Helping others was Meishusama's primary concern, and a feeling of gratitude and love were at the core of his dream of creating a Paradise on Earth.

Growing primarily out of Meishusama's spiritual revelations, Shumei also has some roots in the Shinto tradition of Japan. Shinto is an integral part of the cultural heritage of Japan, and to this day influences many of its attitudes and customs. Shumei shares Shinto's deep reverence for nature, and it incorporates some of Shinto's ritual practices and chants in its various religious services. Although Shumei has some religious traits, its principle mission is not otherworldly; it seeks to help build an ideal world here on earth. It is in harmony with all religious traditions that promote peace and happiness. In other words, it is a comprehensive, practical approach to bringing spiritual growth and overall happiness to people. Many members find that their association with Shumei enhances and deepens their current religious beliefs and spiritual practices.

Today, there are over 300,000 members of Shumei worldwide, with centers in over a hundred cities throughout Japan, as well as in North and South America, Europe, and Southeast Asia. Under the leadership of Ms Hiroko Koyama (whose formal title is Kaicho-Sensei), Shumei has expanded its global work for world peace through its three main activities: Jyorei, Natural Agriculture, and the arts. In recent years, believing that the twenty-first century offers critical opportunities to realize the Founder's vision of global peace and world citizenship, the organization has taken a more active role in international activities. Shumei's goal is not only to raise the individual to a more enlightened level of consciousness, but also to create a world of peace, health, and prosperity.

Historical Background

Shumei was originally formed under Meishusama's guidance in 1949 in Kyoto, Japan, by one of his foremost students, Mihoko Koyama, whom Shumei members respectfully refer to as Kaishusama (meaning "the organizational founder" or "most revered leader").

Mihoko Koyama was raised in a family with a pious faith in Kannon, the Buddhist deity of wisdom and compassion, and was also deeply inspired by Christian educators in her latter school days. During this time, she acquired both the spirit of humanism and a faith in God. Her first encounter with Meishusama was in 1941, about a year after her initial experience of Jyorei through a student of his. In those days, Jyorei was called the Okada Style Spiritual Acupressure Treatment. This initial experience occurred during World War II, while her husband was overseas fighting at the front lines. During those years she had to take care of her three little children all by herself.

In these difficult circumstances, Kaishusama felt fortunate to have been introduced to Jyorei and its healing powers. Putting her full faith in Meishusama, she decided to devote her entire life to serving God's Will and to helping others. As she became active in sharing Jyorei, demonstrating its great effectiveness, and caring for others with love and affection, more and more people were drawn to her. Gradually, a group formed, consisting of those who were attracted by Kaishusama's selfless dedication to helping others and by her loyal devotion to Meishusama. With a sincere heart, and Meishusama's guidance, she worked passionately to create the foundations of Shumei. This name Shumei, meaning "Supreme Light," was the name given by Meishusama to her group in April of 1949.

After World War II, Meishusama established the Japan Kannon Society *(Nihon Kannon Kyodan)* in 1947, and then created the Japan Miroku Society *(Nihon Miroku Kai)* in 1948. Until those two organizations became united under the name of Sekai Kyuseikyo[1] in 1950, Shumei belonged to the Japan Miroku Society. The creation of Sekai Kyuseikyo involved the integration of approximately eighty groups of Meishusama's disciples in various parts of Japan. The groups were of differing sizes, but all shared a self-sustaining power and independence from their mother organization. However, after Meishusama's passing in 1955, Sekai Kyuseikyo began moving toward more standardized policies and centralized direction. As a result, some of the original groups broke away.

From the earliest days of Sekai Kyuseikyo, Shumei, under Kaishusama's leadership, took an active role in sharing Meishusama's teachings with others, and contributed significantly to the organization. As a result of this, in 1967, Kaishusama attained an important administrative position in the organization. However, this new, deeper involvement in the central functions of the Sekai Kyuseikyo soon put her in a difficult situation. She began to witness things that made her feel that the organization was deviating from Meishusama's spirit, and was becoming corrupted by greed and power. Included in her concerns, at this time, was the beginning of an aggressive restructuring of the organization into greater centralization of power. After painful deliberation, she decided, in February of 1970, to separate her Shumei group from Sekai Kyuseikyo along with her original group. She felt this action was necessary to

---

[1] Sekai Kyuseikyo was originally called Sekai Meshiyakyo.

maintain the purity of Shumei. Recollecting the day that she decided to leave the organization created by Meishusama, Kaishusama commented, "It was the longest day in my entire life."

Shumei's withdrawal from Sekai Kyuseikyo was unexpected and shocking to both its affiliated members and to the headquarters of the mother organization. Consequently, it was inevitable for Shumei to face bitter conflicts and turmoil, both among its own members, and with those of Sekai Kyuseikyo. In this whirlwind of chaos, Kaishusama and her first son, Sokichi Koyama, respectfully known as Mikotosama, soon returned to using some of the ritual-related items put aside by Sekai Kyuseikyo after Meishusama's passing. These included the Zengensanji prayer, the Kannon Screen, and the Daikokusama statue (each explained in the following pages). Most importantly, Kaishusama and Mikotosama resumed using Meishusama's original calligraphies as their holy scrolls. At that time, they tirelessly endeavored to console and unite the hearts of members who might have been confused or upset. Although most of Shumei's members had sufficient trust in Kaishusama to willingly follow her in the new direction, others needed time to be persuaded and convinced.

The 1970 break with Sekai Kyuseikyo was one of the most traumatic struggles for Shumei. In accordance with Meishusama's teachings, these struggles were viewed as a purification process rather than a meaningless or unfortunate hardship. During these dark and painful times, Kaishusama and Mikotosama reaffirmed the spirit of Meishusama, and firmly resolved to stand on their conviction that the Founder's spirit was still alive and well among them. Three months after giving initial notification of independence from Sekai Kyuseikyo, Shumei gained legal independence as an organization. Thus, Shumei was born again, and began to further Meishusama's legacy with even greater dedication. (The word *Shinji*, which means Divine Love, was added to the name *Shumei* at the end of 1970.)

In order to bring Shumei's members back to the original spirit of Meishusama's teachings, Kaishusama and Mikotosama strongly encouraged them to actively introduce Jyorei to the people of the world. Soon, members began going door-to-door, offering Jyorei to people in their homes. Others stood in public places, including parks, train stations, and college and university campuses, inviting passers-by to receive Jyorei. The members exhibited a great deal of passion and dedication at this time, and the membership continued to grow rapidly. In particular, many young people became involved with Shumei, drawn by all the excitement and powerful spiritual experiences so many of them were having.

For those who followed Kaishusama's and Mikotosama's spiritual guidance, it was obvious that the power of Jyorei, instead of weakening, as claimed by some, had become much more potent. Various miraculous events occurred through Jyorei. Shumei members interpreted these abundant miracles as a divine message, indicating their strong connection with the spirit of Meishusama.

Blessed by the Divine Light of Jyorei, Shumei recovered its vigorous momentum, and in 1972 purchased the vast forested land in the Shigaraki Mountains, east of Kyoto, which was later transformed into their primary sanctuary called Misono. With great courage and determination, Mikotosama inspired members to support the construction of Misono, which he personally directed during the final ten years of his life. The most magnificent building in Misono is Meishusama Hall, where members attend regular services (sampais) to chant and exchange Jyorei. Its creation in 1983 was a truly remarkable achievement. In July of the next year, at the age of forty-eight, Mikotosama left this world. But his spirit lives on and still touches the hearts of everyone who visits there.

After his passing, under the spiritual guidance of Kaishusama, the seeds of faith Mikotosama had sowed and cultivated, particularly in youth members, blossomed into new leaders who continued to share Meishusama's teachings with the world. Consequently, the membership steadily increased and, in addition to the centers in Hong Kong and the United States, new centers were later opened in many other countries. To succeed Mikotosama, his younger sister, Hiroko Koyama, worked closely with Kaishusama in supervising the entire Shumei community. In 1992, Kaishusama began promoting Natural Agriculture as well as planning the construction of the Miho Museum. In 1994, Hiroko Koyama became the third president of Shinji Shumeikai, and was given the formal title of Kaicho-Sensei.

Beginning in 1997, after years of intense activity focused on bringing Jyorei to people's homes and to public places, Shumei decided it was time to redirect its efforts toward promoting greater balance within individuals as well as throughout the organization. It was felt that in order to better help others, Shumei needed to focus more on self-cultivation, Natural Agriculture, and art.

Following the opening of the Miho Museum in late 1997, Shumei began to establish a public presence that continues to this day with lectures and seminars, interfaith activities, and performances of taiko drumming. In 2002, with the opening of Shumei International Institute in the state of Colorado,

USA, Shumei's three sacred sites were completed: the other two being Misono, high in the Shigaraki Mountains, and the Center on Kishima Island, in the midst of the Seto Inland Sea, to the west of Osaka, Japan. In 2003, the Shumei Natural Agriculture Network was established to bring the principles and techniques of Natural Agriculture to the general public. In 2004, Shumei acquired consultative status as a Non-Governmental Organization (NGO) with the United Nations.

After a long and meaningful life dedicated to Meishusama and his vision of universal enlightenment, Kaishusama left this world in November of 2003. Her enormous achievement, in the face of formidable obstacles, of creating Shinji Shumeikai and vastly expanding its membership, is a living testament to the greatness of her character. Her love, inspiration, and guidance is constantly felt and appreciated by many throughout Shumei.

Our organization wishes to bring harmony to all mankind and to make the whole world into one family. Because we believe in this kind of pacifism we recognize all religions as our colleagues and will link hands with them in mutual amity as we go onwards. – Citizens of the World. HT

Three Sacred Grounds

In line with Meishusama's teachings concerning the significance of the three spiritual elements, Shumei has constructed centers at three special locations: Misono, representing fire; Kishima, representing water; and Crestone, representing earth. The centers serve as sacred pilgrimage sites where visitors can commune with the unique spiritual energies found at each location.

Misono

Shumei's international headquarters moved from Kyoto in 1983, and assumed permanent residence in Misono in the Shigaraki Mountains east of

Kyoto. Misono, meaning "Sacred Garden," was created to serve as an archetype of the heavenly world that Meishusama envisioned. The site on which Misono stands has been considered sacred since ancient times, when five Shinto shrines occupied the area and protected its serenity. The foremost architects, artists, engineers, and craftsmen collaborated in creating this sanctuary of beauty and spirituality. At Misono, nature, art, science, and technology come together to form an archetypal prayer for peace, prosperity, and beauty for mankind and the world.

In the beautiful surroundings of Misono, one of the most outstanding pieces of architecture is Meishusama Hall. Completed in 1983, it was designed by Minoru Yamasaki (1912-1986), who also designed the World Trade Center's Twin Towers in New York City (lost in 2001). Resembling the shape of Mt. Fuji, the structure is supported, amazingly, by just four curved pillars. The structure is sixty meters in width, ninety meters in length, and fifty meters in height. This masterpiece by Yamasaki was realized with the aid of his engineering partner, Yoshikatsu Tsuboi (1907-1990), a leading authority on structural dynamics. It stands as a symbol of peace, happiness, and well-being for all mankind.

> Entering the sanctuary of Meishusama Hall, you will see a vast, light-filled space. The structure enclosing this space is supported by four gracefully arching pillars that rise to a height of fifty meters. Nature's beauty is forever a presence within the Hall as the glass walls that encircle most of the interior allow one to enjoy the surrounding gardens and mountains. So, both man-made and natural beauty are entwined in the ambiance of this great building.[2]

Misono functions as: Shumei's primary spiritual center; a sacred pilgrimage site; the organization's international administrational headquarters; a spiritual training facility for young *hoshishas* (volunteer workers who learn how to selflessly dedicate their lives to God and Meishusama). One of the major events that Misono periodically hosts is a spiritual gathering referred to as the Monthly Sampai. At these events, and others, Misono welcomes mem-

---

[2] Kaicho-Sensei, "Shumei's Three Sacred Places," *Shumei Magazine*, vol. 255 (Jan./Feb. 2005).

bers and guests from all over the world. Especially during the Grand Sampai in early May, members from different countries visit Misono to celebrate the legacy of Meishusama and the birth of Shumei.

Meishusama Hall

Because Misono is located high up in the mountains—where the spiritual Light is most intensely focused—it is generally regarded as an embodiment of the element of fire. Fire is warm and bright, with its flames rising upward to the heavens. It burns impurities in order to create new beginnings. Fire is sacred because its light illuminates our daily existence.

Heaven's Portal

Kishima Island

Located in a designated nature preserve in the midst of Seto Inland Sea, west of Osaka, Japan, Kishima Island is blessed with abundant scenic beauty. Shumei originally acquired some of the island in 1962 as a place where children and young people could cultivate their inner nature by getting in touch with nature.

The construction of our first Center on the island began soon thereafter. It was built by volunteers who hand-carried the construction material to the highest point on the Island. In 1989 a new center sanctuary was built to replace the original structure. The exterior of the building is shaped like a seashell, in acknowledgement of the sea that surrounds it. The interior of the sanctuary is unique in that it is constructed of concrete, stainless steel, and glass. Through the large windows you can see the vast expanse of the sea, including a spectacular view of the evening sunset. After the sanctuary's completion, Kaishusama said, "Kishima Island is surrounded by the sea, and the sea is what connects us to the whole world." She envisioned the island as a base from which Shumei's message would spread over land and sea so that one day all people could benefit from the values and ideals that Meishusama promoted.

Since Shumei's purchase, the island has also been devoted to the research and practice of Natural Agriculture. Fields of crops can be seen throughout the island, demonstrating the wonderful variety and wholesome quality of food produced by this natural practice.

There are two camping villages on the island. A series of camping trips for children, including one for the physically and mentally challenged, are held each summer. Young Shumei members experience the natural splendor of Kishima by attending summer camp on the island, and by learning the art of Natural Agriculture throughout the year. Kishima is also being developed into an environmental research center that will host conferences on conservation and the promotion of an environment free of industrial chemicals. Increasingly, Kishima is serving as a spiritual retreat center, hosting various workshops on communication, personal growth, and spiritual development.

As a place surrounded by water, Kishima Island is generally regarded as an embodiment of the spiritual element of water which flows laterally and accepts all things by permeating and dissolving them into itself. Water is sacred because it is the source of all life.

Shumei International Institute

Shumei International Institute (SII), a non-profit organization, was created in 2002 in the community of Crestone, Colorado. It is located on a thirty-five acre site, 8,300 feet above sea level, in the Sangre de Christo Mountains of the San Luis Valley. Shumei was drawn to this location by its natural beauty and spiritual energy. Other spiritual and religious groups from throughout the world also have felt this place's special allure and built ashrams, monasteries, and retreat centers along the mountainside.

> Crestone is a place where many religious and spiritual centers have sprung up; among them are Christian, Buddhist, and Hindu sanctuaries. Each tradition represented there has its own goals and activities. Yet, despite their differences, these diverse people in Crestone have become friends and live in harmony with one another. They do not close themselves off from the practices and values of others. They truly engage in interfaith activities.[3]

Inspired by the teachings of Meishusama, SII helps people of the world—through broad educational exploration—in all areas realize that they are citizens of the world. The Institute's headquarters, which are also used as the Shumei Crestone Center, provides an environment for spiritual growth through interfaith activities, the practice of Jyorei, and Natural Agriculture, as well as art, environmental, and cultural events. It offers programs for training young people in leadership skills, caring for our precious natural environment, and respecting the diversity of cultures and people.

Because SII is dedicated to the ecological concerns of the environment, and is located in the largest high-altitude valley on earth, SII is generally regarded as an embodiment of the element of earth. In line with this symbolism, it was built using the best available regenerative technologies to sustain the earth and to show respect for the surrounding environment. Earth is heavy,

---

[3] Ibid.

dense, and solid. It provides the physical matter from which all material things are created. It is sacred because it supports and sustains our manifest existence.

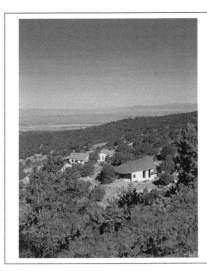

Crestone center

With the completion of SII in Crestone, Shumei's three sacred sites were established embodying the elements of fire (Misono), water (Kishima), and earth (Crestone). According to Meishusama, when all three of these elements are harmoniously combined, a dynamic, creative energy is unleashed. Since the establishment of this third sacred site, many have noticed an increased level of Light within Shumei, as well as a trend towards greater openness and creativity. The opening of SII was thus a significant milestone in Shumei's ongoing mission to disseminate Meishusama's message and to create an ideal world here on earth.

The Miho Museum

For someone who has knowledge of art and literature, to gaze at the flowers of spring, the autumn leaves, or a view of the mountains or sea, is delightful.
– Religion and Art. HT

Shumei's commitment to encouraging the arts led to the creation of the Miho Museum in 1997. Meishusama wanted everyone to experience art, not only for its spiritual benefits, but also for its pure pleasure and enjoyment. He taught that, "A museum is a symbol of an ideal world."

Inspired by Meishusama's ideals, Kaishusama initiated the planning and construction of the museum, guiding the process every step of the way. She received enormous support from her daughter, Hiroko Koyama, who oversaw all the practical details of the project. The word "Miho," in Japanese, means 'excellence in beauty,' and it is also the first two syllables of Mihoko Koyama's (Kaishusama's) first name. Thus the word serves two purposes: to honor the creator of the museum, and to highlight its key theme.

Located in the Shigaraki Mountains an hour and a half drive from Kyoto and less than a mile from Misono, the Miho is a stunning design and engineering achievement. In addition to Kaishusama's private collection of traditional Japanese art (now housed in the North Wing), the museum's collection has expanded to include thousands of ancient masterpieces from throughout Eurasia and Egypt (located in the South Wing). It is now considered one of the most impressive art collections in Japan. A visitor here has the combined benefit of viewing an outstanding array of traditional art, a building of dramatic yet elegant beauty, and an exquisite natural setting of mountains, trees, and sky. Not only does the surrounding landscape add to the beauty of the museum, but it also contributes to its spiritual influence. Meishusama called the world of nature "God's Art."

Designed by one of the world's greatest architects I.M. Pei, the Miho Museum evokes the image of a traditional Japanese temple while embracing the aesthetics of modern design. Of significance is the quantity of light that floods into the building through the glass walls and skylights, which are supported by large metal beams arrayed in strikingly geometric patterns. Through the abundance of glass, the building seems to expand to the outside surrounding landscape, allowing the art of nature to contribute to the collection.

With eighty percent of the structure contained within the mountain slope, the Miho Museum is not intrusive, but instead blends harmoniously with the landscape. This consideration for the inherent beauty of the land is a reflection of Meishusama's love and respect for nature. This unity and harmony with nature is a source of inspiration for visitors who come to the Miho Museum.

In addition to welcoming visitors from around the world, the museum holds special exhibits, symposiums, seminars and lectures for children and adults. The Miho promotes art and beauty as a transformative experience for humanity's spiritual advancement.

A visit to the Miho might call to mind a spiritual pilgrimage, in which a traveler seeks out a remote place to find contemplative peace and spiritual guidance. Here, both transcendence and aesthetic enjoyment come together in a seamless harmony that is heavenly as well as down to earth.

Miho Museum

Entrance Hall

Waterfall in Misono

The primary source of Jyorei, as described in earlier chapters, is the spirit of fire, which is one of the three fundamental spiritual elements in the universe. It dispels spiritual clouds accumulated in our spiritual body just as fire burns combustible material. In line with this, Jyorei is often referred to as purification by fire.

In addition to the healing of Jyorei, Shumei offers another distinctive form of healing, one that clearly symbolizes the power of the spirit of water. Water has been commonly used as an important medium for purification in religious communities throughout the world, including the two main religious traditions in Japan, Shinto and Buddhism. In both of these traditions, people who come to visit their temples or shrines are customarily advised to rinse their mouths and wash their hands before entering the sacred area. Water is used to purify the defilements of people, which they accrue during their daily life, and to help them prepare for moving into the sacred dimension.

In Shumei, water also has this value, and it is also used for the same purpose as mentioned above. There is usually a stone fountain or spring at each Shumei center for a simple purification ritual: rinsing the mouth and washing the hands.

Such places where water purification occurs are called mitarashi. Among the many places where it is practiced, the Shumei Kyoto center (former international center) and Misono (present and permanent international center), in particular, are quite noteworthy because of the remarkable healing properties found in the water.

The healing by water first appeared in the Kyoto center's mitarashi, a stone fountain designed in the shape of a five-petaled plum flower. It was around the beginning of 1975 that the first report of its healing effects first came to light, and since then a number of healing incidents have been reported, among which are healing from brain tumors, gastric ulcers, lung cancers, skin diseases, impaired hearing, toothaches, rheumatism, burn injuries, etc.

When Shumei's headquarters was transferred from Kyoto to Misono in 1983, Misono's mitarashi, called 'Kumo Ga Taki', began showing similar healing properties, and its water is now regarded as highly sacred.

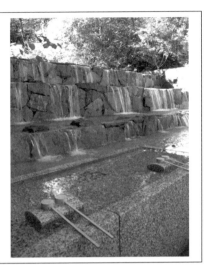

Waterfall in Misono

It seems natural for one to compare this miraculous water in Misono with that of Lourdes in France. Interestingly, the healing effects of mitarashi at the Kyoto center emerged after a group of Shumei members led by Kaishusama visited Lourdes, following which Kaishusama had an audience with Pope Paul VI in May of 1974.

Although we have no explanation as to why and how such 'miracles' started, the effect of healing is undeniable, and members of Shumei take it as a divine gift from God and Meishusama.

Shumei's Symbol of Light and Power

The history of the world, up until today, has been characterized by two different cultural traditions: Eastern culture, which leans towards spirituality, and Western culture, which leans towards materialism. And, since both cultures veer toward extremes and are not integrated with each other, nothing goes well for them. This situation does not bring any real solutions to humankind's suffering and the unstable condition of the world never seems to end. Observing this, I believe that the creation of an ideal world culture is not possible without the harmonious union of the vertical and the horizontal. So what concerns us is when, if ever, these two aspects will be united, and to your surprise, that the very moment is now. Our mission is to assist this important event, which is perfectly symbolized by the design of our organization's emblem.[4] *– KW*

Shumei's official symbol is a circular form with four curved shapes extending out from a central circle. The horizontal axis of these shapes represents water, the element that flows and spreads horizontally, and the perpendicular axis represents fire, the element that burns vertically. Fire represents shojo (conservatism), and water represents daijo (liberalism). The circle in the middle represents the spirit of Izunome, the balance and harmony between these two opposite principles. It relates to Meishusama's analogy of the point within the circle, indicating spirit within matter—that which animates all living things.

These two elements of water and fire combine to produce Light, which radiates out from the spiritual presence located within the center of the circle. This spiritual presence is the Light of Jyorei.

The curvature of the four curved shapes indicates movement, and symbolizes spirit in motion. The overall form is bending clockwise, symbolizing the power to establish truth, virtue, and beauty in the world. It is the divine power of God manifesting in the realm of time and space.

The Official Symbol of Shinji Shumeikai

[4] Meishusama, "Vertical and Horizontal," *Shumei Magazine*, vol. 269 (May/June).

We will start a civilization that revolves clockwise. Our task is to establish a completely civilized world, a world of Light.[5] – *KW*

The Shumei Taiko Ensemble

Taiko drums are Japanese musical instruments traditionally used to help celebrate religious festivals and special occasions. They are also used in traditional Japanese plays and in martial arts events. Shumei's taiko performances are non-verbal prayers for world peace. Shumei often uses taiko drums during Sampai to strengthen and amplify chanting through the agency of their powerful vibrations.

The dynamic rhythms and invigorating sounds of the taiko clears the mind, bringing people's awareness back into the present moment. This heightened presence allows for greater receptivity to the spiritual influences of chanting and Jyorei. The abrupt, sharp sounds of taiko heighten the contrast between sound and silence, while simultaneously uniting them through the experience of pure beauty. Many people discover an inexplicable feeling of deep serenity amidst the booming intensity of the taiko.

Since the Shumei Taiko Ensemble was founded in 1982, it has come to occupy an eminent place in the world of Japanese performing arts. Acclaimed for its mastery of traditional taiko technique, the Ensemble has built upon these techniques to create a pure, strong, and exhilarating form of taiko performance that is modern and original.

Recently, the Ensemble has performed not only in Japan, but also in other countries at events such as the Parliament of World Religions in Cape Town, South Africa (1999) and Barcelona, Spain (2004), and the World Peace Summit for Religious and Spiritual Leaders at the United Nations headquarters in New York City (2001). The Shumei Taiko Ensemble continues its mission of uniting the hearts of people around the world through the captivating sound of taiko.

---

[5] Meishusama, "Creating the World of Light," *Shumei Magazine*, vol. 251(May/June 2004).

During the "World Festival of Sacred Music" in Cape Town in 1999, the group performed in front of 5000 people. This event was initiated by His Holiness the Dalai Lama to mark the approaching millennium with a message of peace, cultural understanding, and spirituality.

Shumei Taiko Ensemble

Recently, many local Shumei centers have been forming taiko groups of their own. These groups have been especially popular amongst youth members. Beyond the obvious esthetic experience, involvement in these groups also helps promote character development, stressing self-discipline, reliability, and cooperation.

Shumei Taiko Ensemble

14 SHUMEI'S RITUALS

The Purpose of Rituals

Some people question the functional purpose of rituals and wonder if they have any relevance in this modern, scientific day and age. Yet even such questioners would probably feel a little disappointed if they attended a birthday party where no one sang "Happy Birthday," blew out the candles on a cake, or gave presents. The same would also apply to weddings and funerals, which rely on rituals to channel emotions in a meaningful way. All of these events are organized to publicly acknowledge an important social event, and their various rituals provide people with a feeling of satisfaction and completion. Important gatherings, such as inaugurations and award presentations, are often highlighted by colorful rituals or ceremonies. They transform what could be a mundane occasion into a special event. Thus, to omit these rituals would result in an unfocused and meaningless event that would have no emotional impact.

The purpose of sacred rituals is to reinforce certain thought and behavior patterns. They are very powerful ways to focus the mind. When we bow upon entering a Shumei sanctuary, we are reminding ourselves to value and respect the sacred objects and activities that occur there. Bowing reinforces reverence and gratitude, and helps to integrate these attitudes into the physical body by converting subjective thoughts into objective action. Sacred rituals also harness the power of symbolism, which communicates higher truths to the subconscious mind. Through repetition, ritual encourages character development and induces spiritual experience.

Scroll of Light

Located on the altar within each Shumei sanctuary is a sacred Scroll of Light containing an exact reproduction of original calligraphy done by Meishu-sama. The Scroll of Light at most local centers has two Chinese characters inscribed on it: one signifying "Bright" and the other signifying "Divine Light." Centers that operate as regional headquarters each have a Scroll containing three characters that indicate "Great Bright Light." As an embodiment of Divine Light, the Scroll of Light is an object of deep veneration for members of Shumei, although what is actually focused on during Sampai is the energy and ideas behind these symbols rather than the visible characters, themselves.

It is customary for the Scroll to be enshrined behind a special screen that is only opened during Sampai. In Misono, an original Scroll created by Meishusama himself is located behind Meishusama Hall, housed in a special eight-sided annex called "The Octagonal Shrine" (Shinden).

Scroll of Light

Usually, there is a floral arrangement to the side of the Scroll, affirming Shumei's belief in beauty as a form of spiritual nourishment, and also a picture of Meishusama, in honor of his role as the "Bringer of Light." Beneath the Scroll is an offering stand, a pair of candles, and a flower arrangement. The stand is also used for daily offerings of gratitude consisting of water, rice, and salt. These humblest of foods constitute the essence of nourishment, and it is these essences that are offered to God, whose spiritual presence is intensified in the altar area.

Sampai

Sampai is a Japanese word meaning "going to a higher, spiritually pure place for spiritual purposes." Specifically, Sampai is a form of ritual that, through its structure, provides a sense of order and serenity to the mind. (In Shumei, a Sampai can be conducted either individually or collectively, and will include the sharing of Jyorei when more than one person is present.) Each Shumei center has its own daily scheduled Sampai gatherings, with at least one in the morning and one in the evening. In addition, every month a larger group gathering, called the Monthly Sampai, is held at each center during which a sensei (teacher) gives Jyorei en masse to everyone who attends on that day.

Sampai is, in essence, a precious moment of communion with the Divine, and a process of purification attained through prayer, chanting, and Jyorei. The more often one comes to a Sampai, the more one's spiritual cords connecting to God and Meishusama will be strengthened. Receiving Jyorei during a Sampai heightens the power of the energy, thereby accentuating healing and spiritual growth.

Collective Sampais, such as the Monthly Sampai, are especially significant because the more people who attend, the greater the energy becomes. The monthly gathering is meant to readjust and improve one's relationship with God and Meishusama, and to function as a joyous celebration. Even though the Monthly Sampai is designed with a large group in mind, it is usually maintained as a simple ceremony.

Those members who have smaller-sized Scrolls of Lights enshrined in their homes also conduct public or private Monthly Sampais there. It is an honor and a blessing to have a scroll installed in one's home, as it brings much Light into the area. Having a scroll enshrined in one's home entails a good deal of responsibility on the part of the recipient. It is both an honor and a mark of dedication to the ideals that Shumei embraces. Also, in many homes there are altars with Kannon Screens dedicated to deceased family members and ancestors. The Kannon figure on the screen is a copy of a brush painting that was rendered by Meishusama.

Maintaining a Kannon screen is an act of reverence for our departed loved ones who exist in the spiritual realm and who often help us from that invisible location. The positive energy that we send to our ancestors by honoring them with gratitude and sacred chants before this special altar helps to purify and uplift their consciousness. This benefits us as well as them, because the higher their spiritual level, the greater their capacity to help us in times of need.

In your house, you should perform respectful services of enshrinement in front of the altar, which insures the purification of the entire household's spiritual form.

– Fire and Jyorei. HT

Otamagushi

Otamagushi, a financial offering given before attending a Sampai, is a Japanese word meaning "pure human heart (or pure intentions) aligned with the heart of God." An alternate meaning is "a pure human soul and God's Spirit joined as one." Offering Otamagushi is an essential part of the Sampai, equal to washing the hands and rinsing the mouth, and it helps prepare our minds for contemplation and prayer during the Sampai. Whether small or large, what is put in a white envelope to offer at the front of the Sanctuary is important if it comes with gratitude for all the blessings given to us by God. If one does not have the financial means for giving Otamagushi, then an act of hoshi at the center, such as washing the sink, sweeping the grounds, or mopping the floor, can be an appropriate substitute. Both are good ways to express the sincerity of one's gratitude. The intent behind Otamagushi is to give back to God a portion of what has been given to us. One whose heart is full of gratitude comes to realize that all things are gifts from God.

Shumei Chants

The Amatsunorito

The Amatsunorito, which literally means the Prayer of Heaven, is the basic chant recited during Sampai. "Amatsunorito" is comprised of two words, "amatsu" and "norito." "Amatsu" means "heavenly," and "norito" refers to a type of ancient Japanese ritual-prayer that stems from the Shinto tradition.

According to Meishusama, the universe is filled with invisible ether through which inaudible sounds are carried. In many ancient cultures the belief has existed that the manifest world was created by the frequencies of these sounds. Meishusama explains that there are seventy-five primal sounds in the universe that are in continual vibratory motion.

In addition, there are five root syllables that are considered to be the essential conveyors of spiritual power. When these five sounds are vibrating out of harmony, the universe is thrown into disarray. The Amatsunorito incorporates all five syllables throughout its length, and when chanted with the correct tone and rhythm, and with pure intent, balance and harmony are restored in the world.

The power of chanting is based on the underlying principle of Kototama, the concept that every word has a spiritual power inherent in its sound, irrespective of its actual meaning. The idea of certain root sounds having special divine power is similar to the Eastern concept of Mantras, which are used for meditation and inner transformation. The Amatsunorito, in particular, with its unique combination of sounds, is used to purify the spiritual world, the condition of which affects the physical world. Meishusama believed that this chant was a particularly powerful means of purification. In accord with the principles of Kototama as well as his own spiritual insights, Meishusama slightly refined this ancient prayer to make it even more potent.

The origin of the "Heavenly Prayer" is ancient and obscure, the author or authors are unknown. Its language is archaic, and most modern Japanese cannot comprehend the words. This is comparable to a modern English speaker attempting to understand the original text of the Beowulf epic, which roughly dates to the same time as the Amatsunorito. To understand the Amatsunorito's literal meaning, the following background in Japanese myth is helpful.

The demigod or kami, Izanagi, defiled himself by entering the underworld to bring his dead wife, Izanami, back to the world of the living so they could continue to create the land in which they and their descendants were to live. When he found her on the other side of the gates of the palace of the dead, she told him with deep regret that he had come too late. For she had already eaten the fruits of the underworld—literally from the ovens of hell—and could not return to the land of the living without permission. She made him promise to wait for her and not follow or even look at her until she safely returned to him. She left Izanagi and went to plead with the rulers of the underworld to release her. A very long time passed as Izanagi waited. Finally, impatient, he broke his pledge and entered the netherworld to find his wife. When he did, he looked at her and saw that her flesh was putrefied and consumed by maggots, and the sounds of every kind of thunder emitted from her head and limbs. She cursed him for his betrayal and sent hoards of demons to pursue him. He picked up three peaches, imbued with divine power, and threw these at the demons, chasing them away. Once he reached the realm of the living again, his wife appeared one final time on the other side of death's gates. So, man and wife, Izanagi and Izanami, stood at opposite sides of the border between life and death, she respectfully threatening to kill all his descendants, he with due courtesy pledging to produce more progeny than she could ever manage to kill. Finally, after much conflict, he rolled a boulder over the maw of Hades and left.

Although escaping death, entering the kingdom of the dead had left him impure, and so he washed himself in the waters near the small mouth of a river surrounded by a field of evergreens at Himuka Tacibana (Tachihana) in Tsukushi. And as Izanagi bathed, from out of his body sprang numerous newly born deities.

The story is, of course, fantastic. Yet, it has universal implications that echo in legends and myths throughout the world. Westerners might recognize similarities in Izanagi's story with that of the primal father Adam and his first wife Lilith, or that of Orpheus following Eurydice into Hades. All these stories are meant more to entertain and fill the listener with wonder than to be literally believed. Yet, as legends and metaphors they express more than a little truth. As all Izanagi's children eventually would stand on one side or the other of the portals of life and death, so do all humanity's children. And we all are capable of breaking pledges, going against the natural order of things (as

Izanagi did by venturing into the realm of the dead while still alive), or being tainted by circumstances beyond our control. And we all need purification from time to time. As such, chanting this prayer is a great means of being made clean.

The poem opens with an image related to its meaning: Kamurogi and Kamuromi on the heavenly plane. Shinto scholars have often identified "Kamurogi" and "Kamuromi" as collective nouns representing male and female ancestral deities. Both can be thought of as universal principals, rather like yin and yang, or as universal forces that constantly purify the world.

A loose translation of this prayer follows:

Prayer of Heaven

On the highest planes of heaven

Primeval Kamurogi and Kamuromi live.

And in accord with them, Izanagi,

In a grove of pine at Tsukushi,

Bathed at a river's clear mouth.

As he bathed, purifying spirits were born.

Of them we ask that all fault,

Baseness, and filth be washed away.

Humbly, we plead that they be dispelled

And we be made pure.

Please, divine spirits,

Legions of heaven and earth,

Answer our plea.

And just as the dappled horses of heaven

Perk their ears at the slightest rustle,

Hear our meek prayer.

In Shumei, the exact meaning of the chant is not considered to be as significant as its overall intent. In general, the Amatsunorito is a supplication to God and Meishusama to dispel all our negativity and wrong actions, which are the main causes of misfortune and suffering. It asks for protection as well as blessings for supreme happiness and spiritual growth.

Chanting the Amatsunorito aligns us with the purpose, power, and rhythm of the universe. It is one of the principal means for bringing us into harmony with God and nature. Just as a musician tunes an instrument before playing it, so too, does chanting tune the instrument of the self by harmonizing one's individual vibratory expression.

The purity of the individual reciting the Amatsunorito chant greatly affects the degree of power emitted by the words. The higher a person's spiritual level, the greater their ability to affect the world. Words spoken with virtuous intent emit high vibrations and dispel spiritual clouds, whereas words spoken harshly or with lack of awareness do the opposite.

Chanting the Amatsunorito follows a ritual sequence comprised of: (1) bowing, (2) three handclaps, (3) chanting the Amatsunorito, and (4) concluding with three handclaps.

The bowing, which is typified by three bows (one shallow and two deep), both initiates and finalizes the chanting. The first shallow bow is to acknowledge and open our hearts to God. The second and the third deep bows are expressions of respect and gratitude.

The clapping of the hands is also done three times, symbolizing God's Realm, the spiritual world, and the physical world, respectively. Alternate terms for this could be spirit, mind, and body. The abrupt, brisk sound from the clapping clears our minds, making us more receptive to the spiritual blessings of Jyorei.

Kamigoto

Kamigoto, like the Amatsunorito prayer, came from the Shinto tradition, and it literally means "words of Kami," or "divine words." This chant has the great capacity to purify our spiritual clouds, rejuvenate our spiritual energies, and align us with higher truth. Chanting either of these prayers generates a strong sound vibration that purifies the atmosphere in the area and prepares one to receive Light.

Although the Kamigoto sounds different from the Amatsunorito, it can be regarded as a longer version of the latter. Unlike the Amatsunorito, it is generally chanted only on special occasions. While the Amatsunorito is chanted during all daily Sampais, the Kamigoto prayer is typically chanted three times a year, on February 3, June 30, and December 31.

Individual members may choose to recite the Kamigoto when they feel the need for a special purification, or as a means to make a new resolution in response to some regrettable situation they may have caused. Everyone makes mistakes occasionally, and unfortunately, sometimes these mistakes hurt others. At such times, it is only natural to feel remorse for one's thoughts, words, or actions. Chanting Kamigoto, with sincerity, helps one to maintain an open heart by dissipating some of the spiritual clouds generated by wrong actions. In cases where we have hurt or offended someone, we should, as a demonstration of our sincerity, apologize to them, as well as chant Kamigoto. It is always important to understand the reason for chanting, and to take full responsibility for our actions. This is the true test of our sincerity. When we chant with such sincerity, and with correct resolution, the solution to our problems will sometimes spontaneously come to us. This is because the sound of Kamigoto naturally purifies our mind so that we can see things more clearly.

The Kamigoto chant has a loose story-like narrative that relates a request for divine intervention to purify the land, the body, and the spirit because of some major indiscretion. The chant calls on kami-deities to come in and dissipate the resultant spiritual negativity. The various kami-deities then intervene to dissipate the spiritual pollution, which is carried by the wind, rivers, and ocean, until finally it is flushed down into the underworld, where it is purified and transformed.

In the final refrains of the Kamigoto, both Miroku Omikami (the Ultimate God of Divine Light) and Meishusama are called upon to cleanse the chanters' bodies, minds, and spirits of the world's pollution, and to protect and bless them with happiness and spiritual growth.

The Zengensanji

"Zengensanji" literally means "The Good Words of Praise." In contrast to the Amatsunorito and the Kamigoto, both of which originated from the Shinto tradition, the Zengensanji is based on Buddhist scriptures.

Just prior to the official commencement of the Japan Kannon Society in 1935, Meishusama asked one of his students to bring him a copy of chapter twenty-five of the Lotus Sutra, entitled "The Universal Door of the Bodhisattva Who Listens to the Sounds of All the World." This is popularly called the Kannon Sutra. Following a series of profound mystical experiences with Kannon, Meishusama was led to this sutra, from which he drew inspiration and borrowed some key terms based on their spiritual power.

The Lotus Sutra is one of the most influential of all the sacred scriptures of Mahayana Buddhism. The author of this sutra, the place where it was initially composed, and the language in which it was originally written are all shrouded in the misty past. It is believed that the sutra was used in China in the middle of the third century, more than seven centuries after the Buddha's passing. This sutra, which is comprised of 28 chapters, depicts a drama of cosmic scale in which the Buddha gave teachings to an assembly of humans and heavenly beings.

Kannon is a Buddhist name referring to one of the most important Bodhisattvas of the Mahayana tradition. A Bodhisattva is a being, either supernatural or human, who seeks Buddhahood, but who, upon attaining perfect virtue, renounces entry into the final state of Nirvana until all other beings are saved first. Kannon Bodhisattva is said to be "One Who Hears the Outcries of the World." She has been worshiped and revered for many centuries for the qualities of compassion and wisdom that she is felt to embody. It is popularly believed that these divine qualities of Kannon manifest in the world as a power that can rescue people from their sufferings.

The Kannon Sutra presents a scene in which the Buddha, responding to a question about the name 'Kannon Bodhisattva,' describes in detail, as well as allegorically, Kannon's divine nature. The beautiful description of Kannon, along with the power of salvation believed to be embedded in the text, has inspired the creation of a variety of paintings and sculptures of this deity which are widely revered as both sacred symbols and beautiful artworks.

Meishusama describes Kannon in one of his poems: "From infinite love and compassion God becomes Kannon Bodhisattva in order to rescue the world." *(Kannon Bodhisattva. MK)* Kannon is a manifestation of God's compassionate love, appearing for the salvation of the world. To Meishusama, the salvation of the world is identical with the construction of a paradise on earth. Kannon, with her wisdom, compassionate love, and divine power, is seen as the active agent helping humanity to bring about this ideal state of the world. Furthermore, Kannon is representative of cosmic principles beyond ordinary human comprehension. Meishusama writes, "The underlying force that maintains the eternal flux and transforms the universe from instant to instant is that of Kannon." *(Henri Bergson. HT)*

The Zengensanji does not directly share the same depicted scenes and tones as the Kannon Sutra. While Sutras in Japan have been traditionally written in Chinese, and chanted with Chinese sounds, the Zengensanji is a mixture of both Chinese characters and Japanese. It is not chanted with the same rhythm as Sutra chanting. In this sense, the Zengensanji, rather than being categorized as a Sutra, can more accurately be viewed as a norito prayer about the paradise that Meishusama perceived during his divine revelation.

The Zengensanji emits a powerful vibration by its words, and is therefore considered to have the same kind of effect as the Amatsunorito and Kamigoto prayers. However, in contrast with those prayers, when chanting the Zengensanji it is important to understand the general meaning of the prayer and to create an image or feeling based on that understanding.

Meishusama stresses the importance of the power of will. If we do not have sufficient will power, or if our will to approach an ideal world is weak, then how can we make real progress? The Zengensanji is a prayer that describes the ultimate state of the world, and chanting it helps to strengthen the prayer by evoking vivid images. Chanting is a way to align ourselves with Kannon's wisdom, compassionate love, and divine power, as well as to manifest God's Will on earth.

Yet, if visualizing scenes of world redemption is difficult, there is no need to struggle, because as long as we idealize and yearn for the living reality of a paradise on earth, that feeling is sufficient. What's most important is one's intention to join hands with God in helping to create an ideal world here on earth. With this altruistic attitude, one can receive great benefit from the Zengensanji.

Daikokusama

It was 1933. I had been in debt for some time and was becoming a little dispirited. A bank employee who sometimes visited me had an ancient figure of Daikoku [the god of wealth], which he offered to give me. I accepted it gratefully and placed it in front of my hanging scroll, on which is painted an image of Kannon. From that month on, my financial problems ended and money began to roll in. – *Daikoku, the god of Wealth. HT*

Meishusama attributed the dramatic turnaround in his financial problems to the acquisition of a statue of the Japanese folk deity, Daikokusama. Thus began an inner relationship with this deity that lasted to the end of his life. As Meishusama began collecting statues of Daikokusama, his financial situation continued to improve.

All Shumei centers now have a statue or picture of Daikokusama within their premises. At the headquarters in Misono, there is a special shrine dedicated to him located on the edge of the Great Plaza outside of Meishusama Hall. He appears as a chubby, elderly man with a gentle smile on his face, holding a small mallet in one hand, and carrying a large bag of rice over his shoulder. Historically, Daikokusama symbolized financial wealth, health, longevity, and wisdom. Meishusama advised people to keep a statue or picture of this deity in their homes to promote wealth and abundance. In order to enhance the blessings, he volunteered to strengthen the spiritual presence within each of their statues. Some Shumei members honor this deity by chanting a modified version of the Amatsunorito in front of this statue or picture.

15 CONCLUSION

The Spiritual Significance of Meishusama

When people have asked, just who was Meishusama? We reply that he was a healer, a mystic, a prophet, a humanitarian, a visionary, a saint, or more. We say that he was a unique manifestation of God. It is a difficult question to answer because to those who knew and loved him, he did not easily fit into any single classification. Many would say that to some degree, he exhibited all of these traits because his talents and range of interests were so numerous. And, those in touch with his spirit can easily say that, because the deepest truths of God's being are beyond the reach of the mind, our intellectual understanding of Meishusama's true identity must also be limited. However, to really understand Meishusama, we would need to get inside the man.

On a purely biological level, he was simply a man. The outer man was an author, a healer, a prophet, an artist, a businessman, a humanitarian, a spiritual guide, farmer, and husband. He was a success in these and many other roles, but in our loving analysis of him, this is just the outer man.

We can recognize three distinct identities in Meishusama. There is the human who loved friends and family, who had personal feelings and interests. Then there is the man who was subject to the cultural influences of the time and place where he lived. And, finally, there is the universal, spiritual dimension to his identity, which transcends time and space. Concerning these aspects of his being, Meishusama himself writes, "When I think about myself, I see that I am a man but not man, God but not God." *(Meishusama II. MK)*

Despite his spiritual status, he was still a Japanese man who spoke Japanese and lived through a period of great change and turmoil in that country. Although he had a critical view of Japanese society at times, and despite the global scope of his universal philosophy, he was of course personally influenced by the customs and values surrounding him. His identity did not just transcend the local conditions in which he lived, but also included them. He embraced the people and the beauty around him, which was an expression of his profound love for others. Meishusama's life story was a living demonstration of the power to heal and grow through spiritual purification. He lived and breathed the principles that he taught, which gave authenticity and lent authority to his voice.

Meishusama never lost sight of the distant stars that beckoned him onward despite all the rocks encountered along the road. Each person's health or spiritual needs was cared for to the best of his ability, and each business or organizational problem was attended to as effectively as possible. Yet, beyond life's day-to-day concerns, he also remained true to his grand vision for the spiritual transformation of the world, and to his deepening inner relationship to God. In this way, it can be said that Meishusama's life exemplified the ideals and principles of Kannon's Way, the way of dynamic balance.

Moving on to an understanding of the spiritual dimension of his identity, we need to explore the nature of Spirit, and its relationship to the world of nature and man, as taught by Meishusama himself. Spirit is the inner dimension of God. Miroku-Omikami is the principle that God's Presence is everywhere and within everything. From this principle, it follows that God resides within all people as their divine spirit. The direct perception and inner realization of this fact is the final goal of evolution and spiritual growth. But because of the clouding of our spiritual vision, we see only separation everywhere and therefore cannot perceive the underlying unity and perfection of all of creation. This spiritual blindness also seems to cut us off from much of God's redeeming grace.

We can assess the wisdom in a person by the way he or she treats others. The more spiritually evolved a soul becomes, the more they exhibit the spiritual qualities of honesty, love, friendliness, humility, kindness, and integrity in their behavior. These attributes come from Spirit, and reveal the degree to which a person has purified his or her soul from the inner clouds of darkness. Meishusama exhibited all of these positive characteristics. His life was surrendered to a Higher Will. He was inspired by God to work for the salvation of humanity, and despite tremendous obstacles and suffering, went on to accomplish great things.

Having conquered physical attachments, I see not a cloud in the sky of my heart.
– Meishusama VI. MK

God works through everyone because we all have God's Spirit within us. For most of us, though, this influence is heavily blocked by the presence of spiritual clouds. But when someone has merged sufficiently with God's Will, then it is the Supreme Being's identity that is more clearly revealed through him or her, rather than a subjectively-based personality.

I am merely a vessel of God, proceeding according to God's will.
– Meishusama II. MK

Meishusama was just such an inspired individual. The Light of God shone brightly through him, and could actually be seen and felt by others. Because of this Light, and its tremendous impact on people's lives, many considered him a living embodiment of God. In Meishusama, this Spirit was not only inner, but also outer. In him, it was brought out to the surface, and affected everything he thought, said and did. Indeed, he claimed that there was no longer any separation between divinity and himself—they were fused together completely. Thus, many felt that to approach Meishusama was to see God in action.

Although divinity is essentially formless, it can descend into the world through the agency of an archetypal form, such as Kannon, the popular Buddhist deity of compassion, who, in turn, will act through a spiritually transformed individual, such as Meishusama. The Divine Light of God shines through such great souls for the spiritual benefit of humanity. Kannon was often seen standing and moving near Meishusama. He claimed that she made use of his body to serve others. Within his abdomen she placed a bright orb of golden light, which became the source of his healing and blessing power.

Through Kannon's mysterious power filling my body, transformation is here for all people. – Meishusama I. MK

Meishusama had a deep and profound relationship with Kannon. She literally entered into and took over Meishusama's body, and then began using it for the healing and upliftment of all who came into contact with him. About this condition, Meishusama writes:

> I later realized with a shock that the spirit of Kannon had been constantly by my side, and from that moment on, miracles connected with Kannon began to happen. As a result of this, I finally came to know that she appeared in this world as a manifestation of God in order to help humanity, and she will eventually revert back to her original form when the proper time has arrived.
>
> Since the year 1926, I have been physically possessed by Kannon in this way. She has told me a variety of things and given me many orders. Indeed, Kannon has used my body with perfect freedom as a physical vehicle to aid all living things.
>
> As I have said, I did not attain my present state through a belief in Kannon. Quite contrary, it was Kannon that used me as her tool. I am, one could say, a physical and masculine embodiment of Kannon. I am used completely as my divine master thinks fit, and have none of the freedom of an ordinary person, but I have a freedom that he or she does not have. This spiritual state is very difficult to explain, as it is beyond our everyday imagination." *My Testament. HT*

Deities such as Kannon are manifestations of God's power. Each deity tends to manifest a particular spiritual quality, such as compassion, truth, wisdom, peace, or joy. All deities are inwardly one with God, yet separate in terms of outer appearance. If God is invisible, then deities are the clothes that He wears in order for people to see Him. Because deities have a discernable form, it is easier for many to feel closer to them than to something as incomprehensible as God.

Both little children and valiant men adore and yearn for Kannon's merciful eyes.
– Infinite Compassion. MK

Kannon, in particular, is known in different countries by different names: in China she is called Kwan Yin, in Tibet she appears as a male deity named Chenrezig, and in India she is also regarded as a male deity named Avalokitesvara. In Japan, Kannon is sometimes perceived as female, while at other times male. This reflects the fact that God, as Miroku Omikami, is essentially beyond gender. Although Spirit transcends duality, it supports the manifestation of all dualities and qualities within the realm of time and space, much like a prism refracts light to create various colors and shapes. The soul is also, in its essence, neither male nor female, although it takes on these gender specific attributes from one lifetime to another during the long course of its evolution.

At a certain point in the soul's evolution, it will begin to identify less with the conventional personality and more with the spiritual presence at the core of its being. When this happens, the individual becomes truly humble and selfless. Its former identity is transcended and is replaced by deep inner silence and peace. Although the personality still remains, it now operates more like a superficial mask rather than as a personal identity. And if the soul continues to evolve further, it may discover that various spiritual qualities and powers begin to manifest through it. Kannon is one of these powers, and the more a soul surrenders to God the more she or another divine form will use it to serve others. In Meishusama, the surrender was complete, which resulted in his soul merging completely with Kannon Bodhisattva.

Kannon descends from heaven in a cloud of golden light.
– The Descending of Kannon. MK

Thus is revealed the great mystery of God in human form; a paradox of the human and divine, the physical and spiritual. In truth, there is only one, undivided reality—not two—and all of creation partakes of this divine unity, although few have the ability to perceive it. Meishusama was one who did perceive it, and it was his sacred mission to open our eyes to the spiritual world, and to help manifest a "World of Light."

The Light of Miroku Omikami softens and appears in the world as Kannon.
– Kannon Bodhisattva. MK

The Mysticism of Three

Every tension of opposites culminates in a release, out of which comes the "third."
In the third, the tension is resolved and the lost unity is restored. – Carl Jung

A common pattern one discovers in Meishusama's teachings is the constant reference to groups of three. Here is a list of examples: Currently we live in a world of sickness, poverty, and strife, but—through the cultivation of love for others, gratitude, and makoto—we can help usher in a world of truth, virtue, and beauty. Through the three spiritual practices of Jyorei, Natural Agriculture, and the appreciation of Art, we can transform our spirit, mind, and body, as reflected in our thoughts, words, and deeds. His universal philosophy embraces both the subjective realm of thoughts, feelings, and intention, as well as the objective realms of science, religion, and art, to bring us into harmony with God's Realm (the world of the ultimate mystery), the spiritual world, and the physical world. All of these trinities manifest through the symbolic substances of fire, water, and earth. And finally, the spiritual development of our soul is dependent on its relationship of the three spirits: the divine spirit, the animal spirit, and the guardian spirit.

This emphasis on 'three' reflects Meishusama's intention to reconcile mankind's history of dualistic conflict. The number two is the basis for opposition and conflict. Most of Western Philosophy is based on the dialectics of opposites. Not only is good at war with evil, but also, fate contradicts free will. Faith is at odds with doubt, and reason struggles with emotion. Like a computer, our minds use binary logic. Everywhere, we see opposites. The direction "up" opposes "down", the location "in" contrasts with "out", the temperature "hot" contrasts with "cold."

Meishusama draws on a third factor, a spiritual principle, to bring mediation, reconciliation, and harmony to the world of opposites. A two-legged table is unstable and can easily fall down, whereas a three-legged table is stable and, therefore, remains upright. The third leg adds width to the directions of length and height, thereby creating a volume of space in the middle. This space is the principle of awareness. Introducing an impartial observer into a conflict situation often produces a peaceful resolution because of the added awareness that person brings.

The number three has played a significant role in the mythologies and theologies of the world. Christians believe in the mystery of the Trinity made up of the Father, the Son, and the Holy Spirit. Buddhism emphasizes the importance of the three jewels of the Buddha, the Dharma, and the Sangha (the teacher, the teachings, and the spiritual community). Hindus worship the deities Brahma, Vishnu, and Shiva, who perpetually create, preserve, and destroy the universe. The ancient Egyptians revered the gods Osiris, Isis, and Horus who symbolized the conscious, unconscious and superconscious aspects of the mind, respectively. Taoists cultivate Jing, Chi, and Shen, the three qualities of universal energy.

According to Pythagorean numerology, the number one symbolizes the Absolute, pure unity, unpolarized energy, and the transcendent cause of all things. The number two symbolizes polarized energy, dichotomy, conflict, and opposition. When the absolute unity of God separates into duality to become conscious of itself, the one simultaneously becomes two and three. The objective world is the number two, and the process of becoming conscious of itself is the number three. Two people in a room are not in relationship until they get to know each other. First they must communicate with each other. Number three is thus the principle of communication, relationship, mutual understanding, and love. It combines the perceiver, the perceived, and the act of perceiving. The number three is objective awareness. As the Swiss Psychoanalyst Carl Jung stated, "Three is an unfolding of the One to a condition where it can be known—unity becomes recognizable."

It is clear that Meishusama puts great value on the number three because of the spiritual principle that it introduces. The Age of Night was trapped in the conflict of opposites, and was a world of strife. With the dawning of the Age of Day, it is time to transcend conflicts through love and understanding. This is more than just abstract symbolism, for it has the higher purpose of reintegrating the sacred dimension back into our ordinary, day-to-day lives.

Happiness

While passing through this transient world, create the happiness of eternal life.

– Life and Death. MK

Many people have asked, "What is the connection between the three main practices of Shumei? What do Jyorei, Natural Agriculture, and Art have in common?" The single principle that ties these three together is the universal pursuit of happiness. Meishusama had a great sympathy and concern for people's suffering. Very simply, he wanted, with all his heart, for people to be peaceful and happy. Happiness, to be complete, depends upon both inner and outer harmony. Inner peace contributes to outer harmony, and outer harmony contributes to inner peace. They are mutually supportive.

More than countless riches, happiness is living in safety and health.

– Gratitude. MK

Even a saint would probably not be very happy living in a ruthless, totalitarian country that frequently violates human rights and that practices genocide. Also, his happiness would probably be diminished if he was sick and in terrible pain. Although ultimate happiness comes from Spirit, even great saints have bodies capable of feeling physical pain, as well as minds capable of experiencing emotional suffering. To experience complete happiness on all levels of body, mind, and spirit, not only do we need inner peace, but we also need our outer social and physical environment to be peaceful and whole as well.

Conversely, a person living in a utopian environment would not be very happy if he was inwardly full of anger, fear, or sorrow. How often have we ignored the beauty around us because of a self-preoccupation or problem that was on our mind? Inner peace is essential for us to enjoy the world around us. As we grow in consciousness we become more sensitive, not less, and therefore, our need for a harmonious environment increases even further. The alternative to sensitivity, which is to deaden ourselves to feeling, is not the solution to pain because, in the process, we also dull our ability to experience joy and excitement. Thus, pain medication and psychiatric drugs do not produce happiness either.

Happiness largely depends on both subjective and objective factors. Subjectively, we feel happiest when we are relaxed in the body, quiet in the mind, and peaceful in the heart. In the objective environment, we feel happiest when we have access to good food and decent shelter, as well as a peaceful and loving environment full of beauty and comfort. Wanting to help people at all levels of spiritual development, Meishusama understood the importance of both our inner and outer worlds for fostering a balanced happiness. He wanted to help the average person in very immediate, practical ways. Thus he avoided the trap of overly ascetic spiritual traditions that deny the importance of physical necessities while also recognizing the superficiality of most utopian dreams of worldly fulfillment. This middle path was an expression of Kannon's Way—a balancing of the subjective and the objective, and of avoiding the extremes of asceticism and hedonism.

All three of Meishusama's prescribed activities affect both the inner and outer worlds. Through practicing Natural Agriculture, the farmer begins to develop a spiritual relationship with nature, and begins to feel a profound inner peace and contentment. Outwardly, Natural Agriculture helps to rejuvenate the eco-system through its avoidance of toxic chemicals, and through its respect for the land. It also provides people with pure food that promotes increased levels of health and vitality.

Inwardly, beauty calms the mind, opens the heart, and uplifts the spirit. Outwardly, beautiful environments uplift society and promote social harmony by making the world an enjoyable place. In contrast to this, ugly slum dwellings promote crime, social violence, and despair. The best in people and society is brought out by exposure to beautiful art, music, and architecture, whereas the worst is brought out by ugly art, noisy music, and monotonous buildings.

Jyorei transforms the subjective dimension of experience—thoughts, feelings, and perceptions—as well as the objective dimension of experience—relationships, finances, and health. The inner leads the outer and the invisible precedes the visible. Initially, one may be like a dirty window covered by layers of selfishness and negativity, but over time, through Jyorei, the window will become clean and transparent, allowing greater amounts of light to shine through. As one's spiritual clouds begin to disappear, physical health is revitalized, emotional balance is restored, mental tranquility returns, and, most importantly, spiritual freedom is attained. Meishusama writes: "In Shumei, Jyorei is usually given with the purpose of healing sickness, but really it has a significance far greater than that. This significance is, in short, that Jyorei is a means of creating happiness." *(Jyorei and Happiness. HT)*

Everything exists within God, while, paradoxically, also moving toward God. The more we see the perfection around us the more it becomes a part of our lives. The main objective is to bring about, by means of both the purifying process of Jyorei, as well as through selfless service to others, a dramatic acceleration in our spiritual development. By doing this, we also contribute to the spiritual evolution of the world.

The way to liberate humanity lies in guiding people to the path of eternal life.
– Meishusama III. MK

In this way, Jyorei, Natural Agriculture, and art and beauty, contribute to both inner and outer happiness. Primarily, happiness comes from within. It comes from inner purity and love, as well as from the inner satisfaction gained by helping others to be happy. It comes from realizing our essential unity with the world, in which we do not see ourselves as separate from the people, places, and things around us. Feeling love for others, along with the desire to be of service, transcends mere healing. They are expressions of spiritual maturity. Love and service are also the basis for peace on earth.

Healing the body is not enough. A tyrant filled with selfishness, hatred, and violence, whether physically healthy or not, can still create a "hell on earth" through his destructive actions. He can plunder an economy, oppress the people, or create horrible wars. What the tyrant really needs is deep spiritual transformation, not just physical healing.

Meishusama's primary objective is the creation of a Paradise on Earth, which he describes as a world of truth, virtue, and beauty. These values and qualities will be the true foundation for world transformation. True Paradise on Earth will come from universal peace and love, not from political revolutions, social campaigns, or financial reforms. Although quite necessary, these efforts toward change must be based on peace and love, not conflict and hate. Therefore, the primary goal and activity of Shumei is soul evolution, which healing serves. Healing is secondary and supportive to this primary goal.

What Jyorei, Natural Agriculture, and art and beauty have in common is that they all promote human happiness, both on a relative level and on a spiritual level. On a mundane level, happiness tends to increase when the outer conditions in our lives improve. But on a spiritual level, happiness comes from a deeper inner peace and harmony. These deeper inner levels require and naturally involve spiritual transformation. Jyorei promotes spiritual growth, beauty elevates the soul, and Natural Agriculture fosters love and respect for all things. Together, they contribute to a better world by bringing Light to it.

After thousands of years of waiting, a bright, shining age now draws near.
– World of Light, MK

Epilogue

Meishusama is still with us in the invisible spiritual world. Many people feel his divine guidance and support as a constant influence in their lives. The three main activities that he promoted continue to expand throughout the world. Jyorei, as a spiritual practice, has spread to all four corners of the world; Natural Agriculture is replacing chemically based farming in many areas of Japan, and interest in this approach to farming is spreading from one country to another; and, the Miho Museum is gaining increased international attention each year.

With these activities, we hope more people may benefit from personal healing and spiritual awakening. The road to increased happiness begins when one embarks on a program of purifying one's body and soul, and most importantly, when one takes the major step of deciding to live for God by serving others. This step is no small matter, but is the crucial step one must take to lead a truly spiritual life.

Since receiving a new life, his eyes have become gentle, his face radiant and bright. – Faith. MK

It is a paradox that the more self-serving we are, the more miserable we become, whereas the more we serve others, the happier we become. True happiness comes from expanding our sense of self to include the world around us. By serving others we also serve God. We should not, however, in our minds exclude ourselves from the greater unity. We also serve God by taking care of our own needs, which, in turn, enables us to better serve humanity. How can we help others be happy if we, ourselves, are miserable? How can we aid others financially if we are destitute? How can we feed others if we are hungry?

God's presence can be found both within and without, because that which is beyond boundaries cannot be divided or confined. God is everywhere, like the space between atoms and molecules. With our limited imaginations, we tend to categorize reality, putting everything into mental boxes. This creates division where there is really only unity. Love blossoms from seeing Spirit everywhere. God's spirit is in the trees, the water and the sky; in the animals that roam the earth; in the fish that swim in the sea; and in the birds that soar through the heavens. Both our friends and our enemies are God's children. All have God's presence within them.

By serving others, we find that we are actually serving our own selves, because all of us have the same spirit within us. Service of others purifies our desires, opens our hearts, and allows God's Power to work through us. It was Meishusama's heartfelt desire to see everyone happy and fulfilled, free of the three maladies of poverty, sickness, and strife. Our sacred task is to help transform the world with love and Light, into the fulfillment of his dream.

Just as Meishusama was inspired by Kannon's infinite compassion, may each of us be so inspired. May we also come to realize that love and gratitude are their own reward.

Thinking of the happiness that my transformation has brought me, how can I refrain from giving myself, body and soul, to returning what I have received?
                                                          – Gratitude. MK

Glossary

Amatsunorito:
Ancient chant, derived from the Shinto tradition in Japan, for divine blessings and purification. It literally means the 'Heavenly Prayer.'

Ancestor Spirit:
Spirit of one's deceased ancestor, also referred to as the *Guardian Spirit*.

Animal Spirit:
Spiritual being who works on human's basic desires and instincts for their survival and propagation. It is also referred to as the *Secondary Guardian Spirit*.

Aura:
A spiritual radiation that reflects the condition of the soul.

Bodhisattva:
One who dedicates himself to the salvation of others.

Daijo:
A term of Buddhist origins adapted by Meishusama. It is horizontal in nature and represents a spiritual expression that is tolerant, adaptable, and inclusive.

Daikokusama:
A demigod of financial wealth, health, longevity, and wisdom.

Divine Light:
Spiritual radiance. *Jyorei*.

Divine Spirit:
The eternal, unchanging, divine spark located within each person.

God's Realm:
The highest level of the spiritual world. Also referred to as the World of Ultimate Mystery.

Guardian Spirit:
An *Ancestor Spirit* selected to watch over and assist a person from within the *spiritual world*.

Hoshi:
Selfless service to others, while dedicating the results to God.

Hoshisha:
Members of Shumei who perform *hoshi* on behalf of Shumei's mission to promote the betterment of humankind.

Izunome:
The perfect harmony and balance between *Daijo* and *Shojo*. It also represents the spiritual essence of *Kannon's Way*.

Jyorei:
A spiritual healing method for purification and spiritual growth introduced by *Meishusama*, also referred to as *Divine Light*. The word *Jyorei* literally means "purification of the spirit."

Kaicho-Sensei:
Current president of Shinji Shumeikai, Ms Hiroko Koyama.

Kaishusama:
Organizational founder and the first president of Shinji Shumeikai, Ms Mihoko Koyama.

Kamigoto:
Chant for atonement and purification.

Kannon:
Buddhist deity of compassion and wisdom. (See a footnote on page 23.)

Kannon's Way:
A flexible, moderate, and balanced approach to life that includes patience and tolerance, and brings harmony to one's life. (See *Izunome*.)

Kototama:
A spiritual power inherent in the correctly pronounced sounds of words.

Main Spirit:
(See *Divine Spirit*.)

Makoto:
A fundamental character trait that includes such higher qualities as sincerity, truthfulness, altruism, reliability, and integrity. A person has makoto when his actions are in alignment with his words and ideals. Essential to the practice of makoto is the consideration for others and for the will of God.

Meishusama:
A spiritual teacher who introduced *Jyorei* and *Natural Agriculture* to the world. "*Meishusama*" is an honorific, meaning "Master of Light," commonly used by Shumei members when referring to *Mokichi Okada*.

Miho Museum:
A museum dedicated to Meishusama's vision of beauty.

Mikotosama:
The second president of *Shinji Shumeikai*, Mr. Sokichi Koyama.

Misono:
Shumei's International Center located in the mountains in Shiga prefecture, Japan.

Mokichi Okada:
The birth name of *Meishusama*.

Miroku Omikami:
All-encompassing presence of God.

Natural Agriculture:
A spiritually based form of farming. The essence of this practice is having reverence for nature and cultivating the food crops in a manner close to how plants thrive in a natural setting.

Ohikari:
Silk amulet worn when transmitting Jyorei. It consists of a small parchment bearing calligraphy by *Meishusama*.

Otamagushi:
Monetary offering given in gratitude prior to *Sampai*.

Possessing Animal Spirit:
Evil spirit of discarnate animals which like to put people under their control, and can possess human bodies.

Primary Guardian Spirit:
(See *Guardian Spirit*.)

Purification:
A natural mechanism and process to cleanse the *spiritual clouds* accumulated in one's spiritual body. Depending upon the degree and type of *spiritual clouds*, it can appear in various forms and intensities.

Sampai:
In Shumei, it means 'coming to a Shumei center to chant and receive Jyorei.'

Secondary Guardian Spirit:
(See *Animal Spirit*.)

Sensei:
A Japanese word meaning 'teacher.' It is a title given to those who have achieved a certain degree of skill and knowledge in a certain field of endeavor. Shumei's senseis are authorized by the organization to teach, counsel, give spiritual guidance, perform rituals, and oversee administrative work.

Shinji Shumeikai:
Spiritual fellowship following Meishusama's teachings. It is often referred to as *Shumei*.

Shojo:
A term of Buddhist origins adapted by *Meishusama*. Shojo is vertical in nature and represents a spiritual expression that is principled, restrictive, narrow, and disciplined. It is conservative, introspective. It is the complementary principle of daijo. *Meishusama* taught that both horizontal *daijo* and vertical *shojo* must be in harmony for a spiritual pursuit to succeed. The symbol of such harmony is the equilateral cross.

Shumei:
(See *Shinji Shumeikai*.)

Soul:
That which carries a person's deepest individual characteristics from lifetime to lifetime and capable of evolving spirituality.

Spirit:
The innermost essence and source of all things. Within individuals it is referred to as Divine Spirit. (See *Divine Spirit*.)

Spiritual Body:
The immaterial body that influences the mind and affects the physical body.

Spiritual Clouds:
Impurities caused by one's negative thoughts, words, and deeds that obscure our spirit and darken our soul. They are the source of all human misery.

Spiritual Cords:
Invisible, spiritual bonds between people, places, and things.

Spiritual World:
The invisible, spiritual dimension of existence that exerts a profound influence on the physical world. It is also referred to as the world of deceased spirits.

Toku Energy:
The spiritual wealth gained by doing good works and making others happy. Not only does one profit from the accumulation of this energy, but it also benefits one's friends and family members as well. Although good always comes from amassing *toku energy*, its specific benefits ultimately are in the hands of God. *Toku Energy* is sometimes referred to as 'Grace.'

The World of the Ultimate Mystery:
The highest level of the spiritual world. Also referred to as *God's Realm*.

Zengensanji:
Special chant composed by Meishusama for envisioning an ideal world.

Illustrations

Diagrams

Drawings

Bibliography

Appleton, Nancy. *The Curse of Louis Pasteur*. Santa Monica, CA: Choice Publishing, 1999.

Braden, Gregg. *Awakening to Zero Point: The Collective Initiation*. Belleview, WA: Radio Bookstore Press, 1997.

Combs, Allan. *The Radiance of Being: Understanding the Grand Integral Vision; Living the Integral Life*, 2d ed. St. Paul, MN: Paragon, 2002.

Dauncey, Guy. *"Ten Reasons Why Organic Food is Better," Common Ground Magazine*. Vancouver, Canada: Common Ground Publishing Corp, August 2002.

De Chardin, Teilhard. The Phenomenon of Man. Translated by Bernard Wall. New York: Harper & Row, 1959.

Deguchi, Kyotaro. The Great Onisaburo Deguchi. Translated by Charles Rowe. Tokyo: Aiki News, 1998.

Donelan, Peter. *Growing To Seed*. Willits, CA: Ecology Action, 1999.

Enby, Erik, Peter Gosch, and Michael Sheehan. *Hidden Killers: The Revolutionary Medical Discoveries of Professor Guenther Enderlein*. Austin, TX: Sheehan Communications, 1990.

Francis, Raymond, with Kester Cotton. *Never Be Sick Again: Health Is a Choice, Learn How to Choose It*. Deerfield Beach, FL: Health Communications, Inc., 2002.

Fromm, Erich. *The Art of Loving*. New York: Harper & Row Publishers, 1956.

Fukuoka, Masanobu. *The One–Straw Revolution: An Introduction to Natural Farming*. Emmaus, PA: Rodale Press, 1978.

Goble, Frank G. *The Third Force: The Psychology of Abraham Maslow*. New York: Simon & Schuster, 1970.

Hall, Edward T. and Mildred Reed. *Hidden Differences: Doing Business with the Japanese*. New York: Anchor Books/Doubleday, 1987.

Harman, Willis W. and Elisabet Sahtouris. *Biology Revisioned*. Berkeley, CA: North Atlantic Books, 1998.

Hawkins, David R. *Power vs. Force: The Hidden Determinants of Human Behavior*. Sedona, AZ: Veritas Publishers, 1995.

The Holy Bible, New Kings James Version. Nashville, TN: Thomas Nelson Inc, 1982.

Isaacs, Nathan. *A Brief Introduction to Piaget*. New York: Schocken Books, 1974.

Iwao, Takahashi. *Okada Mokichi ni okeru Shukyo to Geijutsu (Spirituality and Art in the Philosophy of Mokichi Okada)*. Japan: Kazeno Bara, 1984.

Johrei Fellowship. *Reminiscences About Meishu-sama: A Collection of Stories and Anecdotes*. Torrance, CA: Johrei Fellowship, 1996.

Kasulis, Thomas. P. *Shinto: The Way Home*. Honolulu: University of Hawaii Press, 2004.

Kishmoto, Hideo. *"Mahayana Buddhism and Japanese Thought," Philosophy East and West*. University of Hawaii Press. October, 1954.

Genku. Kimura, Yasuhiko. *"Beauty as a Path of Peace," The Journal of Integral Thinking for Visionary Action*. Anaheim, CA: Vision in Action™ Newsletter.

———. (Translator) *Lao Tzu: The Book of Balance: Lao Tzu's Tao Teh Ching*. University of Science and Philosophy, 2002.

Kropotkin, Peter. *Mutual Aid: A Factor in Evolution*. London: Freedom Press, 1998.

Lipton, Bruce. *The Biology of Belief: Unleashing the Power of Consciousness, Matter and Miracles*. Santa Rosa, CA: Mountain of Love/Elite Books, 2005.

Lovejoy, Arthur. *The Great Chain of Being*. Cambridge, MA: Harvard University Press, 1936.

Mitchell, Stephen. (Translation) *Tao Te Ching*. New York, NY: Harper and Row, 1988.

Naka, Masao. *Michi Hitosuji:Shinji Shumeikai no Ayumi (Going Straight into a Path of Faith: Development of Shinji Shumeikai)*. Tokyo: Time Life Books, 1983.

MOA Publications. *The Light from the East: Mokichi Okada, Volume two*. Atami, Japan: MOA Publications, 1986.

Mother Teresa. *The Joy in Loving: A Guide to Daily Living*. Compiled by Chaliha, Jaya, and Edward Le Joly. New York: Penguin, 2000.

Okada, Mokichi. *A Hundred Teachings of Meishusama* 1st ed. Japan: Shinji Shumeikai, 2001.

———. *Foundation of Paradise*. Torrance, CA: Johrei Fellowship, 1984.

———. *Fragments From the Teachings of Meishu-sama*. Torrance, CA: Johrei Fellowship, 1998.

———. *Gokowaroku (The Guiding Light: A Collection of Oral Teaching by Meishu-sama Vol. 1)*.Translated by Henry Ajiki, Tuson, AZ: Johrei Fellowship, 2003.

———. *Health and the New Civilization*. Torrance, CA: Johrei Fellowship, 1998.

———. *Johrei: Divine Light of Salvation*. Translated by Ichiro Nakamura, Kyoto, Japan: The Society of Johrei, 1984.

———. *Kannon Gyō (Kannon's Way)*. Shigaraki, Japan: Shinji Shumeikai, 2004.

———. *Meishusama Shizen-nōhō Goronbun-shyu (Natural Agriculture Teachings of Meishu-sama)*. Shigaraki, Japan: Shinji Shumeikai, 2005.

———. *Miakarishu: A Collection of Light*. Pasadena, CA: Shinji Shumeikai of America, 1992.

———. *The Teachings of Meishusama*. Pasadena, CA: Shinji Shumeikai of America, 1990.

Oxford University Press. *The Dhammapada*: The Sayings of the Buddha. New York: Oxford University Press, 2000.

S. Perls, Frederick. *The Gestalt Approach & Eye Witness to Therapy*. Palo Alto, CA: Science and Behavior Books, 1973.

———. *Gestalt Therapy Verbatim*. Moab, Utah: Real People Press, 1969.

Picken, Stuart D. B. *Shinto: Meditations for Reversing the Earth*. Berkeley, CA: Stone Bridge Press, 2002.

Philippi, Donald. *Norito: A Translation of the Ancient Japanese Ritual Prayers*. Princeton, NJ: Princeton University Press, 1990.

Prabhavananda, Swami, and Christopher Isherwood. *The Song of God: Bhagavad-Gita*. Hollywood, CA: The Vedanta Society of Southern California, 1951.

Rohlfing, Gerard. *Sincerity and Truth: The Life Story of Meishusama*. Pasadena, CA: Shumei America Publications, 2005.

Sahtouris, Elisabet. *"A Tentative Model of a Living Universe, Part 1 & 2," The Journal of Integral Thinking for Visionary Action*. Anaheim, CA: Vision in Action™ Newsletter.

Scott, Graham G. *The Complete Idiot's Guide to Shamanism*. Indianapolis, IN: Alpha Books, 2002.

Sheldrake, Rupert. *A New Science of Life*: The Hypothesis Formative Causation. Toronto, Canada: Saunders of Toronto Ltd., 1981.

Shumei America. *Shumei's Chants: The Amatsunorito, Zengensanji, and Kamigoto*. Pasadena, CA: Shumei America, 2004.

Smith, Huston. *The Forgotten Truth: The Common Vision of the World's Religions*. New York: Harper & Row, 1976.

———. *The World's Religions: Our Great Wisdom Traditions*. New York: Harper Collins, 1991.

Stafford-Clark, David. *What Freud Really Said*. New York: Schocken Books, 1971.

Stiskin, Nahum. *The Looking-Glass God: Shinto, Yin-Yang, and a Cosmology for Today*. Brookline, MA: Autumn Press, 1972.

Suzuki, David. *"Organic Farming is Realistic, Science Matters" Common Ground Magazine*. Vancouver, Canada: Common Ground Publishing Corp, August 2002.

Talbot, Michael. *The Holographic Universe*. New York: HarperCollins, 1991.

Timms, Moira. *Beyond Prophecies and Predictions: Everyone's Guide to the Coming Changes*. New York: Random House, 1994.

Tolle, Eckhart. *The Power of Now: A Guide to Spiritual Enlightenment*. Novato, CA: New

World Library, 1999.

Tompkins, Peter, and Christopher Bird. *The Secret Life of Plants: A Fascinating Account of the Physical, Emotional, and Spiritual Relations between Plants and Man.* New York: Harper and Row, 1973.

———. *The Secrets of the Soil: New Solutions for Restoring our Planet.* New York: Harper and Row, 1998.

Waters, Owen, *The Shift: The Revolution in Human Consciousness.* Delaware: Infinite Being Publishing LLC, 2006.

Watson, Burton. (Translator) *The Lotus Sutra.* New York: Columbia University Press, 1993.

Watts, Alan. *The Book: On the Taboo Against Knowing Who You Are.* New York: Pantheon Books, 1966.

———. *Tao: The Watercourse Way.* New York: Pantheon Books, 1975.

———. *The Way of Zen.* New York: Pantheon Books, 1957.

Wa'na'nee'che (Renault, Dennis), and Timothy Freke. *Principles of Native American Spirituality (Thorsons Principles Series).* London: HarperCollins Publishers, 1996.

West, John Anthony. *Serpent in the Sky: The High Wisdom of Ancient Egypt.* New York: Harper & Row, 1979.

Wilbur, Ken. *The Marriage of Sense and Soul: Integrating Science and Religion.* New York: Random House, 1998.

Williams, George. *Shinto,* Philadelphia: Chelsea House, 2005.

Yu, Chun–Fang. *Kuan-Yin: The Chinese Transformation of Avalokitesvara.* New York: Columbia University Press, 2001.